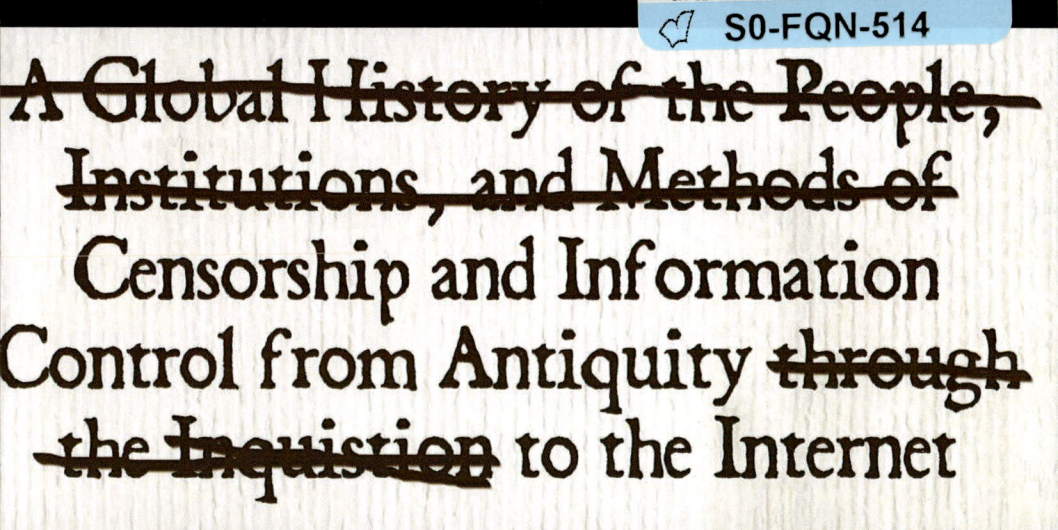

A ~~Global History of the People,~~
~~Institutions, and Methods of~~
Censorship and Information
Control from Antiquity ~~through~~
~~the Inquistion~~ to the Internet

A Global History of
Censorship and
Information Control from
the
Inquistion to the Internet

~~A Global History of the People,~~
~~Institutions, and Methods of~~
Censorship and Information Control
~~from Antiquity through~~
Inquistion to ~~the~~ Internet

Accept Changes?
OK

Censorship and Information Control

Inquitision to Present

September 17-December 14, 2018

University of Chicago

Produced to Accompany the exhibit
"Censorship and Information Control: Inquisition to Present" September 17th to December 14nd, 2018
University of Chicago Library, Special Collections Research Center

Curator: Ada Palmer
Assistant Curator: Julia Tomasson
Editorial Assistant: John-Paul Heil
Art Curator: Samantha Truman
Exhibit Designer: Patti Gibbons

© Ada Palmer 2018

No part of this publication may be reproduced, stored in or introduced into a retrieval system, or transmitted, in any form or by any means) electronic, mechanical, photocopying, recording or otherwise), without the prior written permission of the copyright owner, except by a reviewer who may quote brief passages in a review. Enquiries concerning reproduction outside the scope above should be sent to Ada Palmer, University of Chicago, Department of History, 1126 E. 59th Street, Chicago, IL 60637.

Limited edition of 1500 copies, printed by Swift Impressions in Chicago, USA.

ISBN 978-1-944140-05-2

Original image used for the cover design: *Caxton Showing the First Specimen of His Printing to King Edward IV at the Almonry, Westminster* by Daniel Maclise (1909)

Acknowledgements

Many components of this exhibit were team curated by graduate and undergraduate students in a 2017 course "History of Censorship and Information Control" co-taught by Ada Palmer and Stuart McManus with the help of John-Paul Heil.

Student curators: Adam Biesman, Julian Borda, Peter Chen, ███████ ███████, Anna Christensen, Timothy Cunningham, Hannah Dorsey, Nathaniel Eakman, Jamie Ehrlich, Max Freedman, ███████, Sam Gersho, Henry Hahn, Carolyn Hirsch, Michael Hosler-Lancaster, Caitlin Hubbard, Sam Koffman, Clio Sophia Koller, Sarah Larson, Jillian Lepek, Gautama Mehta, Jasmine Mithani, Morley Musick, Olivia Palid, Lauren Scott, Kyle Shishkin, Katherine Surma, ███████, Julia Tomasson, Hannah Trower, Samantha Truman, Augustin Vannier, Julia Walker, Peyton Walker, Caleb Wang, and Victoria Xing.

With special thanks to librarians Catherine Uecker and Sem Sutter, and to Leo Cadogan, Cheryl Cape, Kyong-Hee Choi, Cory Doctorow, Adrian Johns, Mack Muldofsky, Lauren Schiller, and Jo Walton.

Made possible by projects supported by the University of Chicago Institute on the Foundation of Knowledge, the Neubauer Collegium, Nicholson Center for British Studies, and Kickstarter.

With special thanks to the American Library Association Office of Intellectual Freedom, the Electronic Freedom Foundation, and the Comic Book Legal Defense Fund. We would also like to thank First Aid Comics for supplying our rare comics needs.

TABLE OF CONTENTS

A Note to the Reader..2

Censorship: Expectations and Realities ███████

How do YOU Define Censorship?...................................20

Plural Inquisitions...32
    Censorship Before or After?.................................36
    The Rocky Birth of Copyright Law........................52
    Migrating Print Capitals.......................................60
    What was the Inquisition's Goal?..........................66
    ███████████████████████.....................
    No one Expects the Phillipine Inquisition............84
    With Approval of the King...................................100
    The Church and Art..106

Universal Acids, Toxic Ideas....................................122

Censoring the Classics...132

███████ Censorship in Translation...............146

Censorship in the Soviet Union................................155

The Great Firewall of China.....................................159

Censorship in New Zealand: What does the First Ammendment Really do?...163

Colonial Censorship..168

Censoring Comics...176

███████ Art Censorship in Chicago...................184

Fake News is Not New..190

Internet Censorship: ███████████.................202

Appendix I Banned Bookcase: Tour the Continents..........206
Appendix II: Censor's Desk: Learn What Censoring Feels Like..210
Appendix III: Contributors listed by Case....................213
Appendix IV Further Reading......................................214

A Note to the Reader:

Why do people censor? For ambition? Profit? Fear? This exhibit in the University of Chicago's Special Collections Research Center traces censorship from antiquity to our digital age, showing how information control has worked, thrived, or failed, and how real censorship movements tend to be very different from the centralized, methodical censorship depicted in Orwell's *1984*. From indexes of forbidden books to the subtle censorship of teaching biased histories, the materials in this exhibit will challenge you to answer: how do *you* define what is and isn't censorship?

The exhibit focuses on the human face of censorship, and explores the specific goals and motives of individuals throughout history who have designed or participated in forms of censorship. By introducing readers and viewers to the many different kinds of people who have voluntarily carried out censorship, the exhibit and catalog seeks to explode the common assumption that looking out for censorship means looking for a malevolent, top-down, centralized force, and introduce diverse forms of local, ad hoc, well-meaning, commerce-driven, and bottom-up censorship —forms which easily persist even in societies which, like ours, condemn censorship in the abstract.

This exhibit was conceived as a collection of attempts to understand and define 'censorship,' by first asking—what does censorship look like? The exhibition and catalogue seek to raise more questions than they answer and provide readers with examples and illustrations for their own arguments. Our exhibit in the University of Chicago's Special Collections gallery, and its printed catalog, will accompany the ongoing discussions in an associated seminar series "Censorship and

Information Revolutions" with a visual narrative of the long history of censorship and information control. Our public dialogue series brings together scholars of print revolutions past and present with practitioners working on the frontiers of today's information revolution. These events will not be formal panels with presented papers, but free-form discussions in which experts bounce ideas off each other, discovering rich parallels between our work and sharing them in real time. Taking place from October through November, the eight dialogues will unite historians, editors, novelists, poets, and activists, and will be filmed and shared online, to let the public enjoy and continue the discussions.

By bringing together scholars of premodern publishing and censorship with experts in the current rise of digital media, this collaboration will bridge two disparate arenas of knowledge that can inform each other in symbiotic ways. It will start a conversation about the ways in which the history of information technology can inform how we respond to an ever-changing digital epoch, impacting scholars of the history of censorship, activists, publishers, administrators and legal professionals involved in policy-making, advocacy and legal cases, the University of Chicago campus community's ongoing conversation about academic freedom, and larger nationwide and international conversations about free speech and academic freedom, in which University of Chicago is already an important voice.

For more information see: https://voices.uchicago.edu/censorship/

Reader Be Aware of Editing

Throughout this exhibit, sections of text--especially points where "..." would be used to mark excerpts in quotations--have instead been marked with blackout as if redacted, to simulate the chilling experience of reading in societies where the black marks of expurgation and redaction peppered libraries.

SVMMA CONTRA GENTILES
COMMENTARIA IN SACRAM SCRIPTVRAM
SVMMA

Censorship: Expectations and Reality

> "As good almost kill a man as kill a good book: who kills a man kills a reasonable creature, God's image; but he who destroys a good book kills reason itself."
> – Milton, *Aeopagitica*, 1644

> "The Dell code eliminates entirely, rather than regulates, objectionable material. 'DELL COMICS ARE GOOD COMICS' is our credo and constant goal."
> –A Pledge to Dell Comic Parents, 1956

In George Orwell's *1984*, Winston Smith arrives each morning at the towering, well-funded offices of the Ministry of Truth, to help colleagues falsify news, erase people, and destroy or dumb down literature and language in service of a clearly-defined, multi-decade plan. This vivid tale of totalitarianism and surveillance has become a bedrock of how we think and talk about censorship, but this centralized, top-down, state-directed censorship with stable and defined goals is very atypical of historical realities. This exhibit documents numerous cases of censorship or information control from antiquity to the present, many exemplifying decentralized, grassroots, hastily improvised, unconscious, or unintentional censorship, with motives—from protecting children to maximizing profits—very different from the Orwellian quest for control. As Orwell himself wrote in his 1946 essay "The Prevention of Literature": "Any writer or journalist who wants to retain his integrity finds himself thwarted by the general drift of society rather than by active persecution. To exercise your right of free speech you have to fight against economic pressure and against strong sections of public opinion, but not, as yet, against a secret police force." From the Inquisition and book burnings to film ratings and copyright law, the cases explored here demonstrate that those who seek to understand information control in our society must look out for much more than just Big Brother.

Facing: Works of Aquinas Thwarting Others. Ceiling fresco in the Vatican, Rome. Photograph by Ada Palmer.

Censorship is as old as philosophy itself: The earliest documented endorsement of censorship in the Western intellectual tradition is this passage in Plato's *Republic*, which advocates banning Homer in his ideal city, saying that Homer teaches bad morals and incorrect theology through his unflattering depictions of the gods.

Censorship Today: The American Library Association's Office for Intellectual Freedom tracks when books are banned or challenged, usually when individuals demand that books be removed from libraries or classrooms. 2017's most challenged book was the 2007 young adult novel *Thirteen Reasons Why*, treating depression and teen suicide, which received fresh attention due to its new Netflix TV series. From 2000 to 2009 the OIF tracked 5,000+ book challenges, most from parents or library patrons, with accusations citing sexually explicit content, violence, profanity, "homosexuality," "religious viewpoint," "anti-family" messages, or "occult" or "Satanic" themes, an accusation often levied against the most frequently challenged series of recent decades, *Harry Potter*.

Above: Jay Asher, *Thirteen Reasons Why*, New York: Razorbill, 2007. *Gift of Ada Palmer.*

Facing: Papyri Fragment, *Iliad*, [150 CE-199CE]. Ms. 1063.

Plato on education (Book II: 337b-d):
"Then the first thing will be to establish a censorship of the writers of fiction, and let the censors receive any tale of fiction which is good, and reject the bad; and we will desire mothers and nurses to tell their children the authorised ones only. Let them fashion the mind with such tales, even more fondly than they mould the body with their hands; but most of those which are now in use must be discarded."

"Of what tales are you speaking?" he said.

"███████████ Those, I said, which are narrated by Homer and Hesiod, and the rest of the poets, who have ever been the great story-tellers of mankind."

Many Powerful Acts of Censorship are Unplanned: As the condition of this fragment demonstrates, papyrus, the main writing surface of the Roman Empire, was very fragile, and crumbled after a few centuries of active use. When the fall of Rome cut off access to Egyptian papyrus, Europe's libraries had only a few centuries to copy crumbling books onto parchment (animal skin), which was so expensive that producing one book could cost as much as building a house. Not everything was copied in time, and most now-lost works of antiquity were lost during this process. Since most scribes were monks, they prioritized texts relevant to their lives, which is why more writings of Saint Augustine made the cut than all pagan Latin authors put together.

Keeping Censors Up-To-Date: The Inquisition's famous *Index* strove to help censors and readers keep track of which books and authors were prohibited, or required to have select passages "expurgated" i.e. crossed out. First printed in 1551, the *Index* was updated regularly until the 20th edition of 1948. In 1966, during the reforms of Pope Paul VI, the *Index* was declared to no longer have the force of ecclesiastical law, though to this day it is supposed to have "moral force" for Catholics, warning of "writings which could endanger faith and morality." When this copy was printed in 1938, Catholic students assigned to read Machiavelli or Thomas Hobbes here at the University of Chicago were still expected to request special permission from a priest before doing so.

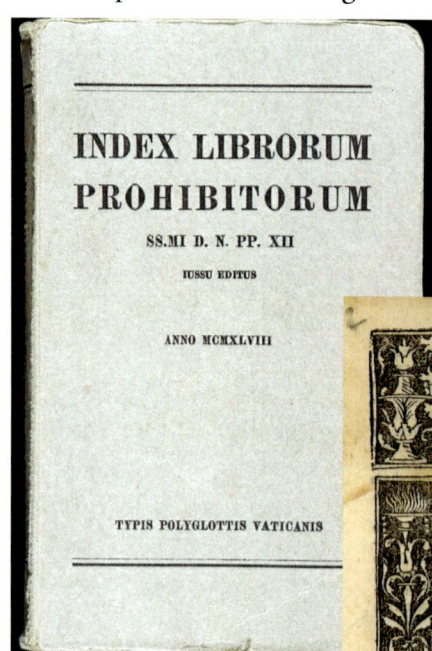

Left: *Index Librorum Prohibitorum: SS.MI D. N. PP. XII,* Italy: Typis Polyglottis Vaticanis, 1948. *Gift of Walter Kaegi.*

Right and Facing: Savonarola, *Tabule Sopra le Prediche del Reveredo,* Venice: Bernardino Benali, 1517. *On loan from Ada Palmer.*

[8]

Crowdsourcing the Inquisition: Unlike the imagined government of *1984*, the Inquisition was never powerful enough to police everyone and everything. One technique for expanding manpower was requiring book owners to cross out condemned passages themselves, as a condition of keeping the censored book. This volume collects the sermons of the firebrand preacher Girolamo Savonarola, burned at the stake in 1498 for his political activities. In 1559 the Inquisition banned his third sermon "Ecce gladius domini," and in this copy—which once belonged to a Jesuit college—someone has loyally cut out the forbidden sermon, and pasted over its remnants.

Right and Below: Francis Blackburne, *Remarks on Johnson's Life of Milton To which are added Milton's Tractate of edvcation and Areopagities.* London: s.n., 1780. PR3581.J7 Rare.

The Sin of "Killing" a Book: John Milton's *Areopagitica* is a foundational text in debates around freedom of expression. Milton had already been a target of censorship for defending divorce, but wrote this impassioned pamphlet—packed with literary references—to oppose a 1643 law mandating that all works be examined and licensed by government censors before they could be printed, as the Inquisition required in Catholic Europe. In 1945 George Orwell attended a celebration of the *Areopagitica*'s tercentenary, and was dismayed to find that speakers shied away from discussing the many books "killed" by wartime censorship in the UK and USA, and even defended the purges then happening in Soviet Russia. This and similar experiences shaped *1984*, which stands beside the *Areopagitica* as a pillar of censorship discourse.

Meticulous Record-Keepers: Jesuit missionary and prolific book-burner Antonín Koniáš assembled this, *A Key to Identifying and Eradicating Heretical Mistakes*, listing Czech language Protestant and anti-Catholic literature to be confiscated or burned. No one else in the period kept records of Czech publishing, so this work is now the foundation of Czech bibliography, and the only record of many works which—partly through Koniáš's efforts—do not survive.

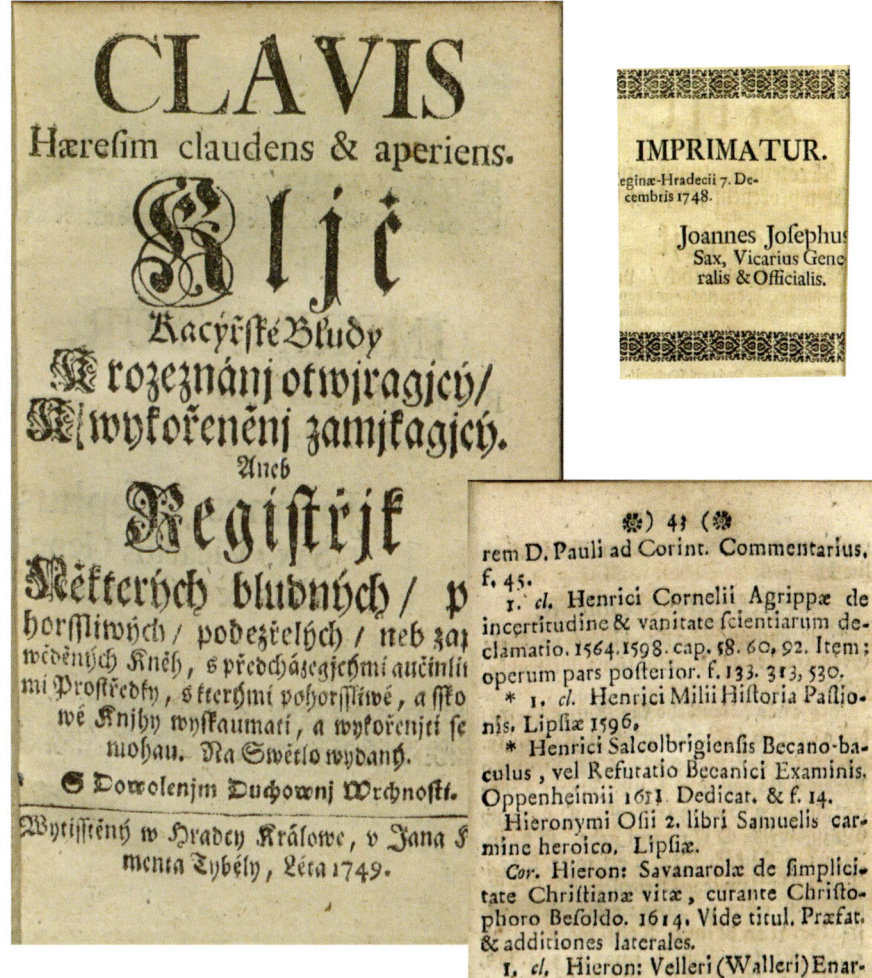

Above; Right: *Clavis haeresim claudens & aperiens*, Hradec Králové: Jana Klimenta Tybély, 1749. Z1019.C53 1749 Rare.

Reflecting Reality: *1984* was less fiction than many readers realize: in addition to satirizing the totalitarian realities of Stalinist Russia, Orwell's ironic Ministry of Truth reflected England's real life Ministry of Information which exerted enormous control over press and publications, justified as wartime necessity even when the war was over. In fact, Orwell's wife Eileen Blair worked as a government censor during the war. Orwell's famous line "We have always been at war with Eastasia" also mirrored the British Communist Party's flip-flopping on Nazism. As he described it:

"For years before September 1939 [a writer] was expected to be in a continuous stew about 'the horrors of Nazism' and to twist everything he wrote into a denunciation of Hitler: after September 1939, for twenty months he had to believe that Germany was more sinned against than sinning, and the word 'Nazi' omitted section had to drop right out of his vocabulary. Immediately after hearing the 8 o'clock bulletin on the morning ████████, he had to start believing once again that Nazism was the most hideous evil the world had ever seen."

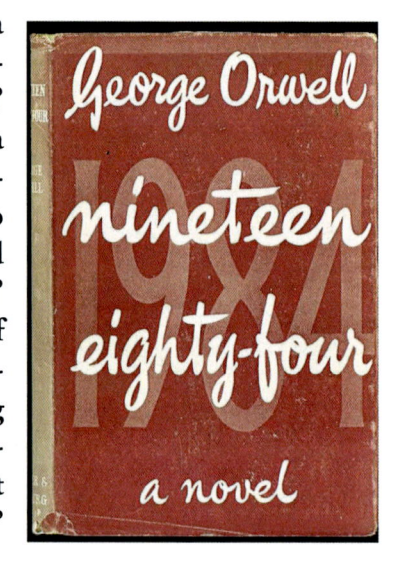

-"The Prevention of Literature," 1946

Above: George Orwell (1903-1950), *1984: A Novel*, London: Secker & Warburg, 1949. PR6029.R9N7 1949a c. 2 Rare.

Facing: George Orwell (1903-1950), *Nineteen Eighty-Four*, New York: Penguin, 2002. On loan from Ada Palmer.

Orwell's Legacy: In 2002 Penguin released this commemorative edition of *Nineteen Eighty-Four*, with the title and Orwell's name blacked out as if censored, as a tribute to the book's unique contributions to discourse about censorship. Orwell's novel cemented dystopia as a genre—joining Yevgeny Zamyatin's *We* (1921) and Aldous Huxley's *Brave New World*, and created new tools and imagery for discussing censorship—such as Big Brother, thought police, thoughtcrime, and doublethink—now in use around the globe.

PENGUIN BOOKS

COMPLETE UNABRIDGED

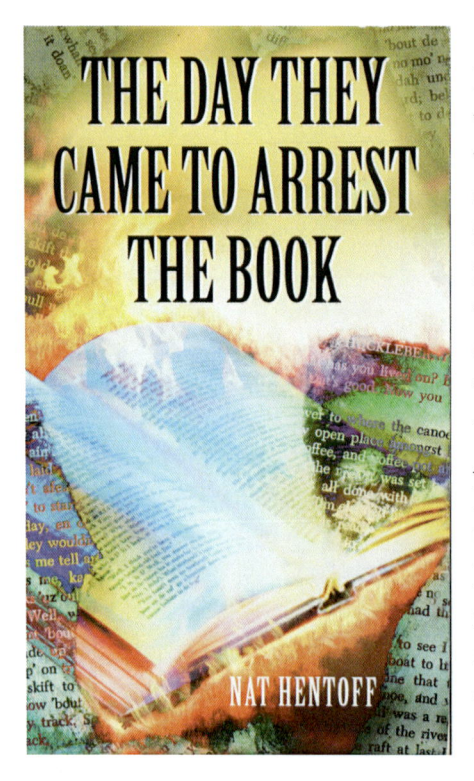

Painful Words: *Huckleberry Finn* was criticized for "coarse" language when first released, while in recent decades it has been criticized for racism. A 1996 lawsuit sought to block it from schools in Phoenix Arizona, while in 2011 controversy dogged a censored edition by NewSouth Books which replaced the n-word with the word "slave." *The Day they Came to Arrest the Book*, by journalist Nat Hentoff, tells a fictionalized account based on real cases when schools have been pressured and teachers fired over *Huckleberry Finn*, which remains among the most frequently challenged books in America, making the top ten in 2002 and 2007.

Above: Nat Hentoff, *The Day They Came to Arrest the Book*, New York: Dell Laurel-Leaf, 1982. *On loan from Ada Palmer.*

Right: Mark Twain (1835-1910), *The Adventures of Huckleberry Fin (Tom Sawyer's Comrade)*, London: Chatto & Windus, 1884. PS1305.A1 1884 Rare.

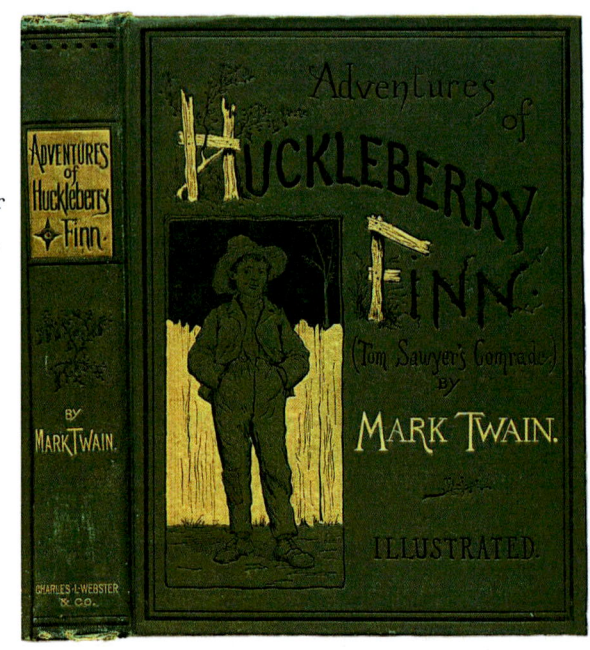

Misc Holds Press Conference With Former Maroon Editor

At an open Press Conference held by the "Misc" last Thursday, Mr. Alan Kimmel, ex-editor of the University of Chicago "Maroon," was called upon to give his views on the controversial issue leading to his dismissal as editor and also to relate some of his European experiences.

Before the guest speaker arrived, Sylvia Bacon presented some of the background material pertinent to the case. Her facts were based upon newspaper accounts of the story and information gleaned at the University of Chicago. Last May Mr. Kimmel was elected editor by the staff of the "Maroon," and published one issue of the paper. During the summer he went to attend the East Berlin Youth Festival of which he was a sponsor. On October 3rd, Mr. Kimmel had still not returned to the campus, and Dean Strozier dismissed him as editor of the "Maroon" on the grounds that "his actions in sponsoring and attending the East Berlin Youth Festival demonstrated his lack of qualification to edit a free and independent newspaper."

The Student Government met on October 5th to take action on the case but came to an impasse trying to decide whether or not Dean Strozier was just in his actions. Out of this impasse grew the compromise of October 10th which reinstated the paper as a legal publication of the University of Chicago and provided that the "Maroon" staff elect a new editor, which they did.

When Mr. Kimmel was about to board a plane at the Moscow airport someone rushed up to him to tell him, for the first time, about his dismissal from the editorship of the "Maroon." He looked at his informant in disbelief, but when he was shown the story in "Pravda," he realized that Dean Strozier had relieved him of his office. On returning to Chicago a few weeks after the college had opened—a perfectly permissible action at that University—he learned the facts of his dismissal.

Consequences

Kimmel's participation at the conference and the resulting involvement of the University in the conference had cost him his post. When questioned by students at the press conference, he said that he had gone to Berlin as an individual. When called upon to speak informally to people at the conference or to organize groups in countries behind the iron curtain, he gave his opinions on American life freely, but did not claim to represent anyone but himself. He spoke of Chicago University as a place where an individual may express himself freely, and described what he believed to be the prevalent opinions of students. He used his position as editor only for identification. Although that position probably helped him to get to the conference and afterwards to Russia and Poland, he said that he did not claim to represent the University. Dean Strozier had argued, he said, that in putting out a pamphlet to publicize the conference last spring, he had allowed his name, college and newspaper to appear on its masthead. Mr. Kimmel said that according to his request under the masthead was printed the words "organization for identification only."

Left: "Misc Holds Press Conference With Former Maroon Editor," Miscellany News, Vassar College, Volume XXVI, n. 11, 12 December 1951. Archives and Special Collections Library, Vassar College.

No Record is Spotless:
University of Chicago takes pride in its record on academic freedom, particularly the fact that it did not purge communist-affiliate faculty during the McCarthy era—a choice which sparked ferocious criticism and brought the university under FBI surveillance. Yet in 1951, Dean of Students Robert Stroizer shut down the student newspaper the *Maroon*, demanding that they replace their editor Alan D. Kimmel, who had attended a Communist World Youth rally in East Berlin. The *Maroon* considered going underground but capitulated, despite fierce campus protests and national coverage. Such cases demonstrate how difficult it is for complex institutions such as governments or universities to apply their own policies consistently, and that, if an apparatus capable of exercising censorship exists, even in the most trustworthy hands, it will likely be used someday.

Suspend MAROON;
Strozier ousts editor

CHICAGO MAROON

University of Chicago, October 5, 1951 — 31

ARE YOU WITH US?

Dean of Students Robert M. Strozier yesterday informed the MAROON that: (1) editor Alan Kimmel has been removed from his post on the MAROON, and that (2) after this issue, publication of the MAROON is to be suspended until Student Government takes steps for holding a new election "based on my recommendations of last Spring."

We feel that Strozier's action was arbitrary and unjustified, and we hereby issue a call to all students and faculty to attend a mass meeting to protest and petition against this move. The meeting will be held Tuesday, Oct. 9, at 7:30 p. m. in Mandel Hall.

Strozier's action raises, at the very least, a number of interesting legal questions. The Student Bill of Rights guarantees student publications freedom from "censorship or other pressure aimed at controlling editorial policy, with the free selection and removal of editorial staffs reserved to the organizations sponsoring these publications." The bill further states, "Where a publication enjoys a monopoly . . . the recognizing authority may properly insist on adequate safeguards in the constitution of the publication to insure that the requirements for membership shall be limited to interest, activity and journalistic ability. The staff of the publication shall institute these safeguards and shall be the sole judge of these qualifications. . . . Recognition shall not be used as a lever to control the purposes or programs of the organization . . . or to dictate its form of organization or procedure."

Strozier's action is an attempt to usurp these safeguards of student freedom contrary to all existing precedent. Strozier himself, in an interview about the MAROON with another newspaper last spring, told the South Town Economist, "The university responsibility is limited to determining that the publication is conducted on a sound financial basis and that it does not violate the law." He is also further reported as saying that the **UC administration has no legal control over the contents or policies of the MAROON.**

Strozier's action in removing Kimmel from his duly elected post as editor-in-chief is a violation of basic civil liberties which guarantee freedom of political thought. Further, it reveals the political motivation behind Strozier's entire course of action. The s t u d e n t code states, "The students of the University of Chicago, as individuals and as members of recognized student organizations, are expected to conduct themselves at all times in a manner which will reflect creditably on the university." In no case can Kimmel's political beliefs be construed as reflecting discredit on the university—**unless the university itself is submitting to the current nationwide pressure against freedom of political beliefs.** Certainly, Strozier's statement in his letter to Kimmel that "your action in sponsoring and attending the East Berlin Youth festival demonstrates your lack of qualification to edit a free and independent newspaper"—certainly this statement is indication enough of the political motivation behind this attack.

We feel strongly, furthermore, that Strozier has no legal basis whatsoever for his action in suspending publication of the MAROON. We are guaranteed freedom to elect our own officers in the Student Bill of Rights. We have fulfilled every requirement set down by the administration regarding campus organizations. By no stretch of imagination can any action by the MAROON staff be construed as justification for suspension of publication. No matter what the legal status of our editor-in-chief is, there is no basis for denying the MAROON the right to cope with this situation in any way it sees fit, as long as it follows university regulations.

Since, in our interpretation of the laws governing student organizations there is no legal basis for Strozier's action, we feel we are within our legal rights in continuing to publish the MAROON as long as it is possible to do so. While doing this, the MAROON will take all legal courses open to it to fight its battle and to retain our legitimate status on campus in accordance with the constitution and Bill of Rights. These courses include appeal to SG and to the Student-Faculty-Administration Court.

However, these courses may not be enough. The final decision as to whether the MAROON shall be forced from the campus at worst, or forced to take part in the establishment of a dangerous precedent at best, lies in the hands of our readers. We hereby appeal to the campus for moral, financial, and political support.

There is much the students and faculty can do. Circulate petitions. Participate in the protest meeting set for Tuesday in Mandel Hall. Protest directly to Strozier. In the forthcoming SG elections, support only those candidates who indicate their support of a press free and independent of administration control.

It's your fight as well as ours. **Are you with us?**

Ex-Editor comments

As a former MAROON editor, I was very much alarmed to hear of the unprecedented action of the Administration. In these times, when it is so important to keep all channels of communication open in the face of repressive influences, it was expected that the campus would remain steady during blows to freedom of expression elsewhere. It is especially significant that Mr. Kimmel was apparently trying in his post as a newspaper editor to further the cause of peace in the world through better communication between East and West. I hope that all who believe in the continuation of the independent spirit of the MAROON will oppose this move. The recent speeches in Chicago by the former La Prensa editors should leave fresh in your mind the penalty of failing to act in this matter.

Charles Garvin
Editor, 1950-51

Call protest meeting; Action comes suddenly

BULLETIN!

As the MAROON went to press at midnight, the executive board of Student Government was considering a proposal made by Merrill Freed and Lou Silverman which, after quoting articles from the Student Bill of Rights of the National Student Association stated that, "The executive board of Student Government condemns the removal of Mr. Kimmel and the suspension of the MAROON
see "Bulletin," page 11

by Fred Winsborg, acting editor-in-chief

The MAROON has been ordered suspended. Al Kimmel, constitutionally elected editor of the MAROON, has been ordered removed as its editor.

Both actions were taken by Dean of Students Robert M. Strozier in a surprise move early yesterday. Strozier handed a representative of the MAROON copies of letters to Kimmel and Student Government at 9 a.m. The reason for the suspension was given as Kimmel's sponsorship of and attendance at the Third World Festival of Youth and Students for Peace held this summer in Berlin. Strozier's letter states that these actions make Kimmel unfit "to edit a free and independent newspaper."

Waits for SG action

Strozier a n n o u n c e d he had

In a move to bring the present suspension controversy to campus, the MAROON is sponsoring a mass meeting, to be held in Leon Mandel Hall Tuesday, October 9, at 7:30 p. m. Admission to the event will be free, with all members of the UC community urged to attend and form opinions on the basis of verbal arguments presented by the participants in the case.

Dean of Students Robert Strozier, author of the decree removing MAROON editor Kimmel, and temporarily suspending the MAROON, has been invited to attend and present his case.

The MAROON viewpoint will be presented by editor-elect Kimmel if he is available at the time, or in his absence, by acting editor Fred Winsborg.

Ample time has been left on the agenda for questions from the floor of the meeting, to be directed toward the various participants.

taken this step pending Student Government arrangements for election of a new editor.

The move had the support of Chancellor L. A. Kimpton who stated, "I approve of Mr. Strozier's action and I do not see that Mr. Strozier could have taken any other action under the circumstances."

Admits lack of precedent

In an interview with the MAROON, Strozier stated that
see "MAROON," page 11

Step distresses students
Faculty found noncommital

MAROON reporters interviewed students on the campus, showing them Strozier's letter.

Nancy Mann—I see no relation between suspending the editor and suspending the paper.

Eva Fishell—What kind of academic freedom is this?

M. Guyan Basset—I have been expecting similar action for a long time.

Jim Redfield—This represents the triumph of American Imperi-
see "Students," page 12

In an attempt to sample faculty and administration opinion on the suspension of the MAROON, and the removal of its editor, the MAROON solicited comments by telephone. The following are representative of those called.

Anatol Rapoport, assistant professor of mathematical biology—"I have read Mr. Strozier's letter to Mr. Kimmel from which it appears that Mr. Kimmel's sponsoring and attending the East
see "Faculty," page 12

Read the documents

Mr. Alan D. Kimmel
1752 W. Albion Avenue
Chicago, Illinois

Dear Mr. Kimmel:

Your prolonged stay in Eastern Europe and failure to return to the University for registration make it necessary for me to write you a letter instead of talking with you about a very important matter.

I find it necessary to remove you immediately from the editorship of the MAROON. Your action in sponsoring and attending the East Berlin Youth Festival demonstrates your lack of qualification to edit a free and independent newspaper.

I am today writing the Student Government to request it to proceed at once with steps for a new election, based upon my recommendations of last spring. After the publication of the October 5th issue of the MAROON, publication is suspended until the Student Government has acted.

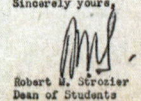

Sincerely yours,

Robert M. Strozier
Dean of Students

Staff to meet

There will be a regular MAROON staff meeting in the MAROON office Monday at 3:30 p.m. weather permitting.

Read the documents

Mr. Alan D. Kimmel
1752 W. Albion Avenue
Chicago, Illinois

Dear Mr. Kimmel:

Your prolonged stay in Eastern Europe and failure to return to the University for registration make it necessary for me to write you a letter instead of talking with you about a very important matter.

I find it necessary to remove you immediately from the editorship of the MAROON. Your action in sponsoring and attending the East Berlin Youth Festival demonstrates your lack of qualification to edit a free and independent newspaper.

I am today writing the Student Government to request it to proceed at once with steps for a new election, based upon my recommendations of last spring. After the publication of the October 5th issue of the MAROON, publication is suspended until the Student Government has acted.

Sincerely yours,

Robert M. Strozier
Dean of Students

Left and Facing: Newspaper article (reproduction), The Chicago Maroon, October 5, 1951.

Below: Newspaper article (reproduction), The Chicago Maroon, October 19, 1951.

THE CHICAGO MAROON

MAROON petitions for hearing in court

A MAROON petition asking for "a declaration of rights" enforced by "an injunction, or other appropriate order" is to be reviewed by the Student-Faculty-Administration Court. The petition, which was drawn up and will be presented by MAROON counsel Merrill Freed, UC law student, states: "Alan D. Kimmel was duly and properly elected editor-in-chief of the MAROON, in accordance with the MAROON constitution. Mr. Kimmel was recognized as ... editor-in-chief by the Office of the Dean of Students...

"Mr. Kimmel became a sponsor of the 'III World Festival of Youth and Students for Peace' in the Soviet zone of Berlin, to advance literature in the following form: 'Alan D. Kimmel, Editor, Chicago MAROON.' Immediately below the list of sponsors, on the same page and in the same type, appeared the following words: 'organizations listed for purposes of Identification only.' Mr. Kimmel also personally attended the said Festival."

Mr. Kimmel receives note On October 3, 1951, the following letter was addressed to Mr. Kimmel by the Dean of Students: "... Your action in sponsoring and attending the East Berlin Youth Festival demonstrates your lack of qualification to edit a free and independent newspaper ..." On October 10, the Student

see Petition, page 8

Maroon charges illegality

"The MAROON charges that the actions of the Dean of Students in removing Mr. Kimmel from the editorship of the MAROON and suspending publication of the MAROON for the reasons stated in his letter ... are

"... later that night, the MAROON staff declared that in view of the fact that Mr. Kimmel had not returned to campus and had thus been absent during the past two issues ... as well as during a time of grave crisis for the MAROON, a vacancy was created as of October 10, 1951, and not before. The MAROON staff proceeded to prepare for the election of a new editor in accordance with its constitution.

"On October 11, the Dean of Students lifted his order suspending the MAROON."

Reporter polls campus opinion; MAROON coverage criticized

by Dave Sher

Because of the "Great Debate" about the MAROON that has been going on for the past few weeks concerning who, what, why, when, and how a campus newspaper should be run, the MAROON this week decided to find out just what people on campus think. The question asked was, "What sort of news do you think the MAROON should carry?"

The answers:

George Sikes, Meadville Theological Seminary: "The MAROON should cover all news of interest to the students. It should primarily carry local news but should also carry news of national and international importance. Basically it should be a community newspaper, but of the community of the University of Chicago where people do think."

Eva Fisher, College: "I think the MAROON should have more coverage of campus events."

Harris Harteler, College: "The MAROON should be confined mostly to school activities. There are ample sources for politics in other than a campus newspaper."

Michael Halasz, Soc. Sci.: "The MAROON should confined itself to student affairs and things of interest to the student body."

Reed Searle, College: "The MAROON should branch out into some coverage of national and international affairs, so that we may get the students' views on them. In relation to what it does now, I appreciate the fact that it reviews downtown shows and movies."

Solvay Hermenson, College: "I think that the MAROON should publish more news of women's clubs."

Lloyd Barr, Bio. Sci.: "I think the MAROON should continue to cover news both outside and on campus, with perhaps two pages devoted to outside news (assuming at least a 12-page paper). This would include editorials on significant outside events. The MAROON should be more than an average college paper, since UC is more than the average college."

Joan Levey, Law: "I think that the MAROON should carry news of the campus and of those organizations, projects, etc., that are of interest to the campus. Campus news comes first."

Louise Schrope, Philosophy Dept.: "The MAROON should carry more news of clubs, campus organizations, etc. The calendar should be expanded."

Howard Bean, Phy. Sci.: "I would like to see more articles on places of interest in Chicago, for example, shows, restaurants, and things of that nature. Also, more news on changes of administration policy that have direct application to students."

T. Peabody, Philosophy Dept.: "I would like the MAROON to print articles on the faculty, based more on what they think and how they teach instead of straight biographies."

Lecture series under way

A series of lectures entitled, "The Western Tradition: Its Ideas and Issues," designed to develop an understanding of the cultural tradition of the Western World, is being given at the University College of the University of Chicago, 32 West Randolph street, beginning Friday, October 12, at 7:30 p.m. and ending in May.

The first speaker of the series will be Alexander Meiklejohn, noted lecturer and educator, who will deliver his talk on "The American Tradition of Freedom."

Succeeding lectures will include:

November 9, Mortimer J. Adler, professor of philosophy of law, University of Chicago, "Liberty: The Free Man and the Free Society";

December 14, Jacob Klein, dean of St. John's College, Annapolis, "Plato's Meno."

Speakers to resume MAROON seminars

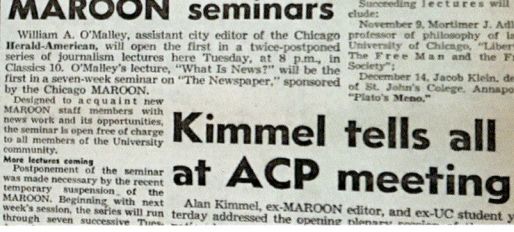

William A. O'Malley, assistant city editor of the Chicago Herald-American, will open the first in a twice-postponed series of journalism lectures here Tuesday, at 8 p.m. in Classics 10. O'Malley's lecture, "What Is News?" will be the first in a seven-week seminar on "The Newspaper," sponsored by the Chicago MAROON.

Designed to acquaint new MAROON staff members with newswork and its opportunities, the seminar is open free of charge to all members of the University community.

More lectures coming
Postponement of the seminar was made necessary by the recent temporary suspension of the MAROON. Beginning with next week's session, the series will run through seven successive Tues...

Kimmel tells all at ACP meeting

Alan Kimmel, ex-MAROON editor, and ex-UC student yesterday addressed the opening plenary session of...

[17]

2018: University of Chicago students protest the invitation of Trump associate Steve Bannon to speak on campus. In 2018, as in 1951, institutions like the University of Chicago have been both deeply split and internally inconsistent in their responses to the challenge of maintaining academic freedom in a heated political climate.

Above: Photograph, "Bannon Invitation Provokes Protest in Chicago," From Socialistworker.org, by Anthony Cappetta, 2018.

Below: University of Auckland *Capping Book*, 1950.

Students Under State Censorship: Not all students enjoy the protections (and challenges) of America's First Amendment. In 1950, students at the University of Auckland in New Zealand produced the annual magazine, shown on the opposite page, for capping, an annual event which celebrates graduation with pranks, satirical shows, and a parade. Their 1950 issue was considered too much, inciting public outrage and an order for the magazine's destruction. "Crudeness" was the common accusation, but one journalist mentioned that the magazine was also political, depicting an Orwellian future New Zealand conquered by America and exploited to develop new weapons of mass destruction. The crudest image in the magazine, a pornographic image of a young woman, is open facing a pre-written outraged letter, satirizing in advance the criticism student authors intended to incite. The letter is written in "madlib" style, with multiple choices to fill in each line; one set of selections yields a letter signed "MOTHER OF 10" who thought it was her "public duty" to register her extreme disgust at the "deplorable" student activities including the Capping Carnival and Procession which served as the "lowest example of student immorality"; the Capping Concert of which she notes that "such trash that should be banned from the public stage"; the Capping Ball she never went to, but which she heard "from a friend of my maiden aunt's sister that is was a disgusting scene of drunken debauchery"; and most of all *Capping Book* "the most immoral publication ever seen on sale here" which she would like to point out that it upsets her and should upset her country that "able-bodied men should waste time to produce such an indecent excrescence." The real backlash for the publication resulted in public demands for state intervention (possible under New Zealand law), and for stripping student funding and canceling future events. With their funds at risk, the Auckland students (like the 1951 *Maroon* editors) capitulated and (unlike the *Maroon* editors) apologized, and the majority of media coverage of the incident attacked student free speech instead of defending it. Most of the books were destroyed, but *Capping Book* continued, inciting another storm of censorship in 1969. In a May 1, 1969 article "Capping Book Is In Obscenity Game" in *the University of Auckland Student Magazine*, a student connected the 1950 and 1969 events, writing that, "[*Capping Book*] is not designed to assuage mothers of 10... We have no doubt, however, that mothers of 10 will buy *Capping Book*, even if only to engage in tut-tuting with a neighbor over the book fence." For more on New Zealand's censorship, and the impact of First Amendment's absence on a culture similar to the USA, see page 161.

NELVANA
www.nelvana.com
Pioneer
CARDCAPTORS
Power Match
DVD
VIDEO

How Do YOU Define Censorship?

"Informal censorship is often fiercer, tougher, and more violent than official censorship, and its inherently voluntary and curious nature is the most accurate word."
– Ghazi Abdul Rahman Al Gosaibi, *Bye Bye London and Other Articles*
2007

"If the human body is obscene, complain to the manufacturer!"
– Larry Flynt, *Sex, Lies & Politics: The Naked Truth*, 1956

Censorship has blurry edges, cases which may feel a little bit like censorship but not quite, or which seem like censorship to some individuals but not to others. Is it censorship for a library to exclude books that deny the Holocaust? For a bookstore to refuse to stock books based on their price? For an editor to rewrite a story for a new audience? Is there some information that should be restricted? Hate speech? Bomb designs? Personal records? Misinformation? Pornography? Are some materials inappropriate for certain readers? Questions like these are much of what makes censorship so hard to legislate, or even discuss. The objects in this section are examples of these blurry edges, and challenge you decide where *you* draw the line.

Invasive Editing: *Cardcaptor Sakura* (1996-2000) is a Japanese girls' comic book by the all-female manga group Clamp. A 70-episode TV version aired in Japan from 1998-2000. When it was dubbed into English, instead of 70 episodes American TV aired *Cardcaptors*, a version cut down to 39 episodes. The change? The network thought a male main character would be more popular, so deleted footage of the "magical girl" protagonist and altered the script to make her male rival the central character. The American company paid for the right to edit the series, and let another company release the unedited version on VHS and DVD, so was it censorship? In a clearer act of censorship, the dub turned the series' same-sex couples into "cousins."

Facing: *Cardcaptors*, DVD, 2000. *On loan from Ada Palmer.*

Private Censorship: In these volumes two different seventeenth-century book owners, both in the privacy of their own homes, take opposite responses to the explicit content in Renaissance romantic poetry. In the Pontano, the owner has crossed out naughty words and written criticisms in the margins, without any effort to force this on other copies. Is that censorship? The Petrarch, on the other hand, was printed already bowdlerized, with new clean language carefully inserted to make the poems scan. The owner has pasted over the bowdlerized verses and written the explicit originals in by hand, de-censoring Petrarch but erasing the original lines written by the anonymous bowdlerizer. The latter practice was sufficiently common that some bowdlerized Petrarch editions included notes at the end specifying the altered words, to help the reader restore them if desired.

Facing: Petrarch, *Rime du Mess. Francesco Petrarca*, Venice: Appresso il Remondini con licenza de sup. E Pruiil., 1751. *On loan from Ada Palmer.*

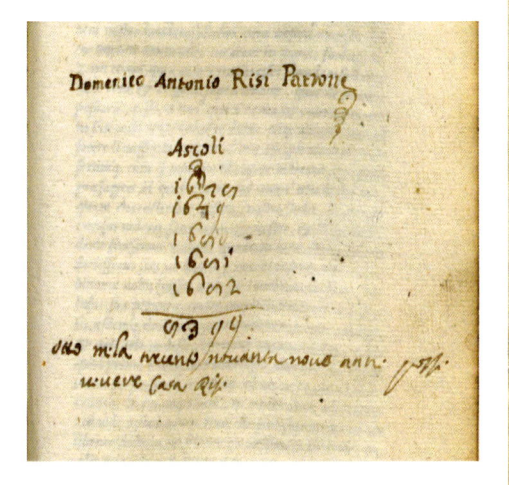

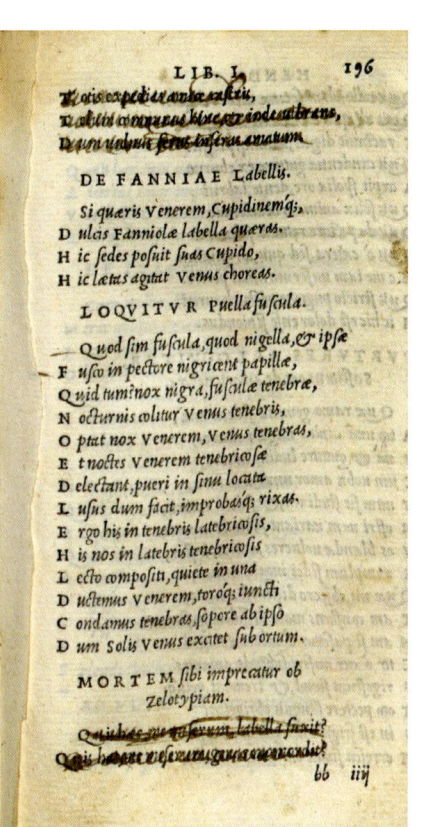

Above and Left: Giovanni Gioviano Pontano (1429-1503), *Pontani Opera*, Venice: Aldus Manutius, 1533. PA8570.P5A16 1533 c. 2 Rare.

To the left, you can see the stubs of pages cut out by the owner.

[23]

Left, Below, and Facing: *Regulae Grammaticae et Rhetoricae.* Ms 99 MsCdx. S.l.: ca. 1450.

Trivial Acts: This Renaissance grammar textbook is peppered with pornographic doodles, likely added by a university student. A later user of the textbook—an expensive manuscript which would have passed through many hands—cut some of the doodles out of the pages, smearing others with ink to obscure them. This microscopic battle in the margins did not have broad consequences like banning a book, but could influence the next student reader's attitudes toward the relative acceptability of censorship and sexual expression. Is such censorship problematic or benign?

[24]

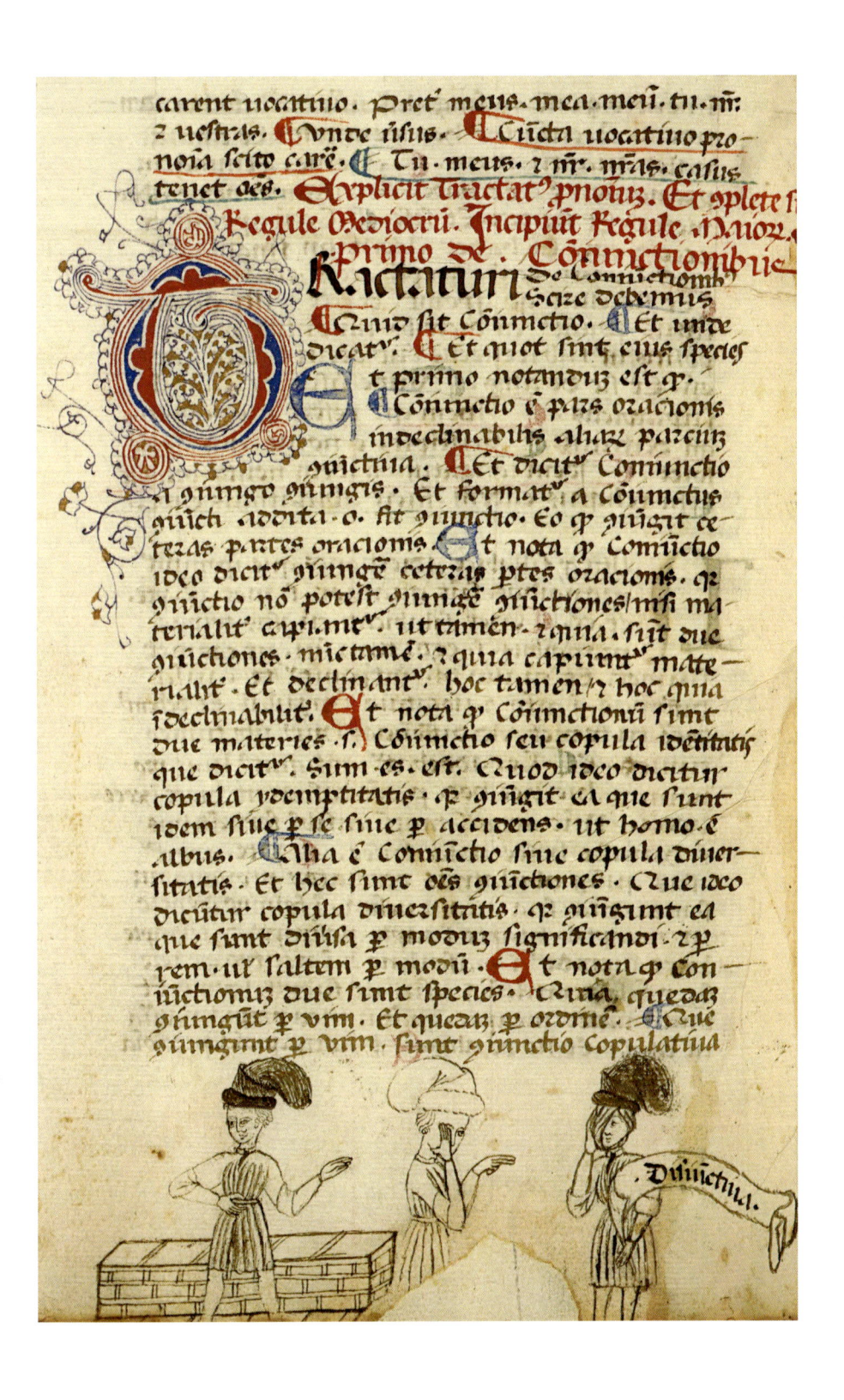

carent uocatiuo. preter meus. mea. meū. tu. m̄:
z uestras. ⁋ Vnde uersus. ⁋ Cuncta uocatiuo pro-
noia scito carē. ⁋ Tu. meus. z m̄r. m̄as. casus
tenet des. ⁋ Explicit tractatꝰ pnoīuz. Et ꝯplete ſ
Regule Mediocrii. Incipiūt Regule Maior.
primo de Coniunctionibuſ

R̄.ictatur de Coniunctionib;
ſcire debemus.
⁋ Quid sit Coniūctio. ⁋ Et unde
dicatur. ⁋ Et quot sint eius species
z primo notandum est q̄
⁋ Coniūctio ē pars oracionis
indeclinabilis aliaȝ parciū
giūctiua. ⁋ Et dicitur Coniunctio
a giūgo giūgis. Et formatur a Coniunctus
giūcti. addita. o. fit giūctio. Eo q̄ giūgit ceteras partes oracionis. ⁋ Et nota q̄ Coniūctio
ideo dicitur giūgere ceteras ptes oracionis. q̄
giūctio nō potest giūgere giūctiones, nisi ma-
terialit̄ capiantur. ut tamen. z quia. sūt due
giūctiones. m̄ tamen. z quia capiuntur mate-
rialit̄. Et declinantur. hoc tamen ⁊ hoc quia
ſ declinabilis. ⁋ Et nota q̄ Coniūctionū sunt
due materies. ſ. Coniūctio seu copula identitatis
que dicitur. sum es. est. Quod ideo dicitur
copula ydemptitatis. q̄ giūgit ea que sunt
idem siue p̄ se siue p̄ accidens. ut homo ē
albus. ⁋ Alia ē Coniunctio siue copula diuersitatis. Et hec sunt des giūctiones. Que ideo
dicitur copula diuersitatis. q̄ giūgunt ea
que sunt diuisa p̄ modū significandi. z p̄
rem. ut saltem p̄ modū. ⁋ Et nota q̄ con-
iūctionuȝ due sunt species. Quia quedaȝ
giūgūt p̄ uim. Et quedaȝ p̄ ordinē. ⁋ Que
giūgunt p̄ uim. sunt giūctio copulatiua

Coniunctiua.

Protecting Innocence: In this children's Shakespeare, "any incident, passage, or even word which might be thought exceptionable by the strictest delicacy, is entirely omitted, and on no occasion has the fair purity of the youthful mind been for one moment forgot." This volume did not aim to replace the original plays, but certainly presented a distorted impression of Shakespeare's works and ideas. Protecting children has been a perennial justification for censorship from Plato's criticisms of Homer to contemporary America, where it motivates 300-500 school and library challenges every year.

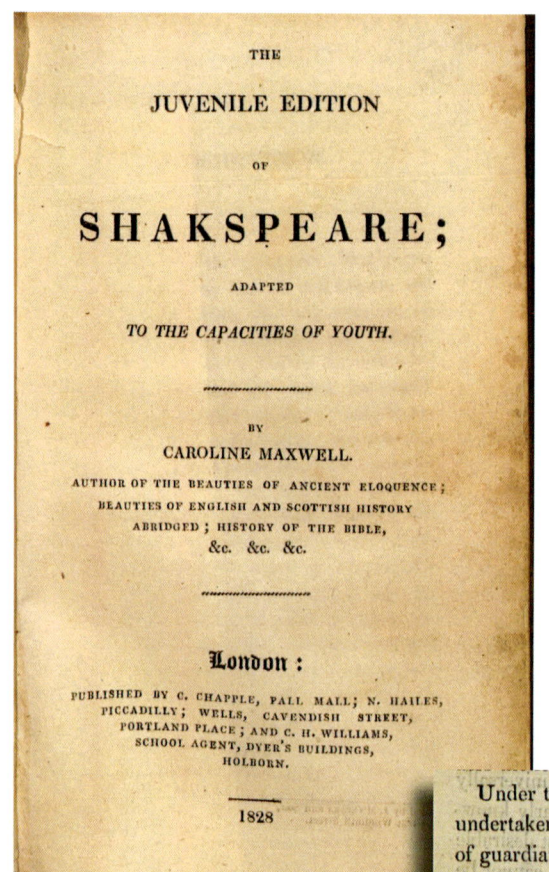

Left and Below: Caroline Elizabeth Sarah Maxwell, *The uvenile Edition of Shakspeare*, London: C. Chapple, 1828. PR2877. M39 1828 Rare. *The ernard Sahlins Collection of Theatrica Works.*

Under these considerations this work has been undertaken, and to the discernment of parents, of guardians, and preceptors, it is submitted for the proof. It may also be necessary to state, that any incident, passage, or even word which might be thought exceptionable by the strictest delicacy, is entirely omitted, and on no occasion has the fair purity of the youthful mind been for one moment forgot, in offering, and in selecting these pages for their perusal.

Relationships of Power: This final volume of the *Twilight* series was the first with explicit sex. In the copy shown below, the mother of the underage reader cut out the pages with the sex scene and obscured related passages with whiteout and sharpie. What was done to this book —removing pages, obscuring remnants—is identical to what was done to the copy of Savonarola's sermons in the adjacent case, but the acts feel different, since that was done by order of the Inquisition, this by a parent. Such contrasts show how the relationship of power between censor and censored is a major factor in how we feel about censorship. Tellingly, the mother was alerted to the sex scene by the reader's elder sister, but the sister did not think to warn the mother about the graphically violent birth scene later in the same book.

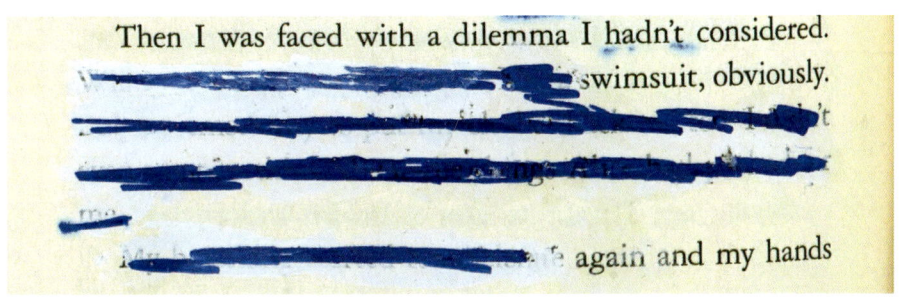

> Then I was faced with a dilemma I hadn't considered.
> ——————————————— swimsuit, obviously.
> ———————————————————————
> ———————————————————————
> ——————————— again and my hands

Wish you could see the whole page? We had trouble clearing the copyright to reproduce the text on the original page, another example of copyright's entanglement with censorship.

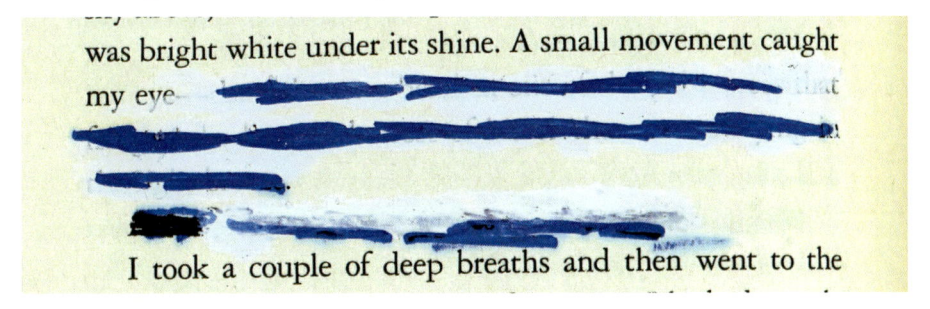

> was bright white under its shine. A small movement caught my eye ————————————————————
> ———————————————————————
> ———————————————————————
> I took a couple of deep breaths and then went to the

Above: Stephenie Meyer, *Twilight: Breaking Dawn*, New York: Little, Brown, and Co., 2008. *On loan from the Palid family.*

Following:: Pollard, Edward Alfred. *The Lost Cause: A New Southern History of the War of the Confederates.* New York, Baltimore: E. B. Treat & co.; J. S. Morrow; [etc., etc.], 1868. E487.P77.

> We shall not enter upon the discussion of the moral question of slavery. But we may suggest a doubt here whether that odious term "slavery," which has been so long imposed, by the exaggeration of Northern writers, upon the judgment and sympathies of the world, is properly applied to that system of servitude in the South which was really the mildest in the world; which did not rest on acts of debasement and disenfranchisement, but elevated the African, and was in the interest of human improvement; and which, by the law of the land, protected the negro in life and limb, and in many personal rights, and, by the practice of the system, bestowed upon him a sum of individual indulgences, which made him altogether the most striking type in the world of cheerfulness and contentment. But it is not necessary to prolong this consideration.* For, we repeat, the slavery question was not a moral one in the North, unless, perhaps, with a few thousand persons of disordered conscience. It was significant only of a contest for political power, and afforded nothing more than a convenient ground of dispute between two parties, who represented not two moral theories, but hostile sections and opposite civilizations.
>
> In the ante-revolutionary period, the differences between the populations of the Northern and Southern colonies had already been strongly developed. The early colonists did not bear with them from the mother-country to the shores of the New World any greater degree of congeniality than existed among them at home. They had come not only from different stocks of population, but from different feuds in religion and politics. There could be no congeniality between the Puritan exiles who established themselves upon the cold and rugged and cheerless soil of New England, and the Cavaliers who sought the brighter climate of the South, and drank in their baronial halls in Virginia confusion to roundheads and regicides.
>
> In the early history of the Northern colonists we find no slight traces
>
> ---
> * It may not be improper to note here a very sententious defence of the moral side of slavery occurring in a speech delivered, in 1856, by Senator Toombs of Georgia, in the Tremont Temple at Boston. It is briefly this: "The white is the superior race, and the black the inferior; and subordination, with or without law, will be the status of the African in this mixed society; and, therefore, it is the interest of both, and especially of the black race, and of the whole society, that this status should be fixed, controlled, and protected by law."
>
> The whole ground is covered by these two propositions: that subordination is the necessary condition of the black man; and that the so-called "slavery" in the South was but the precise adjustment of this subordination by law.

Distortion and Omission: The Lost Cause intellectual movement—named for this book—aimed to legitimize the Confederacy by minimizing slavery's role in the American Civil War and downplaying the harshness of the institution. The movement produced both carefully crafted histories and fiction depicting happy slaves who loved their masters and opposed abolition and the North. Though all histories are shaped by authors' views, the Lost Cause's propagandistic effo ts had consequences similar to information control, obscuring the truth and leaving an enduring stamp on American discourse. But is it censorship? And would removing Lost Cause works from a library be censorship?

Below: Memo to FAS Chapters, "Attack on the AEC," May 25, 1949. Atomic Scientists of Chicago. Records. Box 1, Folder 1.

> The consensus in office discussion (over a hot typewriter or mimeographing machine) goes somewhat as follows. We are not opposed to decent, sober Congressional investigations of AEC performance or Lilienthal's record as chairman. There is no reason to whitewash obvious errors. If there has been laxity in security in really sensitive areas they should be tightened up. Likewise, for inefficiency in administration. But none of the charges so far trotted out appear to be important enough to warrant a general indictment of the AEC. The country would be in a better position to judge the situation, as we have pointed out before, if there were less secrecy about many things which do not require it.

> Concerning two of the charges we can speak immediately and with some authority. Freistadt's fellowship could in no way threaten security, the Commission is completely in the clear here, the case is at worst unfortunate. In the Edelman case the Commission will deserve criticism only if they accede to withdrawing the fellowship. There is no evidence to show that he was any more than mildly interested in the Communist Party six years ago when American-Soviet "friendship" was the order of the day. He stoutly asserts his loyalty and anti-Communism. We have a responsibility here to make clear the distinction between disloyalty and failure of clearance for secret work—also, the completely non-sensitive nature of non-secret fellowships. Especially we need to point out the threat to education and science involved in the hysterical, uninformed attitude of certain Congressmen.

"The Problem of Secrecy": The Cold War was a war of information. This caused all sorts of inefficienies and security issues to become of national importance. In the "Attack on the AEC" Chicago scientists express their fear that the new government strictures will needlessly produce obstacles for scientific research. While they agree that sensitive information should be kept secret, they think that to increase all security clearance and to launch mass investigations is a waste of time. In the "Problem of Secrecy" article series, Baldwin warns of the threat of "over-secrecy." Further, he warns that in the ongoing discussions for plans about combatting espionage and "voluntary censorship" will be a "wedge in the door of freedom."

Following: News Clippings, The papers of the Bulletin of Atomic Scientists, Box 1, Folder 8.

"The Problem of Secrecy: Forrestal Is Ready to Discuss Means for 'Voluntary Censorship' of News" by Hanson W. Baldwin, *New York Times,* March 2, 1948.

> "Secrecy and censorship, ordinarily, are incompatible with democracy, yet a new importance has been attached to both—particularly in military minds—during the present tense state of the world, and since the birth of the atomic age. ▬ But the history of mankind shows that fear always has been used to restrict freedom."

> "Take the matter of secrecy," [David E Lilenthal, the chairman of the Atomic Energy Commission] said. "It is generally assumed by those unfamiliar with how scientific and technical progress comes about—especially in a democracy such as we enjoy—that secrecy and (military) security are synonymous***Now the fact is that secrecy, applied in a stupid and hysterical and demagogic way, can actually impair and weaken our security.*** We need ideas if we are to keep our lead (in atomic energy) and increase it. Where will the ideas that will push us ahead rapidly come from? In what kind of soil do new ideas grow? In the past, we have relied upon competition, with the free use of information the broadest kind of competition, and the cross-fertilization of many minds. New ideas require not only inspiration and perspiration but information*** it is vital that the public understand that we pay a price for secrecy in the technical field; that if we were to impose secrecy unintelligently, the price of secrecy in terms of our own military security would then be so high as to impair, rather than strengthen, our own security."

"The Problem of Secrecy: Forrestal, Editors Will Meet Today to Weigh 'Voluntary Censorship' Plan" by Hanson W. Baldwin, *New York Times,* March 3, 1948.

> "'Voluntary censorship' thus can be used—especially when Government-directed and sponsored as in this case—as a powerful restraining influence on the flow of information. Indeed, the formalization of any type of censorship in time of peace—except the censorship, self-imposed, of responsibility to the national interest—can be a wedge in the door of freedom."

Facing: "The Problem of Secrecy: Censorship Cannot Guard our Security Without Infringing Our Basic Freedoms" by Hanson N. Baldwin, *New York Times,* March 7, 1948.

THE NEW YORK TIMES, SUNDAY, MARCH 7, 1948.

The Problem of Secrecy

Censorship Cannot Guard Our Security Without Infringing Our Basic Freedoms

By HANSON N. BALDWIN

The problem of preserving essential military secrecy in the atomic age without infringing basic democratic freedoms cannot be solved by Government censorship, no matter in what guise.

A sense of far greater responsibility to the national interest than ever before in history on the part of all information media is basic to the solution of this problem. The press, the radio, the magazine and the motion picture, individually and collectively, must accept the responsibilities of freedom as well as its advantages.

The advisability of publishing military information must be weighed in each instance in the scales of the national interest and must be viewed against the background of the greatest good for the greatest number.

Press associations, radio organizations and the Government itself must constantly stress and emphasize the responsibility of the media, not only in defending the basic freedoms but in promoting the national security. The industry must police itself.

But the Government, too, has obligations that it must assume if vital military information is not to fall into the hands of potential enemies. These obligations cannot be satisfied by restricting or classifying information or by imposing greater and greater secrecy upon its own employes; reasonable steps of this nature may help, but they will not suffice and they may well reduce efficiency by too much compartmentalization.

First and foremost, the military must eliminate some of their own mistakes. The Poles discovered that we were attempting to take aerial photographs of their terrain from a plane assigned to our military attaché in Poland because Army orders transferring the aerial photographer to Warsaw were misdirected from this country, addressed to "Chief of Staff, Warsaw." The orders were delivered to the Polish Army headquarters.

During the war a similar mistake sent some important "top secret" papers dealing with the projected invasion of Normandy to a civilian address in Chicago.

At Los Alamos, photographs dealing with the atom bomb were taken from the files by some of the Army's own enlisted personnel, who obviously were not well checked, although entrusted with highly confidential work.

Security "checks" of persons engaged in highly secret Government research sometimes are completed after the person concerned has finished the job.

In other words, the information media of the country are not responsible for many of the most important "leaks"; Government's own inefficiency and carelessness are often to blame.

Threat of Espionage

The other major threat to the country's real military secrets is espionage. Espionage rings ordinarily are subject to reasonable surveillance and control; today they have become more dangerous than ever before, because they are aided within the country by Communists and Left Wingers whose strange philosophy of "loyalty" puts Moscow before Washington. To meet treason, disloyalty, the termitic tactics of communism and espionage, more deftness and skill and effort than ever before are necessary.

The Federal Bureau of Investigation is entrusted — properly — with this counter-espionage and counter-treason mission, and the bureau must have ample funds and facilities to carry out its work.

But the FBI is primarily a criminal investigation agency and it has often applied these methods to the far more delicate task of counter-espionage. Improvement in its tactics and techniques and quieter and less self-advertising methods are essential to a sound security. The bureau may need the help of modified legislation, but any such proposals ought to be examined with the greatest of care, for espionage acts, improperly legislated, can have grave consequences to freedom.

The FBI also has been entrusted with the important and difficult job of making "loyalty checks" of Government employes. In pursuance of this task the FBI has insisted that its reports and records cannot possibly be open to those it accuses and its position has been upheld. This ruling is repugnant to American tradition, which believes that the accused has the right to face the accuser and to examine the evidence against him. Perhaps equally important, it assumes on the part of the FBI an infallibility and efficiency which the FBI has not always had.

Check of FBI Is Urged

The failure to subject the "evidence" of the FBI to examination and cross-inspection in "loyalty check" cases can encourage sloppy investigative work; shadowy accusations, rumors and hearsay might tend to substitute for fact. Secrecy of some of the FBI records is, of course, essential to sound counter-espionage and counter-treason work. But to promote the efficiency of that work as well as to protect American basic freedoms, the FBI, now endowed with this new grant of power, ought to be subject to the same sort of quiet close Congressional scrutiny to which the Atomic Energy Commission is subject. Only by some such means can we both safeguard our liberties and increase the efficiency of our spy-catching organization.

But these means, rather than attempts to abridge or restrict the flow of information, should be the real safeguards of our vital military secrets. "Freedom of the press" is a basic freedom; it must be guarded well, for eternal vigilance is the price of all freedom. We have few real secrets, but we should keep them well. If we are strong we need not fear spies or "leaks." Super-secrecy, and censorship—tacit or actual—is not only inimical to freedom; it may be revelatory of something wrong within the Government. It is a sign of weakness, not of strength.

As Byron Price said in discussing his wartime experience as head of the Office of Censorship:

"No one who does not dislike censorship should ever be permitted to exercise censorship. The first and last principle to be remembered * * * is that censorship should come into being solely as an instrument of war."

Frontispicio. Tom. 1. y 2.

EL INGENIOSO HIDALGO
DON
QUIXOTE DE LA
MANCHA.

Antonio Carnicero la inv.y dibujó. Fernando Selma la gravó en Madrid 1780.

The Plural Inquisitions

No censoring body in history captures our imagination like the infamous Catholic Inquisition. Despite its claims of universality, the real Inquisition was a far cry from the centralized and all-pervasive institution its architects aspired to create. A world where it took weeks to ride from town to town or months to sail from shore to shore made truly universal information control an impossibility. While Rome declared its authority on paper, numerous centers of Inquisition activity multiplied across Europe and beyond, spearheaded by local authorities from kings, queens, and dukes to monastic orders, universities, city governments, colonial governors, and individual bishops. The Roman *Index of Banned Books* raced to keep track of new authors condemned by distant branches, and rival indexes were printed by other Catholic authorities, such as Spain and Portugal. Inquisitors also depended on local governments to cover the considerable costs of arrests, jails, torturers, and executions, and civil powers used their control over infrastructure and purse strings to manipulate local Inquisitions, wielding them against personal and political enemies while protecting friends and favorites. The inconsistency of these plural Inquisitions had very different impacts in different corners of the globe.

Created in Haste, Repurposed in Crisis

The Inquisition transformed repeatedly in response to perceived crises. The first inquisitors were created in the 1100s when secular and religious authorities demanded a legal framework to combat the spreading Cathar and Waldensian heresies. Monastic orders, especially the scholarly Dominicans, were trusted with the process, and by 1252 the pope authorized the use of torture in interrogations. This decentralized system was soon adapted to new uses, including witchcraft trials and policing public morals. The next crisis came with the expulsion of the Jews from Spain. Anxious that Jews who had converted to avoid expulsion were secretly returning to Judaism,

Ferdinand of Aragon and Isabella of Castile established the Spanish Inquisition in 1478, which—thanks to royal funding and enthusiasm—was far more powerful and active than Rome's. Portugal established a similar Inquisition in 1536. Two more crises joined these. First the printing press let books proliferate by the thousand, which led Rome to issue a bull in 1515 requiring that all books be examined by a Church authority before they were printed. Then the advent of the Protestant Reformation in 1517 explosively increased Rome's fears of printed heresy, leading to the founding of the Holy Office of the nquisition in 1542. Early Catholic lists of prohibited books were printed in the 1530s-1540s in the Netherlands, Paris, and Venice. Rome's first *Index*, which claimed authority over all Christendom, was printed in 1557, but quickly replaced by the expanded Index of 1559 which focused on Protestantism. Over the next centuries, the Inquisition continued to transform in response to sequential crises, first scientific attacks on Aristotle, then the Enlightenment, communism, Darwinism, and others.

A Brief History of Book Burning

We can largely divide book burnings into three kinds: eradication burnings which seek to destroy a text, collection burnings which target a library, and symbolic burnings which intend to send a message, but do not aim to destroy a text. The earliest known book burnings are one mentioned in the Hebrew Bible (Jeremiah 36), then Qin Dynasty China (213-210 BC). Christian book burning began after the Council of Nicea, when Emperor Constantine ordered the burning of works of Arian (non-Trinitarian) Christianity. After 1450 the movable type press made eradication burnings of published material effectiely impossible unless one seized the whole print run before copies disseminated, but even the Inquisition rarely succeeded in such interventions. Instead the Inquisition practiced frequent symbolic book burning, especially in the Enlightenment, when a condemnation from Rome required Paris to publicly burn one or a few copies of a book, while all knew many more remained. When the beloved *Encyclopédie* was condemned, French authorities tasked to burn it burned Jansenist theological writings in its place, a symbolic act two steps removed from harming the original. Since print's advent eradication burnings have diminished, though collection burnings continue, often targeting communities—such as Protestant or Jewish communities—language groups—such as indigenous texts in Portuguese-held Goa (India)—or state or institutional archives, which contain unique content even in an age of print. Regime changes and political unrest have long been triggers for archive burnings, such as the burning of the National Archives of Bosnia and Herzegovina in 2014. Some book burnings were the result of smaller scale conflicts, as in 1852 when Armand Dufau, in charge of the school for the blind in Paris, ordered the burning of all books in the newly-invented braille system, of which he disapproved. Nazi burnings of Jewish and "un-German" material employed eradication rhetoric but were mainly collection burnings, as when youth groups burned 25,000 books from university libraries in 1933, or symbolic burnings, performing destruction to spread fear among foes and excitement among supporters while many party members retained or sold valuable books stolen from Jewish collections rather than destroying them. Archived documents and historic manuscript collections remain most vulnerable to eradication burning, such as those burned in Iraq's national Library in 2003, in two libraries in Timbuktu in 2013, and others recently burned by ISIS. Large-scale book burnings in America include New York Society for the Suppression of Vice (founded 1873) which boasted of burning 15 tons of books and nearly 4 million "lewd" pictures, and symbolic burnings of comic books in 1948 and communist material during the Second Red Scare of the 1950s. Since then, most book burnings in the USA have been small-scale symbolic burnings of works such as *Harry Potter*, books objected to in schools or college classrooms, or Bibles or Qur'ans. In a rare 2010 case of an attempted eradication burning, the Pentagon bought and burned nearly the whole print run of Anthony Shaffer's *Operation Dark Heart*, which—they said —contained classified information.

Der schelmē zūfft

Die schelmen zunfft hatt mich erwelt
Und für eyn schreyber har gestelt
Für sy alle vornan oran
Den ich eyn schelmen kenen kan

Censorship Before or After?

"That no book be Printed, unlesse the Printers and the Authors name, or at least the Printers be register'd. Those which otherwise come forth, if they be found mischievous and libellous, the fire and the executioner will be the timeliest and the most effectuall remedy, that mans prevention can use."

–Milton, *Aeropagitica*, 1644

"Licensing and Persecution of Conscience are two Sisters that ever go hand in hand together, being both founded upon one and the same Principle: Therefore to Asperse the one, permit me to Defame the other." – Charles Blount, *A Just Vindication of Learning*, 1678

As the Reformation heated up, both Protestant and Catholic regions created diverse laws aiming to control and label the dizzying produce of the still-multiplying printing press. Catholic lands, and some Protestant ones, required all books to receive a license or imprimatur ("let it be printed") before they were printed, effectively pre-banning all works. Others allowed free printing but would ban and confiscate books afterward and prosecute printer and author if the work was judged to be dangerous. Such policies often banned anonymous works, and required all books to include the printer's address. Thus in his *Aeropagitica*, subtitled "For the Liberty of Unlicenc'd Printing" Milton was not defending full freedom of expression as we understand it today, but defended prosecuting after publication rather than censoring before. While we would call both an unfree press, Milton argued that censorship before publication twisted the author into writing for the censor rather than for the public. He also feared that there would be a scarcity of people "both studious, learned, and judicious" qualified to judge books. In many real cases of pre-pub-lication censorship in England and elsewhere, we see censors—usually scholars themselves—take great liberties, sometimes letting radical mate-rial slip through if they themselves were sympathetic, other times making changes to content or style which had no connection to ideology or policy.

Facing and Following: Thomas Murner (1475-1537), *Der Schelmen Zunft*, [Frankfort]: s.n., 1512. PT1749.S3 1881 Rare.

Word and Image: *The Great Lutheran Fool,* by the Catholic satirist Thomas Murner, was banned and confiscated by the Protestant authorities of Strasburg. The pamphlet's woodcut prints demonstrate the inflammtory potential of combining printed text with images, especially when visual literacy far exceeded textual literacy.

Practical (Anti-)Magic: Composed in the early 1360's by Inquisitor General of Aragon Nicholas Eymerich, the *Directorium Inquisitorum* compiled then known witchcraft treatises along with practical guides confiscated from suspected heretics throughout the Iberian peninsula. Eymerich's work highlighted the demonic workings inherent in all heretical rituals and described various means of torture thought to elicit a confession from those accused of participating in such rites. The *Directorium* remained highly influential for the Spanish Inquisition well into the seventeenth century.

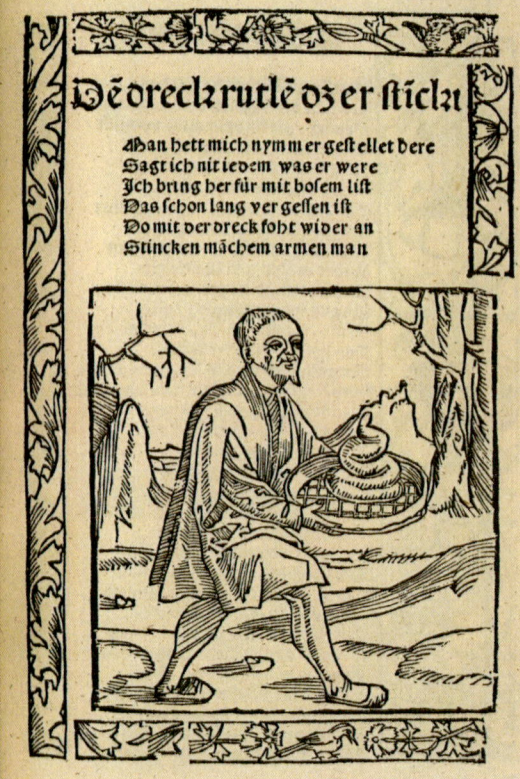

[38]

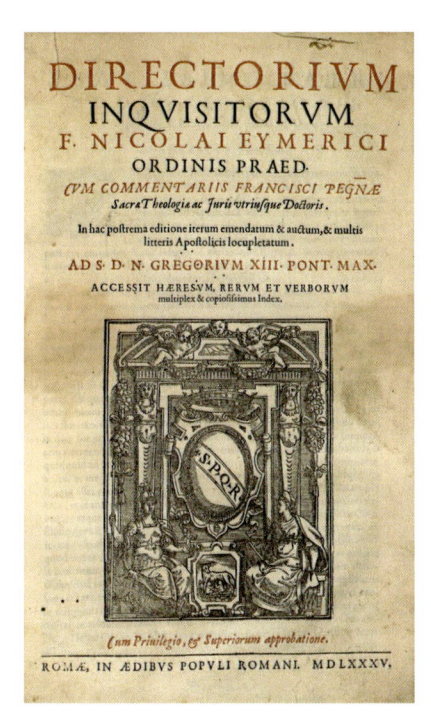

Left and Below Nicolbas Eymerich (1320-1399), *Directorium Inquisitorum* , Rome: In Aedibus Populi Romani, 1585. fBX1710.E9 Rare.

Dealing with the Devil: Whether viewed as superstitious and cruel, or dutiful servants of God, the inquisitors who set out to rid Christendom of the heresy of witchcraft, were well armed come the 1487 publication of the "how-to" guide the *Malleus Maleficarum*. Written by Heinrich Kramer (Institutoris) and Jacob Sprenger, the Malleus details the ceremonies by which witches swore allegiance to the devil and provides a framework for detecting and adjudicating the accused. The sordid history of the Malleus, its use and long-standing popularity (second only to the Bible in terms of numbers printed for roughly 200 years) is testament to the Roman Inquisitions determination to censor heretical knowledge, and the disastrous effects it carried for individuals. Heinrich Kramer and Jacob Sprenger, authors of the *Malleus Maleficarum*, were by no means alone in their assessment that the heresy of witchcraft was running rampant in German-speaking regions of Europe. Book Five of Johannes Nider's Formicarius, first printed in 1475 after having been circulated in the 1430's, recounts the inquisitor Peter of Greyerz's tale of having interviewed a male witch, who described in detail some of the more gruesome aspects of the heresy of witchcraft, such as the ceremonial murder of children.

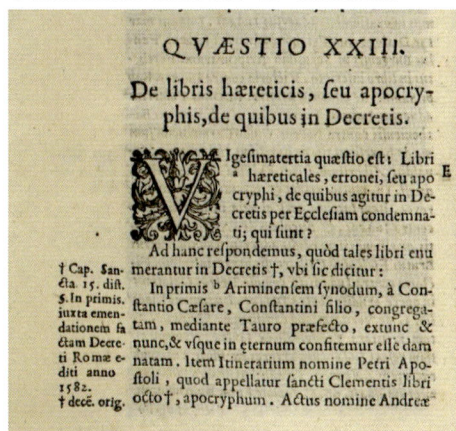

Facing: Johannes Nider [1380-1438], *Incipit Prologus Formicarii Iuxta Edico[n]nem Fratris Iohannis Nider Sacre Theologie*, Auguste: Per Anthonium Sorg, [1484]. alc f Incun1484.N66 Incun.

Below: Heinrich Institoris (1430-1505), *Malleus Malefica um, Maleficas et Earum Haeresin Framea Conterens,* Lyon: Sumpribus Claudij, Landry [1620-1621]. BF1520.I67 1620 v.1-2, pt. 1 Rare.

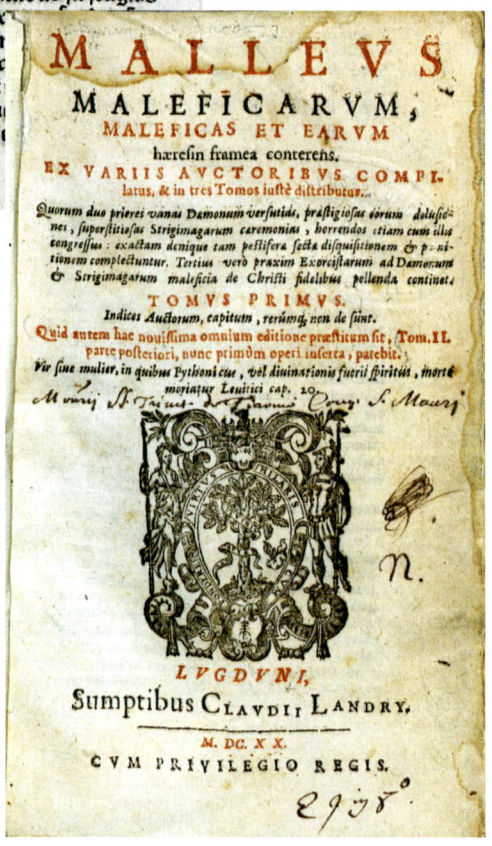

Below; Walter Lawry (1793-1859), *A Second Missionary Visit to the Friendly and Feejee Islands,* London: J. Mason and C. Gilpin, 1851. BV3680.F5L3 Rare.

Rival Missions: Protestant empires too undertook programs of conversion and control. Hoole's narrative of his missionary travels documents the extent of Christianization among indigenous peoples, celebrating that many had given up their "idols." He depicts conflicts between Catholic and Protestant missionaries and emphasizes the importance of making the bible widely accessible to natives—the opposite of the Catholic strategy.

---

104   LAWRY'S SECOND VISIT.

a man come to teach us: and that I was called to the work of the Lord at this time, I am giving thanks.

I am
AMELIA MONGA.
(Assistant Teacher, aged twenty-five.)

I have also received from the King a letter, which I shall place among these papers; and one from Shadrach, whom Tubou, before his inauguration to the throne, proposed to be King instead of himself. Shadrach is now the Supreme Judge of Tonga, an eloquent Preacher, and probably the most learned man in the King's dominions. I have also received a letter from Jone Soakai, whose father I knew well: his name was Oheela, a man of good sense, who, from my first landing, showed an acute mind, favourable to the *lotu.* He was wrecked near Feejee, and swam in the ocean, with a shark attacking him, three days and nights; and from this deliverance, he told me, he was sure that the Great God cared for him. His son, John Soakai, is a lad of about seventeen years old, and an Assistant Teacher in our Institution at Nukualofa.

KING GEORGE'S LETTER.

NUKUALOFA, *July* 16*th,* 1850.
O MR. LAWRY,

I WRITE to you to make known my mind concerning the things you were inquiring about.
The good which I have received through the Christian religion is, that I know the truth of the Gospel, and its preciousness and value to my soul. I have received the

---

FRIENDLY ISLANDS. TONGA.   105

forgiveness of my sins, and am justified by the blood of Christ. God has adopted me as His son, and made my soul anew. I have a hope beyond death, because of Christ. The benefits of this religion to Tonga are, that it has brought peace to our land. Its present settled and happy condition we all attribute to religion's influence. All the Chiefs and people acknowledge this. This *lotu* leaves every one in his proper sphere. A Chief is a Chief still. A gentleman is a gentleman still. A common person is a common person still. So it was not formerly [on account of rebellion and conspiracy]. Our former state was only evil. Our land was verily bad; very different from the blessedness and goodness of these days.

I am very, very pleased in my mind with Mr. Amos's Institution; and my will is that these Schools of Mr. Amos's teaching shall ever abide in this land, and be handed down for [the benefit of] our seed after us. I *fakamonua* ["move the gift to my forehead, in token of reverent thanksgiving"] the love of Britannia to me and my kingdom, inasmuch as they have given up their children to bring the glad tidings to the Tonga Islands.

I wish that many copies of the Sacred Book may be printed in England, that they may be brought for our people to read; by which they will know the truth of this religion, and be preserved from the Popish religion, which prowls about to scatter the people who are ignorant of the Scriptures. I desire that these Missionaries may remain perpetually in this land. This is my will. If there should ever happen a time when the Lord would remove the Missionaries from the Friendly Isles, it would be a painful dispensation to us.

O that the Lord would at once grant that long may be your life, Mr. Lawry! that you may again come to this land! for beneficial is your visit: and if there is any thing which we would wish repeated, it is your visit.

I am
GEORGE TUBOU.

F 5

[41]

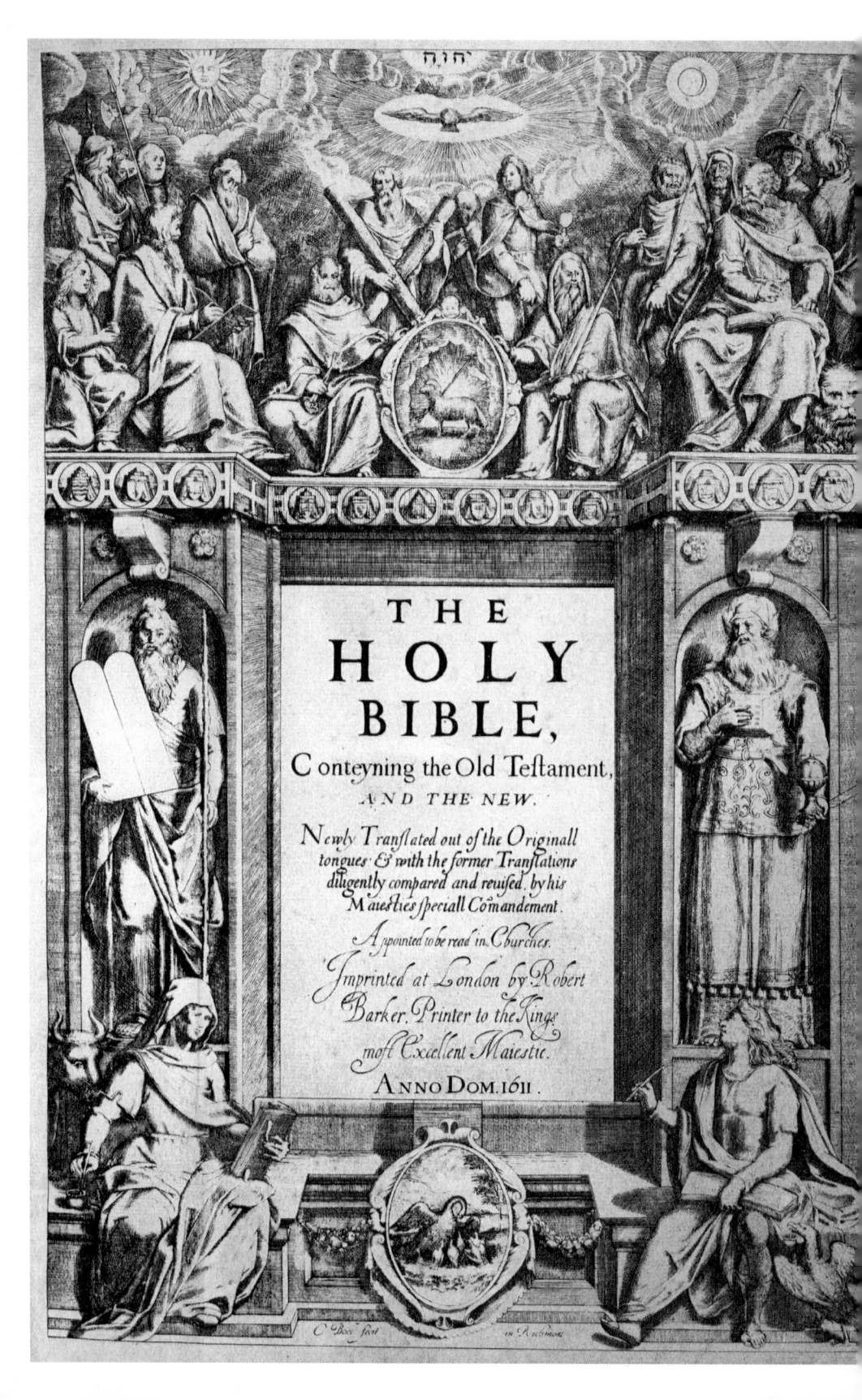

THE HOLY BIBLE,

Conteyning the Old Testament, AND THE NEW.

Newly Translated out of the Originall tongues: & with the former Translations diligently compared and reuised, by his Maiesties speciall Comandement.

Appointed to be read in Churches.

Imprinted at London by Robert Barker, Printer to the Kings most Excellent Maiestie.

ANNO DOM. 1611.

Pages 42-44: *The Holy Bible*, London: Robert Barker, 1611. fBS185 1611 c.2 Rare mq5335875.

The Most Dangerous Book: The best known English Bible translation, completed in 1611, the King James Bible includes an introduction decrying Roman Catholic censorship of translations of the Bible into vernacular languages. Translated Scripture was one of the Inquisition's greatest fears, since it facilitated unsupervised reading and plural interpretations. Some versions of the *Index* proclaimed that reading any part of the Bible in translation (other than Latin of course) resulted in instant damnation without the possibility of repentance or redemption.

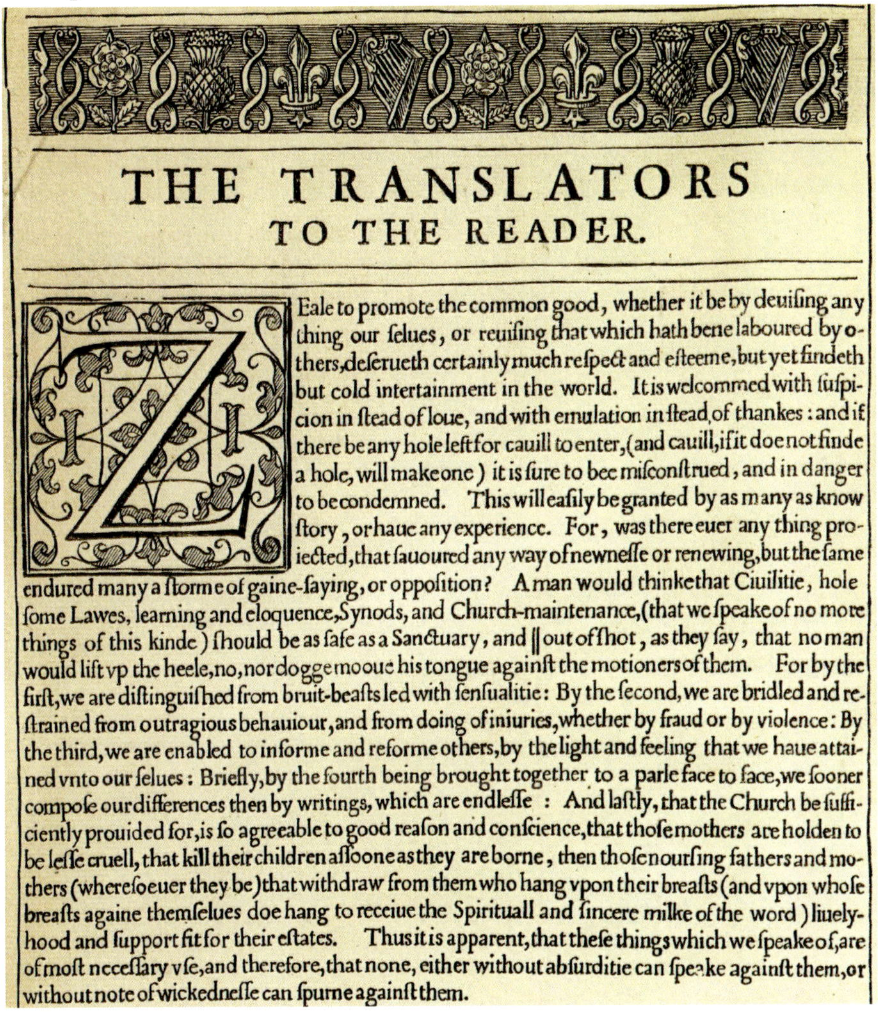

THE TRANSLATORS
TO THE READER.

ZEale to promote the common good, whether it be by deuiſing any thing our ſelues, or reuiſing that which hath bene laboured by others, deſerueth certainly much reſpect and eſteeme, but yet findeth but cold intertainment in the world. It is welcommed with ſuſpicion in ſtead of loue, and with emulation in ſtead of thankes: and if there be any hole left for cauill to enter, (and cauill, if it doe not finde a hole, will make one) it is ſure to bee miſconſtrued, and in danger to be condemned. This will eaſily be granted by as many as know ſtory, or haue any experience. For, was there euer any thing proiected, that ſauoured any way of newneſſe or renewing, but the ſame endured many a ſtorme of gaine-ſaying, or oppoſition? A man would thinke that Ciuilitie, hole ſome Lawes, learning and eloquence, Synods, and Church-maintenance, (that we ſpeake of no more things of this kinde) ſhould be as ſafe as a Sanctuary, and || out of ſhot, as they ſay, that no man would lift vp the heele, no, nor dogge mooue his tongue againſt the motioners of them. For by the firſt, we are diſtinguiſhed from bruit-beaſts led with ſenſualitie: By the ſecond, we are bridled and reſtrained from outragious behauiour, and from doing of iniuries, whether by fraud or by violence: By the third, we are enabled to informe and reforme others, by the light and feeling that we haue attained vnto our ſelues: Briefly, by the fourth being brought together to a parle face to face, we ſooner compoſe our differences then by writings, which are endleſſe: And laſtly, that the Church be ſufficiently prouided for, is ſo agreeable to good reaſon and conſcience, that thoſe mothers are holden to be leſſe cruell, that kill their children aſſoone as they are borne, then thoſe nourſing fathers and mothers (whereſoeuer they be) that withdraw from them who hang vpon their breaſts (and vpon whoſe breaſts againe themſelues doe hang to receiue the Spirituall and ſincere milke of the word) liuelyhood and ſupport fit for their eſtates. Thus it is apparent, that theſe things which we ſpeake of, are of moſt neceſſary vſe, and therefore, that none, either without abſurditie can ſpeake againſt them, or without note of wickedneſſe can ſpurne againſt them.

Continued on the next page...

ted the Bible as carefully, and as skilfully as he could; and yet he thought good to goe ouer it againe, and then it got the credit with the Iewes, to be called ἀκριβῶς, that is, accuratly done, as Saint *Hierome* witnesseth. How many bookes of profane learning haue bene gone ouer againe and againe, by the same translators, by others? Of one and the same booke of *Aristotles* Ethikes, there are extant not so few as sixe or seuen seuerall translations. Now if this cost may bee bestowed vpon the goord, which affordeth vs a little shade, and which to day flourisheth, but to morrow is cut downe; what may we bestow, nay what ought we not to bestow vpon the Vine, the fruite whereof maketh glad the conscience of man, and the stemme whereof abideth for euer? And this is the word of God, which we translate. *What is the chaffe to the wheat, saith the Lord? Tanti vitreum, quanti verum margaritum* (saith *Tertullian*,) if a toy of glasse be of that rekoning with vs, how ought wee to value the true pearle? Therefore let no mans eye be euill, because his Maiesties is good; neither let any be grieued, that wee haue a Prince that seeketh the increase of the spirituall wealth of Israel (let *Sanballats* and *Tobiahs* doe so, which therefore doe beare their iust reproofe) but let vs rather blesse God from the ground of our heart, for working this religious care in him, to haue the translations of the Bible maturely considered of and examined. For by this meanes it commeth to passe, that whatsoeuer is sound alreadie (and all is found for substance, in one or other of our editions, and the worst of ours farre better then their autentike vulgar) the same will shine as gold more brightly, being rubbed and polished; also, if any thing be halting, or superfluous, or not so agreeable to the originall, the same may bee corrected, and the trueth set in place. And what can the King command to bee done, that will bring him more

The Translators

An other thing we thinke good to admonish thee of (gentle Reader) that wee haue not tyed our selues to an vniformitie of phrasing, or to an identitie of words, as some peraduenture would wish that we had done, because they obserue, that some learned men some where, haue beene as exact as they could that way. Truly, that we might not varie from the sense of that which we had translated before, if the word signified the same thing in both places (for there bee some wordes that bee not of the same sense euery where) we were especially carefull, and made a conscience, according to our duetie. But, that we should expresse the same notion in the same particular word; as for example, if we translate the *Hebrew* or *Greeke* word once by *Purpose*, neuer to call it *Intent*; if one where *Iourneying*, neuer *Traueiling*; if one where *Thinke*, neuer *Suppose*; if one where *Paine*, neuer *Ache*; it one where *Ioy*, neuer *Gladnesse*, &c. Thus to minse the matter, wee thought to sauour more of curiositie then wisedome, and that rather it would breed scorne in the Atheist, then bring profite to the godly Reader. For is the kingdome of God become words or syllables? why should wee be in bondage to them if we may be free, vse one precisely when wee may vse another no lesse fit, as commodiously? A godly Father in the Primitiue time shewed himselfe greatly moued, that one of newfanglenes called κοιτών μιυρος, though the difference be little or none; and another reporteth, that he was much abused for turning *Cucurbita* (to which reading the people had beene vsed) into *Hedera*. Now if this happen in better times, and vpon so small occasions, wee might iustly feare hard censure, if generally wee should make verball and vnnecessary changings. We might also be charged (by scoffers) with some vnequall dealing towards a great number of good English wordes. For as it is written of a certaine great Philosopher, that he should say, that those logs were happie that were made images to be worshipped; for their fellowes, as good as they, lay for blockes behinde the fire: so if wee should say, as it were, vnto certaine words, Stand vp higher, haue a place in the Bible alwayes, and to others of like qualitie, Get ye hence, be banished for euer, wee might be taxed peraduenture with S. *Iames* his words, namely, *To be partiall in our selues and iudges of euill thoughts*. Adde hereunto, that nicenesse in wordes was alwayes counted the next step to trifling, and so was to bee curious about names too: also that we cannot follow a better patterne for elocution then God himselfe; therefore hee vsing diuers words, in his holy writ, and indifferently for one thing in nature: we, it wee will not be superstitious, may vse the same libertie in our English versions out of *Hebrew* & *Greeke*, for that copie or store that he hath giuen vs. Lastly, wee haue on the one side auoided the scrupulositie of the Puritanes, who leaue the olde Ecclesiasticall words, and betake them to other, as when they put *washing* for *Baptisme*, and *Congregation* in stead of *Church*: as also on the other side we haue shunned the obscuritie of the Papists, in their *Azimes, Tunike, Rational Holocausts, Præpuce, Pasche*, and a number of such like, whereof their late Translation is full, and that of purpose to darken the sence, that since they must needs translate the Bible, yet by the language thereof, it may bee kept from being vnderstood. But we desire that the Scripture may speake like it selfe, as in the language of *Canaan*, that it may bee vnderstood euen of the very vulgar.

Below and Upper Following: Saint Thomas ore (1478-1535), *A Frutefull, Pleasaunt, & Wittie Worke…*, London: Abraham Vele [1556]. alcHX810.5.E54 1556.

In Word vs. In Deed: The ideal laws of Thomas More's imaginary *Utopia*, "gave to everye man free libertie and choise to believe what he would. Saving omitted that no man should conceive so vile and base an opinion of the dignite of mans nature, as to think that the souls do die and perish with the bodye; or that the world runneth at all a[d]ventures governed by no divine providence." Yet the Reformation hit England shortly after More published this radical endorsement of religious tolerance in 1520, and as Lord Chancellor he personally condemned and burned numerous Protestants and their books, before he was himself executed for refusing to recant his Catholicism when Henry VIII broke with Rome.

A frutefull pleasaunt & wittie worke, of the beste state of a publique weale, and of the newe ple, called Utopia: written in Latine by the right worthie and famous Syr Thomas More knyght, and translated into Englishe by Raphe Robynson, sometime fellowe of Corpus Christi College in Oxford, and nowe by him at this seconde edition newlie perused and corrected, and also with diuers notes in the margent augmented.

Imprinted at London, by Abraham Vele, dwellinge in Pauls churchyarde, at the signe of the Lambe.

¶ The translator to the gentle reader.

Thou shalte vnderstande getle reader that though this worke of Utopia in English, come now the seconde tyme furth in Print, yet was it neuer my mynde nor intente, that it shoulde euer haue bene Imprinted at all, as who for no such purpose toke vpō me at the firste the translation thereof: but did it onelye at the request of a frende, for his owne priuate vse, vpon hope that he wolde haue kept it secrete to hym selfe alone. Whō though I knewe to be a man in dede, both very wittie, & also skilful, yet was I certē, that in the knowledge of the Latin tonge, he was not so well sene, as to be hable to iudge of the fineties or coursenes of my translation. Wherfore I wente the more sleightlye through with it, propoundynge to my selfe therein, rather to please my sayde frendes iudgemente, then myne owne. To the meanesse of whose learninge I

A.ij.   thoughts

Above: Thomas More's description of *Utopia*'s ban on denial of the immortal soul, with the marginal label, "No vile opinion to be conceaved of man's worthy nature."
Facing: Lucrative Lies...

Lucrative Lies: Hendrik van Cuyck was a Catholic archbishop and papal and royal censor of books in the Netherlands. His *Panegyricae orationes septem. Argumenta versa pagina exhibebit. Addita est: paraenetica in Henricum Bochorinck, catholicae religionis desertorem* is a collection of essays including a defense of censorship of the press. Van Cuyck wrote that it was the invention of the printing press which was responsible for the "pernicious lies" which infected the modern world. He commented that prohibited books themselves had become a lucrative genre for booksellers and printers, naming explicitly the works of Luther, Calvin, Erasmus and Hebrew and Islamic religious texts as being examples of particularly hazardous material for the laity.

CENSVRA.

Hæc de vitandis & eliminandis malis libris, in [...]
gyri Theologicæ Doctoralis aulæ Louanij [...]
Oratio, pia facraquè eruditione referta eft, a[...]
planè quæ typis excufa, ad ædificationem Reipub.[...]
ftianæ omnibus tradatur legenda.

Alteram quoque Panegyricam, veluti fecu[ndam]
atheifmi radicem excindēdam in comitijs Licentiæ [Theo-]
logicæ poni vidi, & auditu excepi: eandemque [...]
prælo deftinatam, attentè legi & probaui; vtpotè f[...]
& piam ad comprobandum humana diuinis poftha[...]
nihilque operi Dei, iuxta S. Benedicti elogium præp[...]
dum effe. Quod atteftor ego

Embertus Eueraerts Arend[...]
facra Theologia Doctor, [...]
tri Louanij Paftor.

O Rationes has doctas, & [...]
las corrigendas, vtiles [...]

I. Ianf[...]
facr[...]

O Rationes has Panegyri[...]
perniciofis; Pofteriorem [...]
re gr*ues*, omnium animis i[...]

Ioan[...]

PANEGYRICÆ
ORATIONES DVÆ.

PRIOR,
DE VITANDIS, ET E
REPVB. PROSCRIBENDIS
Libris perniciofis.

POSTERIOR,
ADVERSVS POLITICOS.

Autore HENRICO CVYCKIO,
facræ Theologiæ Doctore, D. Petri Louanij
Decano, Academiæ Cancellario, & Pontifi-
cio ac Regio Librorum Cenfore.

DE VITANDIS
ET E REPVB. PROSCRI-
BENDIS LIBRIS PER-
NICIOSIS, PANEGYRICA
ORATIO.

QVI primi omnium litteras &
fcribendi elementa inuene-
runt, è quibus memoriæ ful-
citur æternitas, & ab omni
obliuionis iniuria res memo-
ratu dignæ vindicantur: &
qui poft illos primi ediderunt libros (quod
Anaxagoræ Laërtius, & Pififtrato Tyranno
Gellius attribuit; vt femper in fuas laudes Græ-
ci effufifsimi fuerunt; etfi multò ante illos, He-
bræorum antiquifsimi facram defcripferint
hiftoriam, & Sacerdotes Ægyptiorum, atque
etiam Chaldæi, complures in lucem libros pro-
tulerint) & rurfum, qui poft vtrofque, non
multò ante noftrum hoc æuum, nouum fcribendi genus finxerunt; Typographicam dico
artem; qua vno die, ab homine vno tantùm
pingitur litterarum, quantum vix multis men-
fibus, à pluribus fcribi poffet; perutilem omnes

A   in Rem-

Above and Right: Hendrik van Cuyck (1546-1609, *Panegyricæ orationes duæ. Prior, De vitandis et e repub. proscribendis libris perniciosis. Posterior, aduersus politicos,* Louvain: Iacobum Heybergium, 1595. BR120. C89 1595 Rare. *The George Williamson Endowment Fund.*

Non est potestas Super Terram quæ Comparetur ei. Iob. 41. 24.

LEVIATHAN
Or
THE MATTER, FORME
and POWER of A COMMON-
WEALTH ECCLESIASTICALL
and CIVIL.

By THOMAS HOBBES
of MALMESBVRY.

London
Printed for Andrew Crooke
1651

The Bugbear of the Nation: Few books have sparked such fierce responses as Hobbes's *Leviathan*. His description of vicious, distrustful human nature seemed to erode the dignity of government, humanity, even God, yet he argued so masterfully—using the methods of Francis Bacon with which all England was enamored—that, as the broadside above put it, "He with such Art deceiv'd, that none can say, If his b e Errours, where his Errour lay." From 1651 until Locke's refutations of 1689, defeating Hobbes was one the main goals English scholarship, and public and leaders alike called for harsher censorship to make it easier to silence "the Beast of Malmesbury." The broadside above mockingly celebrates Hobbes's long-awaited death: "Leviathan the Great is faln! But see/ The small Behemoths of his Progenie,/ Survive to duel all Divinitie."

Facing: Thomas Hobbes (1588-1679), *Leviathan*, London: Printed for A. Crooke, 1651. JC153.H649 Rare. Below: "An elegie upon Mr. Thomas Hobbes of Malmesbury, lately deceased", London, 1679. 133310 Rare Books. *The Huntington Library, San Marino, California.*

AN
ELEGIE
UPON
Mr. Thomas Hobbes of Malmesbury,
LATELY DECEASED.

IS he then dead at last, whom vain report
 So often had feign'd Mortal in meer sport ?
 Whom we on Earth so long alive might see,
 We thought he here had Immortality.
As he, like what he wrote, could not expire,
Whom all that did not love, did yet admire.
For who his Writings still accus'd in vain,
Were taught by him, of whom they did complain.
Some Authors vented have more Truth's ; but so,
If Truths they be, 'tis more than we can know.
He with such Art deceiv'd, that none can say,
If his be Errours, where his Errour lay.
If he mistakes, 'tis still with so much Wit,
He erres more pleasingly than others hit.
For there are Counterfeits of Truth, which are
In shew more Truths than Truths themselves appear.
As Nature in meer sport hath fram'd some Apes
Neerer to Men, than some in humane shapes ;
All were by him so plausibly misled,
They chose to lose the Way with such a Guide,
And wander pleasantly, rather than be
In the right Way with duller Companie.
 With ill success, some fond Disputers strove,
What Doctrines he had planted, to remove ;
And justly are they blam'd : for that Disease
Is ill remov'd, which more than Health does please.
And who delightful Frenzies entertain,
When undeceiv'd, do of their Cure complain. [vade,
 With such sweet Force he does our Thoughts in-
That where he cannot Teach, he does Perswade.
And we that read his Writings wish them true,
If we do not believe them to be so.
If he be in the Wrong, we hold it still,
Because the Right appears not half so well.
Who so would mend his Faults must make a Blot
May be more Truth, but most will like it not.
For though fair Vertue *Plato* wisht to see,
Yet Vice as fair will please no less than she.
Why are Temptations names for what is ill ?
But that her Charms are most prevailing still.
Or Vice call'd Pleasures ? But to shew alone,
That Vice and Pleasure in effect are one.

Hence came our Wit to think there was no Devil ;
Or if he Tempter was, he was not evil :
And finding him drest in a different fashion,
According to the humour of each Nation ,
And that the *Indians* were in this so civil,
To Whiten him we Blackned for the Devil.
He thought that he was Black or White, and Saint or Devil, according as it pleased the Painter.
And Vice and Vertue both were our Opinion,
And vari'd with the Laws of each Dominion.
To which who did conform was understood,
As their Modes differ'd to be had or ----

EPITAPH.

IS Atheist-Hobbes *then dead ! forbear to Cry* ;
 For, *whilst he liv'd, he thought he could not dy,*
Or *was at least most filthy loath to try.*
Leviathan *the Great is faln ! But see*
The small Behemoths of his Progenie,
Survive to duel all Divinitie.

Whither he's gone, becomes not us to say,
The Narrow upper, or the Broad low way :
For who own'd neither well, may hap to stray.

Most think old Tom, *with a Recanting Verse,*
Must his odde Notions dolefully rehearse
To new Disciples in the Devils Ar----

In fine, after a thousand Shams and Fobbs,
Ninety years Eating, and immortal Jobbs,
Here MATTER *lies,---and there's an End of Hobbes.*

Aliud.
Here lies Tom Hobbes, *the Bug-bear of the Nation.*
Whose Death hath frighted Atheism *out of Fashion.*

FINIS.

Printed in the Year 1679.

PROEM.

May it please you, my Lords and Gentlemen,

This Session of Parliament is of such high Importance to these parts of the World, that Heaven seems to have committed the Universal Fate of Christendom to Your disposal; from whose Proceedings, both France, Spain, Germany, Holland, and this part of the Universe, must take their Measures: Nor will it be a Vanity in me to affirm the same thing of You, which heretofore Tacitus did of the Battavi, 'Who in the time of the Romans (saith he) were able ' to confer a Victory upon whatever Party they ad-' hered to.

The Parliaments of England have ever been Formidable to their Neighbours, but You above all others seem to have been reserv'd by Providence, for those Great and Weighty Affairs which are now in Agitation as well at home as abroad, and for which purpose You are here Convened. You only are able to cast out that Angel of Darkness, with his many Legions, who is at this time endeavouring to destroy our best of Kings and Governments: You only are able to Center this reeling Kingdom, which staggers and groans under the Plurisie of Popery, and which (if not now prevented) may in time attaint and corrupt the whole mass of English Bloud: You only are able to preserve that so necessary Religion, and Sacred Property of our British Isle, by continuing (as there now is) a Protestant Head, upon a Protestant Body; without

A 2   which

Above: Charles Blount (1654-1693), *A Just Vindication of Learning*, London: s.n., 1679. Z657.B65 c. 1 Rare.

Small Behemoths of His Progeny: Hobbes had some admirers among his many enemies, including the deist Charles Blount, who admiringly sent Hobbes a copy of his (anonymous) 1679 essay *Anima Mundi*, which ambiguously reviews but also mocks proofs of the immortal soul. In *A Just Vindication of Learning* he echoes Milton's arguments against the law that books be licensed by censors before printing. Blount also wrote of his frustration at how hasty people were to condemn heterodox faiths such as his own deism.

[50]

READER.

MEthinks *I* already behold some haughty Pedant, strutting and looking down from himself as from the Devils Mountain upon the Universe, where amongst several other inferiour Objects, he happens at last to cast his eye upon this Treatise; when after a quibble or two upon the Title, he falls foul upon the Book it self, damning it by the Name of an Atheistical, Heretical Pamphlet: And to glorifie his own Zeal, under the pretence of being a Champion for Truth, summons Ignorance and Malice for his Seconds: But such a person understands not wherein the Nature of Atheism consists, how conversant soever he may otherwise be in the Practice of it. It were Atheism to say, there is no God; and so it were (tho' less directly) to deny his Providence, or restrain it to some particulars, and exclude it in reference to others. Such are Atheists, who

A 2   maintain

Above: Charles Blount (1654-1693), *Anima mundi*, Amsterdam, [London]: s.n., 1679. BL530.B65.

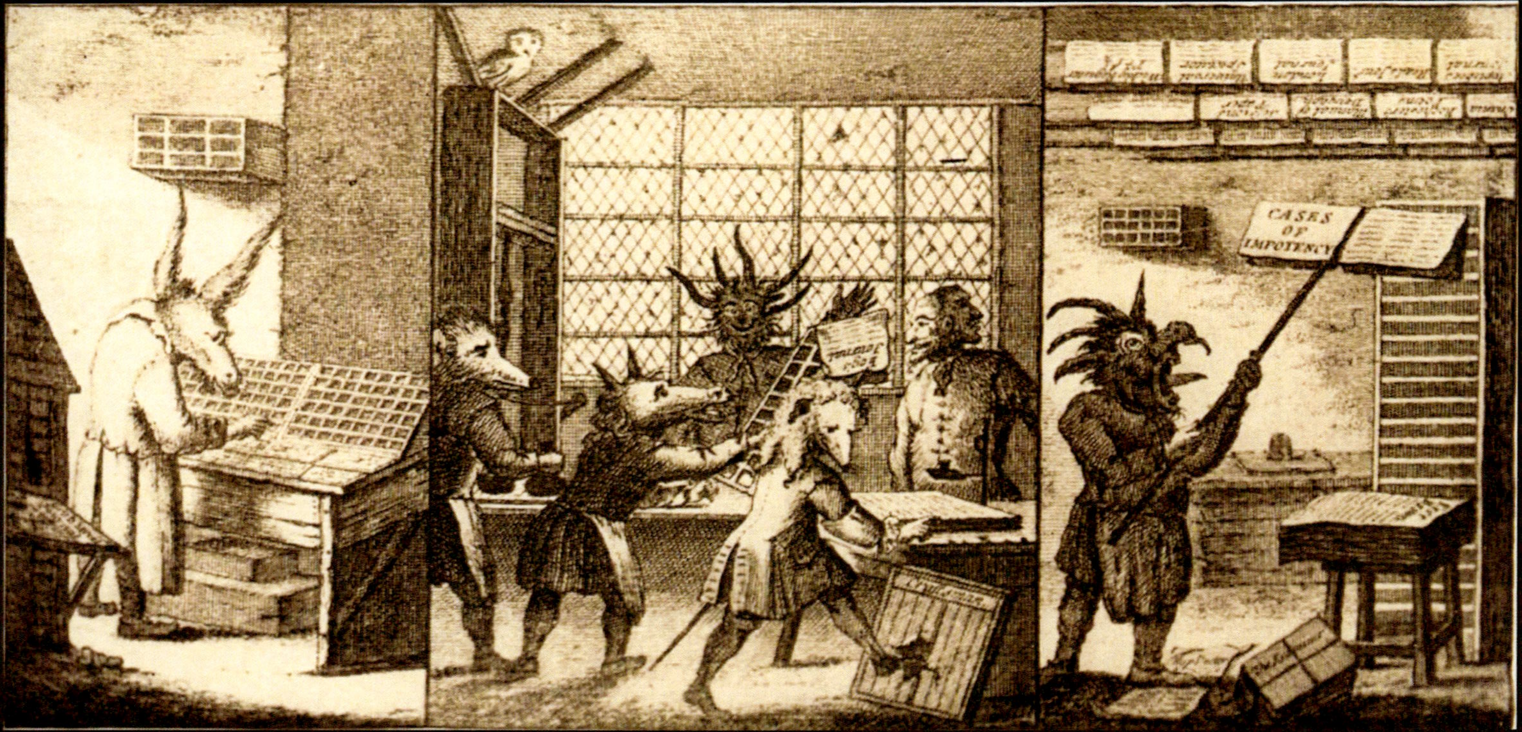
CASES
OF
IMPOTENCY

The Rocky Birth of Copyright Law

> "It cannot be deny'd but that he who is made judge to sit upon the birth, or death of books whether they may be wafted into this world, or not, had need to be a man above the common measure, both studious, learned, and judicious; there may be else no mean mistakes in the censure of what is passable or not."
> –Milton, Aeropagitica, *1644*

> "The censors were so far gone as to find the following sentence obscene: 'The factory gate waited for the student workers, thrown open in longing.' ▮ I could not fathom what he found to be obscene about this sentence. ▮ But for the mentally disturbed censor this sentence was unquestionably obscene. He explained that the word 'gate' very vividly suggested to him the vagina!"
> -Akira Kurosawa, Something Like an Autobiography, *1981*

Copyright, Child of Censorship and Crisis

Many systems of information control are motivated by profit rather than ideology, as those who make money from information seek to control its circulation. Like censoring bodies, copyright policies have rarely been patiently crafted based on philosophical principles. Rather they tend begin as side-effects of other policies, or as hasty legislation penned in the midst of crisis. Innovations in information technology generate or amplify such crises, and modern copyright law is still shaped by policies Europe improvised while facing the tsunami of new materials produced by the printing press. The same process is at work in today's e-book and digital revolutions, whose copyright policies are being shaped by individual legal cases, and the profit-motivated choices of industry giants such as Amazon or Google.

Facing: "The Art and Mystery of Printing Emblematically Displayed," a satire of printing. 'Grub Street Journal', London 1732.

When Printers Profit

The policy Milton opposed so eloquently, The Act for Preventing the Frequent Abuses in Printing Seditious, Treasonable and Unlicensed Books and Pamphlets; and for the Regulating of Printing and Printing Presses, passed in 1662. It ordered "That no Book, pamphlet, or paper shall be henceforth Printed, unlesse the same be first approv'd and licenc't omitted." Licensing was done through the Stationers' Company, an old printing house which thus gained a regulatory monopoly on printing. The Act aimed largely to control political and doctrinal content in pamphlets and newspapers, but many printers and even authors welcomed it since it offered, for the first time, something akin to copyright. Censors granted monopoly licenses to a specific printer, who could then appeal to the law to prosecute others who printed pirated editions which cut into their sales.

Disentangling Censorship from Copyright

On April 5th, 1710, the British Parliament enacted the Statute of Anne, which ushered in modern copyright law and did not also involve a censorship process. The statute granted authors of new books a copyright of fourteen years from publication, with a possibility of one renewal for the same duration. Since then the duration of copyright has been repeatedly extended in the UK and nations like the USA which adopted similar systems. Extensions tend to be triggered when individual companies sue or lobby to prevent particular valuable works from entering public domain. In 1998 the USA passed the Copyright Term Extension Act, secured at great expense by Disney in order to retain its copyright on Mickey Mouse—Mickey's copyright is due to expire again in 2024.

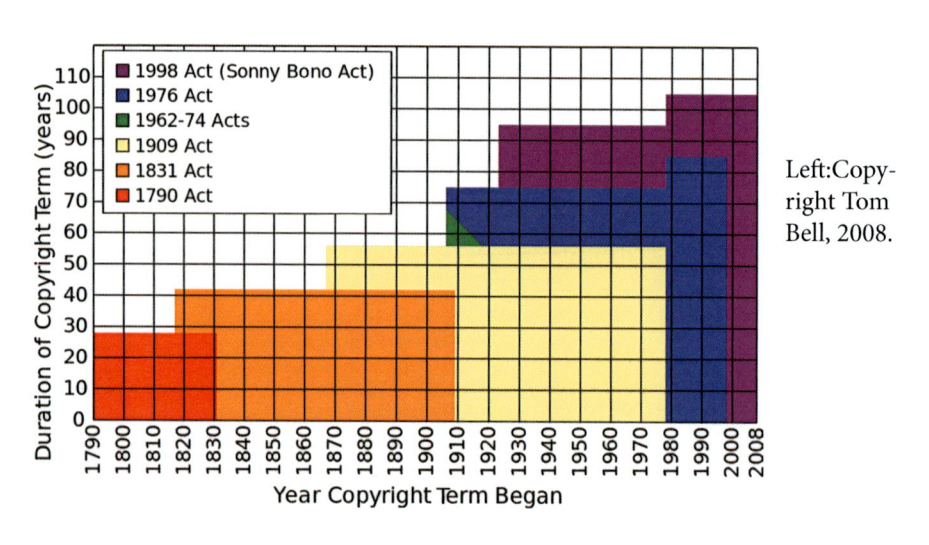

Left: Copyright Tom Bell, 2008.

[54]

Below and Following: John Milton (1608-1674), *Paradise Lost: A Poem Written in Ten Books,* London: P. Parker, 1667. alc PR3560 1667 Rare.

Just One Word: Milton's *Paradise Lost* faced the very licensing system he had protested in his *Aeropagitica*. While the religious content and Satan's speeches, echoing controversial anti-monarchical rhetoric, were left untouched, censors objected to a reference to an eclipse foretelling change in lines 596 to 599 and "Hal'd" (hauled i.e. moved) in line 596 to "hail'd" (summoned) to weaken the implied power of planets. Astrology was a sore spot for Church and Crown because, if the planets dictated Earthly events, that seemed to undermine the power of both God and kings.

```
Book 2.          Paradise lost.
Where Armies whole have sunk: the parching Air
Burns frore, and cold performs th' effect of Fire.
Thither by harpy-footed Furies hail'd,
At certain revolutions all the damn'd
Are brought: and feel by turns the bitter change
Of fierce extreams, extreams by change more fierce,
600 From Beds of raging Fire to starve in Ice
Thir soft Ethereal warmth, and there to pine
Immovable, infixt, and frozen round,
Periods of time, thence hurried back to fire.
They ferry over this Lethean Sound
Both to and fro, thir sorrow to augment,
And wish and struggle, as they pass, to reach
The tempting stream, with one small drop to loose
In sweet forgetfulness all pain and woe,
All in one moment, and so neer the brink;
610 But fate withstands, and to oppose th' attempt
Medusa with Gorgonian terror guards
The Ford, and of it self the water flies
All taste of living wight, as once it fled
The lip of Tantalus. Thus roving on
In confus'd march forlorn, th' adventrous Bands
With shuddring horror pale, and eyes agast
View'd first thir lamentable lot, and found
No rest: through many a dark and drearie Vaile
They pass'd, and many a Region dolorous,
620 O're many a Frozen, many a Fierie Alpe,
Rocks, Caves, Lakes, Fens, Bogs, Dens, and shades of
A Universe of death, which God by curse (death,
Created evil, for evil only good,
Where all life dies, death lives, and nature breeds,
Perverse, all monstrous, all prodigious things,
                                          Abomi-
```

[55]

Below: Henry Sacheverell, *The Tryal of Dr. Henry Sacheverell…*, London: J. Tonson, 1710. xxKD8281.S3 Law. *On loan from D'Angelo Law Library, University of Chicago.*

The Profit Motive: Tonson v. Baker was the first lawsuit filed under the rules outlined by the Statute of Anne. In this case, Jacob Tonsor Sr., the most famous publisher of the day, sued a gang of book pirates led by John Baker for the exclusive right to print this book the trial proceedings of Henry Sacheverell.

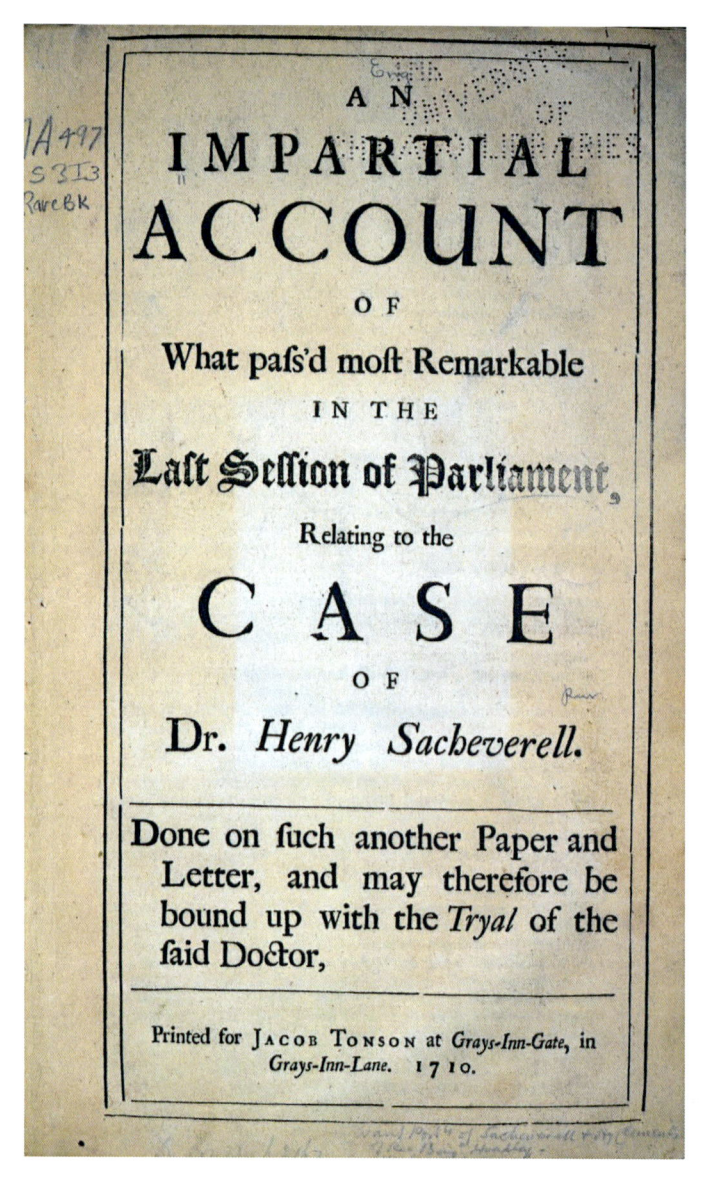

Pages 57-59: *An Impartial Account of What Pass'd Most Remarkable in the Last Session of Parliament…*, [London]: Printed for Jacob Tonson, 1710. DA497.S3I3 Rare.

[56]

Defiance Punished: Despite the elimination of formal licensing with the Statute of Anne, censorship continued in other forms. Henry Sacheverell was a popular preacher at Oxford whose sermons stirred controversy. In November 1709, he gave his most contentious speech, attacking Catholics and dissenters by comparing the failed Gunpowder Plot to the earlier execution of King Charles I. Despite an order banning the printing of this sermon, Sacheverell published it and was put on trial. The final page of the trial proceedings records the outcome.

December the 13th, 1709.

A Complaint being made, this Day, in the House of Commons, of Two printed Books, the one entituled, *The Communication of Sin*; *A Sermon preach'd at the Assizes held at* Derby, August 15, 1709; *By Doctor* Henry Sacheverell: And the other entituled, *The Perils of False Brethren both in Church and State*; *Set forth in a Sermon preach'd before the Right Honourable the Lord-Mayor, Aldermen, and Citizens of* London, *at the Cathedral Church of St.* Paul's, *on the 5th of* November, 1709; preach'd also by the said Dr. *Henry Sacheverell*; and both printed for *Henry Clements*: Which Books were deliver'd in at the Table; where several Paragraphs in the Epistle Dedicatory preceding the first-mention'd Book; and also several Paragraphs in the latter Book, were read:

Resolved,
That a Book, entituled, *The Communication of Sin*; *being a Sermon preached at the Assizes held at* Derby, August 15, 1709: And a Book, entituled, *The Perils of False Brethren both in Church and State*; *Set forth in a Sermon preach'd before the Right Honourable the Lord-Mayor, Aldermen, and Citizens of* London, *at the Cathedral Church of St.* Paul, *on the 5th of* November, 1709; are Malicious, Scandalous, and Seditious Libels; highly Reflecting upon Her Majesty and Government, the late happy Revolution, and the Protestant Succession as by Law Establish'd, in both Houses of Parliament; tending to alienate the Affections of Her Majesty's good Subjects, and to create Jealousies and Divisions among them.

Ordered,
That Dr. *Henry Sacheverell*, and *Henry Clements*; do attend at the Bar of the House to-morrow.

John Dolben, Esq; made the first Motion against the Two Sermons; and was seconded by *Spencer Cowper*, Esq;

They were oppos'd by several Gentlemen, who said, they did not perceive there was any thing in the Sermons, Malicious, Scandalous, or Seditious; nor Reflecting on Her Majesty and Government, the late happy Revolution, and the Protestant Succession as by Law Establish'd; of which they did not observe any Mention; neither had the Paragraphs the least Relation to it. What concern'd both Houses of Parliament, was suppos'd to be the Vote passed four and five Years before, about the Church being in Danger: And as to that, it was affirm'd, the Church was then in Danger, was still in Danger, and, it was to be fear'd, would always be in Danger; not from Her Majesty's Administration, but from Papists on the one Hand, and Fanaticks on the other; from these Her profess'd Enemies, and from *False Brethren*. It was own'd, there were some warm Expressions in the Sermon preach'd at St. *Paul's*: And no wonder that a true Son of the Church of *England* should express himself with some Warmth and Vehemence, against the Liberties that were taken, and with Impunity, to revile the Church, her Doctrines and Ministers, to blaspheme the Name of God, and to insult, and treat with Contempt, every thing that is Sacred. To this, little was return'd, besides bitter Invectives against the Sermons; and particularly, against the Doctrines of *Passive-Obedience* and *Non-Resistance*.

B   December

[57]

December 14.

THE House being inform'd, that Dr. *Henry Sacheverell* and *Henry Clements* attended, according to Order; Dr. *Sacheverell* was call'd in, and, at the Bar, was examin'd touching the Two Sermons yesterday complain'd of to the House: Where he own'd the Preaching, the Directing of the Printing, and Publishing the Sermon preach'd the 5th of *November*, 1709, at the Cathedral Church of St. *Paul*, and the Dedication of it; And also, that the Epistle Dedicatory to the Sermon preach'd at the Assizes at *Derby*, the 15th of *August*, 1709, was agreeable to that which he put to the Impression of that Sermon, which he directed to be printed and published. And being withdrawn, and a Question being proposed, That the said Dr. *Henry Sacheverell* be Impeach'd of High Crimes and Misdemeanors, he was call'd in again, and ask'd, If he had any thing to offer to the House? When he spoke to this Effect: " Mr. Speaker, I am very sorry, I am " fallen under the Displeasure of this House; I did not imagine, any " Expressions in my Sermons were liable to such a Censure as you " have pass'd upon them. If you had been pleas'd to have favour'd " me so far, as to have heard me before you pass'd it, I hope I should " have explain'd myself so, as to have prevented it. And after being heard, he was directed to withdraw. Then the Question was insisted on, for Impeaching the Doctor of High Crimes and Misdemeanors. And several Gentlemen spoke against it, desiring he might rather be prosecuted by the Attorney-General; and if the Sermons were Seditious, if they did reflect on Her Majesty and Government, the happy Revolution, and the Protestant Succession as by Law Establish'd, the Doctor would be convicted, and punished for them according to his Demerits. But if (as common Fame said) the Judges, and the Queen's learned Counsel, had been consulted, and were of Opinion, the Doctor could not be punish'd for them by the ordinary Proceedings in the Courts of Law; they thought it was very Unreasonable, by an Impeachment in Parliament, to endeavour to make a Man Guilty, and a Criminal, that, by the Laws of the Land, was Innocent. However, it was

Resolved,
That the said Dr. *Henry Sacheverell* be Impeached of High Crimes and Misdemeanors.

Ordered,
That Mr. *Dolben* do go to the Lords, and, at their Bar, in the Name of all the Commons of *Great-Britain*, Impeach the said Dr. *Henry Sacheverell* of High Crimes and Misdemeanors, and acquaint the Lords, that the House will, in due time, exhibit Articles against the said *Henry Sacheverell*.

Ordered,
That a Committee be appointed to draw up Articles of Impeachment against the said Dr. *Henry Sacheverell*.

And a Committee was appointed accordingly. And they have Power to send for Persons, Papers, and Records, and to sit *de die in diem.*

Then *Henry Clements* was call'd in, and, at the Bar, was examin'd touching his Printing and Publishing the said Two Books: Which he own'd, and that he had the Copies of them from Dr. *Sacheverell.* After which, he was directed to withdraw.

Ordered,
That the said Dr. *Henry Sacheverell* be taken into the Custody of the Serjeant at Arms attending the House.

Sir

It was then propos'd, that it being impossible the Members could make their Observations on the Articles in such Readings, and the Honour of the House being concerned to have them such as might be justified, a little Time should be allowed, before they were read the second time, to consider them; and to convince others, they intended not Delay by it, they only asked till *Wednesday*. This was order'd; but then it was moved, that no Copies might be taken of the Articles, because it was not proper they should be made Publick in the Coffee-Houses, nor shewed to the Doctor, before they were agreed to, and carried up to the Lords. On the other Hand, it was urged, This was precluding Members of their Right, by unreasonable Suppositions; that they had a Right to take Copies of any Papers before the House, for their Information; and it was not to be imagin'd, they would publish the Articles in Coffee-Houses, or shew them to the Doctor. And, what if they did shew them to him? Were they to be kept a Secret from him! Would he not have a Copy of the Articles order'd him by the Lords, as soon as they were carried to them? And, what Advantage would it be to him, or Disadvantage to the Commons, to see them sooner? But, if Copies were not to be taken of the Articles, it was no Favour, no Benefit to put off the Consideration of them; it had an Appearance of doing what was fair and reasonable, but would, in Truth, be doing nothing; for without taking Copies of them, they could not be consider'd. And it having been said, by one Gentleman, That this was an Extraordinary Thing, and what had never been done before; another reply'd, He thought it Extraordinary, but could not agree, it had never been done before; he remember'd the like, when Sir *J. Fenwick*'s Confessions had been read in the House of Commons; they were order'd to be sealed up by the Speaker, that no Copies might be taken of them. He did not approve that Precedent so well as to follow it; he wished Copies had been taken of those Papers, and that they had been printed; he believ'd, the Kingdom would have been the better for them, at this Day.

After these Debates, this Motion was waved.

This Prosecution gave great Satisfaction to the W----gs in general, to the *Deists*, *Atheists*, and to some among the *Dissenters*; (the Wiser among them disliking it from the Beginning, especially their Teachers, who are used to take greater Liberties in their Pulpits, than the Divines of the Church of *England*) it was very acceptable to those that had no Religion, or that were Enemies to the Church of *England*; they concluding, this was a good Handle either to bring all Religion into Contempt, or to injure the Establish'd. But it pleased God, who has promis'd, that even the *Gates of Hell should not prevail against his Church*, to disappoint the Designs these *Achitophels* had projected; and to shew those that boasted of their Numbers, or that doubted it before, that the Strength of the Nation, among the Nobility, Gentry, and Commonalty, was heartily for our happy Establishment both in Church and State; and that whatever Arts had been used to divide them, and create groundless Jealousies and Fears, of late Years, among them; yet whenever the Rights of the Crown, the Doctrines of our holy Religion, and of the *Church of England*, were attack'd, they would unite for their Maintenance, Support and Defence. There was such a Zeal shewn on this Occasion, and this Matter took such a different Turn from what was expected, that every one wish'd the Prosecution had never been begun; many condemning it; some even of the Man----rs declaring, *They would never be concern'd in roasting a Parson again*; And what was most strange, every one disclaiming the bringing this into Parliament. Which puts me in mind of what a noble Historian says of the great and sudden Change was in this Kingdom upon Sir *J. Greenvile*'s bringing Letters from King *Charles* II. to the Two Houses of Parliament, to the Lord-Mayor, and to the Army and Fleet: " From this time, *says he*, there was such an
" Emulation and Impatience in Lords and Commons, and City, and
" generally over the Kingdom, who should make the most lively Ex-
" pressions of their Duty, and of their Joy, that a Man could not but
" wonder where those People dwelt, who had done all the Mischief, and
" kept the King so many Years from enjoying the Comfort and Support
" of such excellent Subjects.

May it always happen thus! May the same good Providence ever watch over us, to save and deliver the *Church* and *Monarchy* from the Hands of their Enemies! May it *abate their Pride, assuage their Malice, and* not only *confound*, but make them *ashamed* of *their Devices!*

[60]

MIGRATING PRINT CAPITALS

> "███ nothing can be more pernicious consequence than the perusal of bad books ███ The commonwealth of Venice seems to be the only republic that has ever had a just notion of the importance of this maxim ███ her ministers, to this day, enjoy the right of examining whatever books are printed, to prevent their instilling any pernicious doctrines, As for those which were formerly published, occasioned by too great reminissness of the censors, she prevents their being reprinted, to put an entire stop to the evil."
> – Matthew Taylor, *England's Bloody Tribunal, Or Popish Cruelty Displayed*, 1771

> "The Free Use of the Press hath in these parts of Christendom, to the great advantage of Knowledge, been allow'd, till now of late it appears in some places so clogg'd wit un-ingenious Restraints, as Necessitates those who would communicate Fancies not vulgar, either to bury them as an untimely Birth, or else to use them as men do pure Gold, mingling it with base Metal to make it the better endure Minting. But we of the Low-Countries, not thinking any part of our Government so defective, as that our security depends upon the Subjects ignorance, are unwilling to give men any just occasion to quarrel with Learning, by Printing only such books as like Carriers Horses run on in the dirty beaten track of those who went before."
> – Printer's preface to Charles Blount's *Anima Mundi*, 1679

Where to print was an evolving question in the Renaissance and Reformation. In 1450 Gutenberg developed his press in Germany, but he and other early German printers went bankrupt, since print's mass production had no equivalent mass distribution mechanism, and it proved impossible to sell hundreds of copies of the same book when each town had at most a dozen buyers. In the 1480s to 1510s more lucrative print shops flourished in Italy, some founded by Germans who fled south to escape their debts. Venice emerged as a print capital since, as the center of all Mediterranean shipping, it could distribute books through a system not unlike modern airline hubs, while its comparative independence from Rome's Inquisition was another convenience. By the 1520s Paris and Lyon emerged as centers, serving France's large population and universities, while German printing regenerated as a system of book fairs solved the distribution challenge. As the Reformation and Counter-Reformation heated up, and as governments and guilds implemented licensing and other attempts to control what people printed and who could profit from it, publishers turned increasingly to the less regulated presses of Switzerland

and the Low Countries. The absence of a licensing process benefited not only radicals but anyone who wanted to publish quickly without red tape. By the later 1500s Amsterdam—with its port convenient to the increasingly-important Atlantic—accounted for more than a third of all printing, including many condemned works printed to be smuggled into England or Catholic lands. Some branches the Inquisition, unable to keep up with the tide of innovation, simply banned all books printed in Amsterdam.

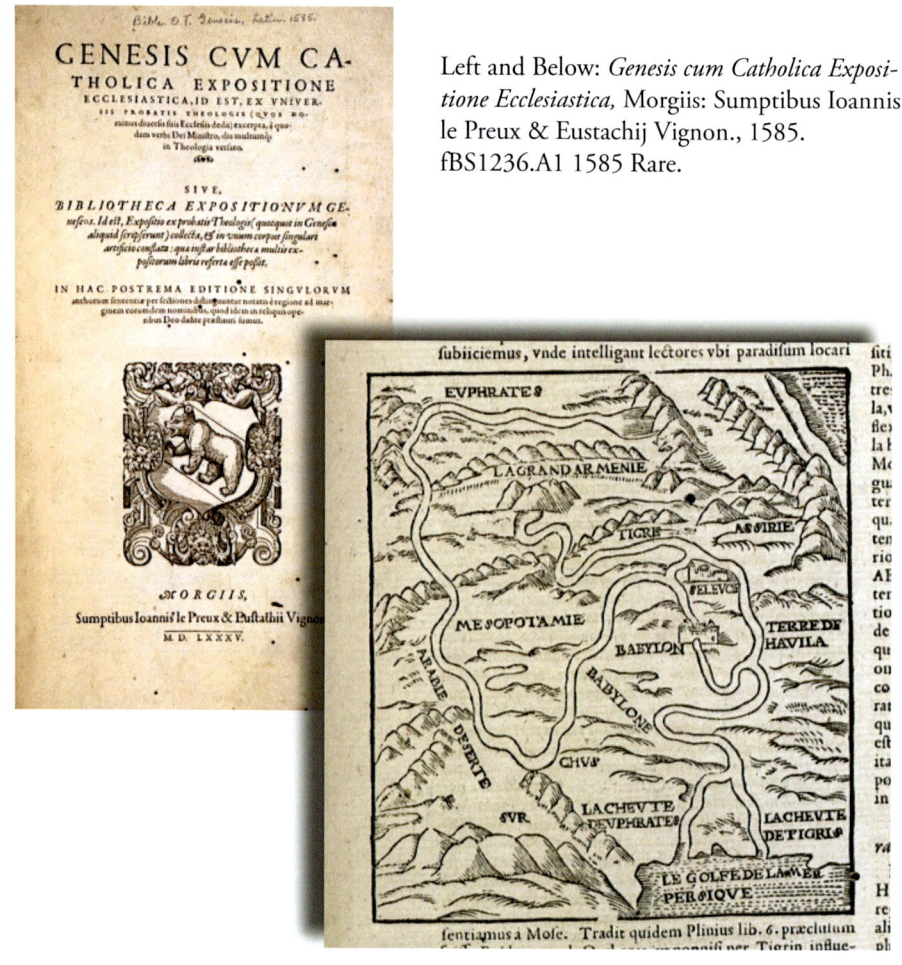

Left and Below: *Genesis cum Catholica Expositione Ecclesiastica,* Morgiis: Sumptibus Ioannis le Preux & Eustachij Vignon., 1585. fBS1236.A1 1585 Rare.

Political Fire: Marlorat was a French Protestant reformer who helped John Calvin write his seminal Institutes of the Christian Religion. His commentary on the *Genesis* cites Reformed, Catholic, and Lutheran sources. Marlorat was burned at the stake in 1562, not for heresy but for treason, since he was one of the leaders of a Protestant rebellion which briefly seized control of the French the city of Rouen, after the Crown denied their petition for permission to practice their faith.

[62]

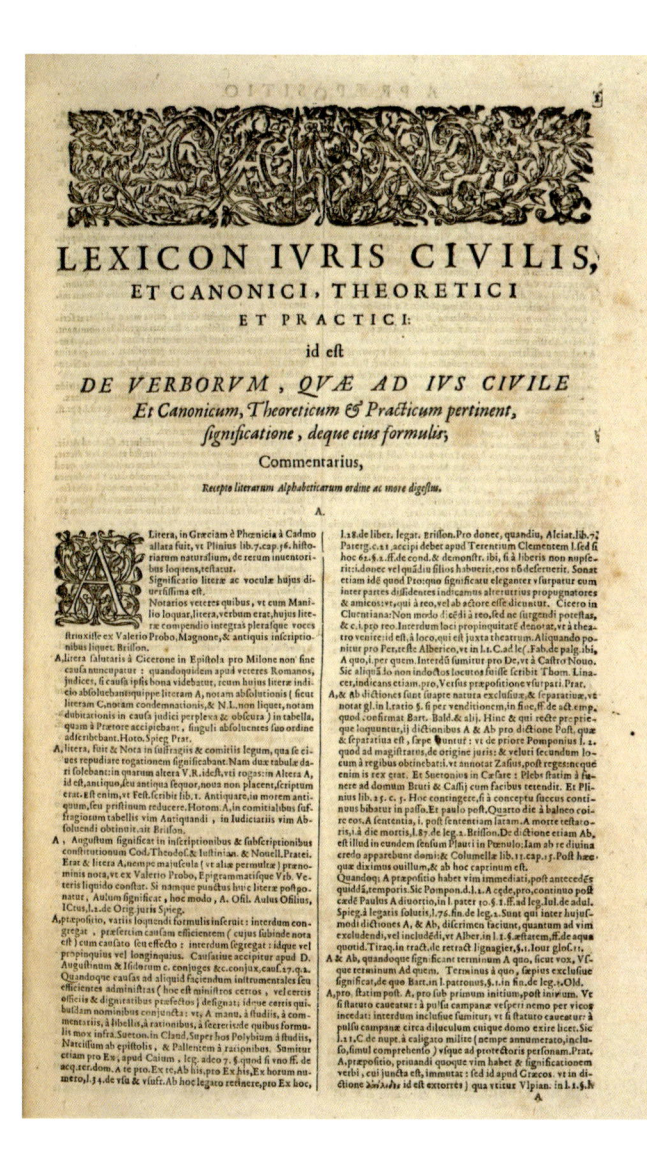

Left: Johannes Calvinus (fl. 1598-1614), *Lexicon Iuridicum Iuris Caesaei Simul* [Hanau?]: Impensis C. Marnii haeredum, I. & A., Marnii, 1610. fPA2387.C2 Rare.

Handling Arch-Heretics: John Calvin founded one of the most powerful and—from its adversaries' perspective—fearsome Protestant denominations: Calvinism. Figures like Calvin led the editors of the Index to diffe entiate "arch-heretics" listed in all caps in some editions. Struggling to keep up with an ever-multiplying list of Protestants, the *Index* sometimes banned all works from a particular place—such as Calvin's Geneva—or all works by associates of a particular person, and at one point all works printed on a printing press that had printed the works of Luther, since such a printer would likely print other Protestants. In this book, Calvin offers his views on civil and canon law.

[63]

Left: Hugo Grotius (1583-1645, *De Imperio Summarum Potestatum circa Sacra*, Amsterdam: Johannem Nicolaum ten Hoorn, 1677. JC510.G86 Rare.

Protestants Persecuting Protestants: Hugo Grotius was a Dutch jurist and an Arminian, believing that faith is a free choice, against the Calvinist position that it is a condition imposed by God. Grotius advocated religious tolerance and angered Holland's Calvinist majority by defending in print the right of the University of Leiden to appoint faculty regardless of their theological positions. When Holland banned Arminianism in 1618 Grotius—age thirty-six—was arrested and sentenced to life imprisonment, but his wife helped him escape hidden in a chest of books. He lived thereafter in exile in France, where he wrote this work on the theological, human, and political complexities of war between Catholics and Protestants.

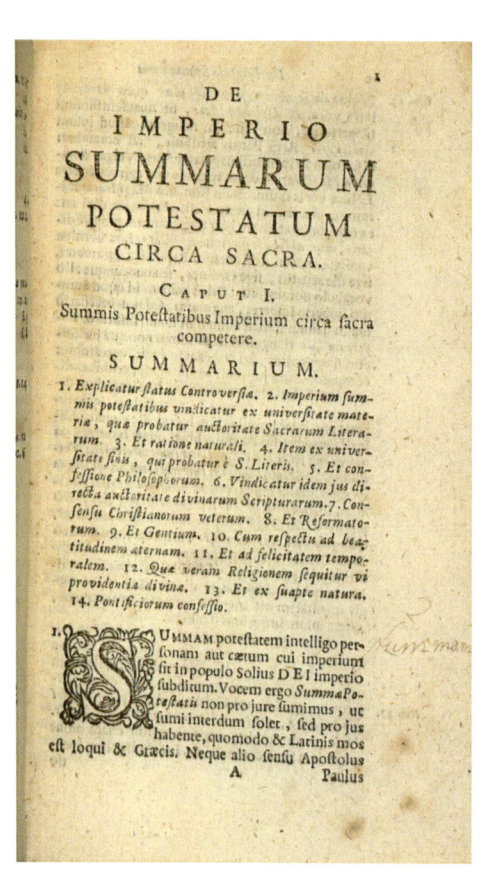

Upper Facing:
Blaise Pascal (1623-1662), *Les Provinciales, ou, Les Lettres Ecrites,* Cologne: Chez Nicolas Schoute, 1669. PQ1876.P8 1669 Rare Crerar. The John Crerar Library.

Friends in the Right Places: While we might expect eighteenth-century Inquisitors to fear Enlightenment innovations such as cultural relativism, deism, atheism, and calls for religious toleration, Inquisitors at the time were far more concerned by Jansenism, a controversial Catholic theological movement which integrated major elements of Calvinism, such as predestination. The mathematician and philosopher Blaise Pascal was a notorious Jansenist, but kept securing permission to publish new works by getting endorsements from influential bishops, whom low-local censors—who were little more than clerks—dared not anger. Here in his *Lettres Provinciales* he laments the results of the Church labeling heretics.

More or Less Condemned: For some authors, such as the Jansenist Blaise Pascal, the Inquisition's Index banned only specific works; for others, such as the John Calvin's associate Augustin Marlorat, it forbade all works on a particular topic, such as theology; for others—such as Luther or Calvin—it banned all works, regardless of the topic. This 1570 update was printed in Antwerp, a print center itself caught in the midst of violent clashes between its Catholic Spanish rulers and Dutch Protestant revolutionaries.

Right: *Index Librorum Prohibitorum,* Antwerp: Ex officin Christophori Plantini, 1570. Z1020.I57 1570 Rare Crerar. The John Crerar Library.

F. THOMÆ CAMPANELLÆ
DE SENSV RE-
RVM ET MAGIA,

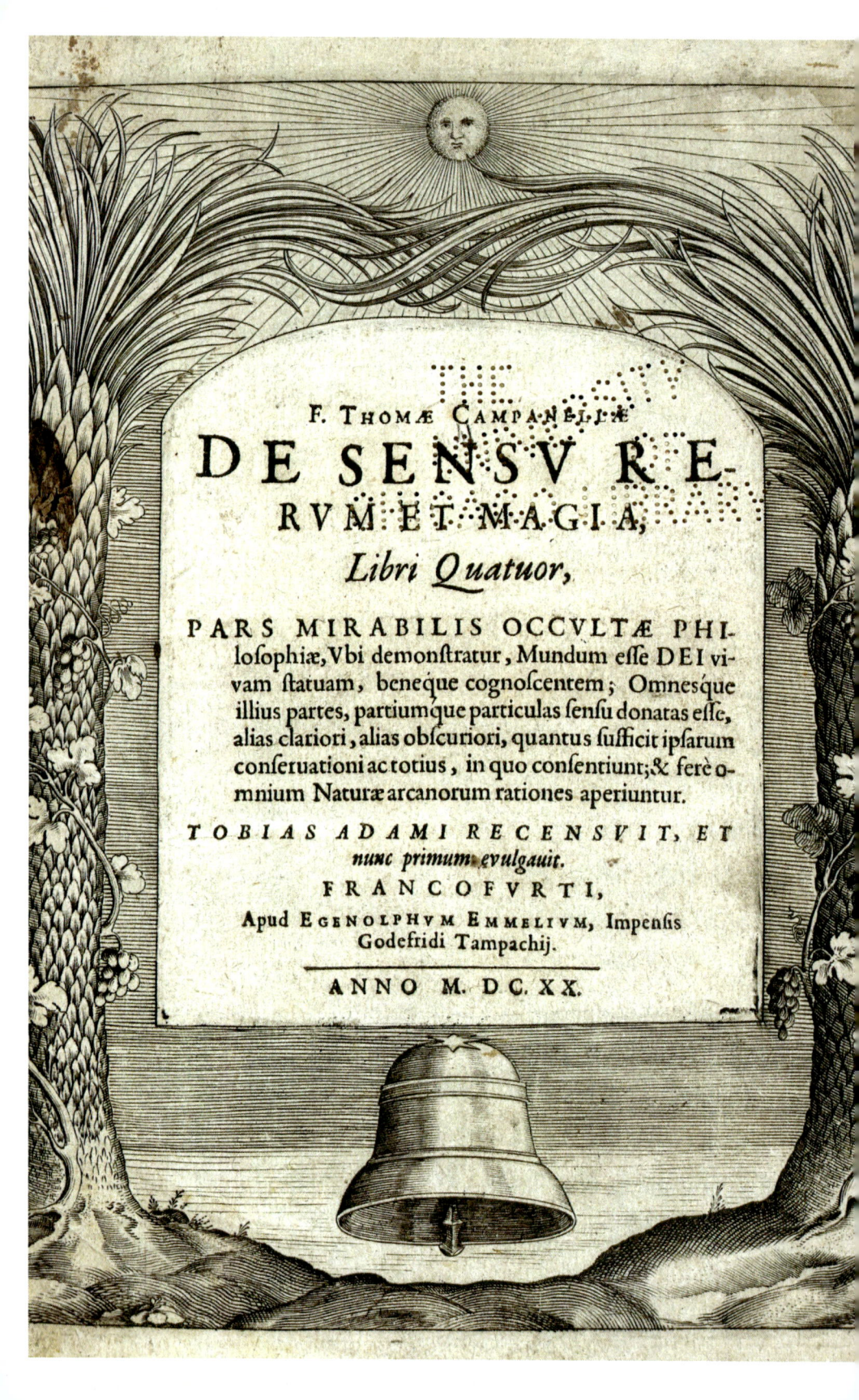

Libri Quatuor,

PARS MIRABILIS OCCVLTÆ PHI-
losophiæ, Vbi demonstratur, Mundum esse DEI vi-
vam statuam, beneque cognoscentem; Omnesque
illius partes, partiumque particulas sensu donatas esse,
alias clariori, alias obscuriori, quantus sufficit ipsarum
conseruationi ac totius, in quo consentiunt; & ferè o-
mnium Naturæ arcanorum rationes aperiuntur.

TOBIAS ADAMI RECENSVIT, ET
nunc primum evulgauit.
FRANCOFVRTI,
Apud EGENOLPHVM EMMELIVM, Impensis
Godefridi Tampachij.

ANNO M.DC.XX.

What Was the Inquisition's Goal?

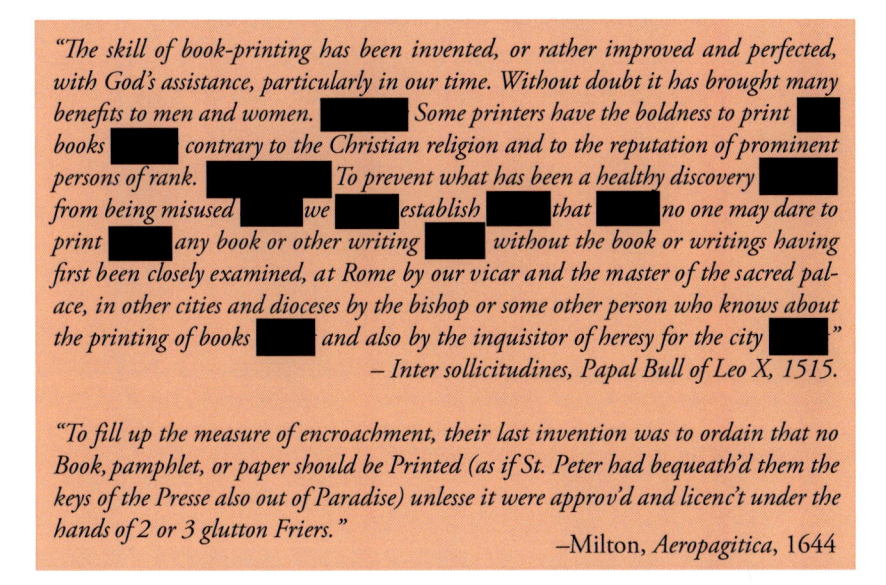

> "The skill of book-printing has been invented, or rather improved and perfected, with God's assistance, particularly in our time. Without doubt it has brought many benefits to men and women. ██ Some printers have the boldness to print ██ books ██ contrary to the Christian religion and to the reputation of prominent persons of rank. ██ To prevent what has been a healthy discovery ██ from being misused ██ we ██ establish ██ that ██ no one may dare to print ██ any book or other writing ██ without the book or writings having first been closely examined, at Rome by our vicar and the master of the sacred palace, in other cities and dioceses by the bishop or some other person who knows about the printing of books ██ and also by the inquisitor of heresy for the city ██ "
> – Inter sollicitudines, Papal Bull of Leo X, 1515.

> "To fill up the measure of encroachment, their last invention was to ordain that no Book, pamphlet, or paper should be Printed (as if St. Peter had bequeath'd them the keys of the Presse also out of Paradise) unless it were approv'd and licenc't under the hands of 2 or 3 glutton Friers."
> –Milton, *Aeropagitica*, 1644

The obvious answer is "to destroy information," but many of the Inquisition's activities were inconsistent with such a goal. Why spend numerous man-hours crossing out the name of the Protestant city where a volume of Homer was printed? Or defacing an author's name without destroying the book's controversial content? Versions of the *Index* carefully delineated works which were more or less forbidden and how each should be handled, rather than treating condemnation as an all or nothing. The Roman Inquisition even kept collections of banned materials, and issued thousands of official licenses granting individuals or libraries permission to own and study condemned books. These practices indicate the Inquisition rarely aspired to fully eradicate texts. Rather it aimed to control who had access to what, and to spread reminders of its authority —from showy trials to tiny black marks in a book—whose presence pressured authors to self-censor, and made readers constantly conscious that they read at their own risk. Thus, while the Inquisition did not keep adversaries' ideas out of Catholic hands, when considering its success or failure we must also consider how many works were never written due to authors' fear, and how many readers' minds were affected by seeing reminders of the Inquisition's presence on every title page.

Page 66 and Below: Tommaso Campanella (1568-1639), *F. Thomae Campanellae De Sensu Rerum et Magia*, Frankfurt: Egenolphum Emmelium, 1620, alcB785.C2D2 1620 Rare.

The Power of the Crown: A Dominican monk, astrologer, astronomer, opponent of Aristotle, and defender of Galileo, Tomasso Campanella faced repeated arrests and imprisonments. First denounced to the Inquisition in 1594 he was held in a convent for three years, but far worse came from secular authorities when the Spanish-controlled Naples charged him with treason against the Crown for his experiments with social communal living. He was tortured seven times and crippled, avoiding execution only by feigning madness. Sentenced to life in prison he still wrote numerous important works and maintained an influential correspondence with philosophers and scientists. After twenty-seven years he was freed by the one force neither Inquisition nor Naples could resist: the personal intervention of even more powerful patrons, first Pope Urban VIII, then king Louis XIII of France and Cardinal Richelieu.

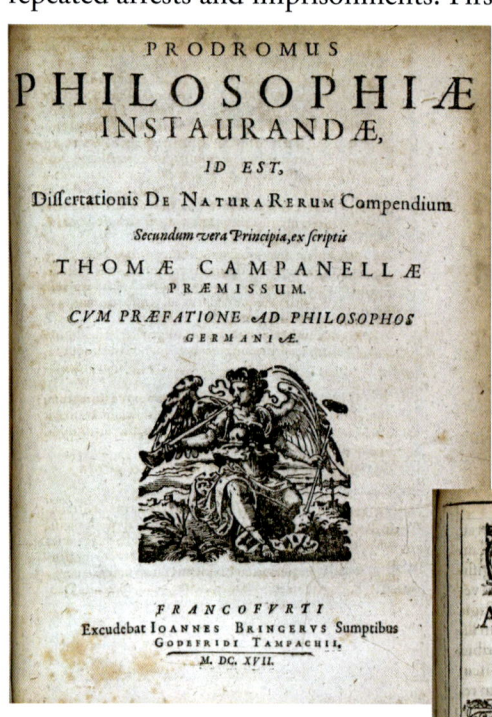

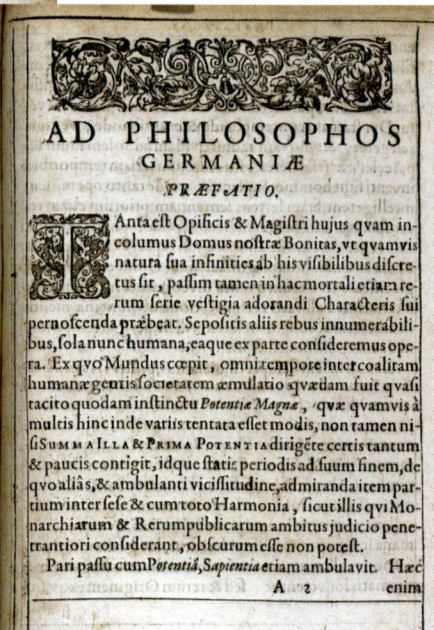

[68]

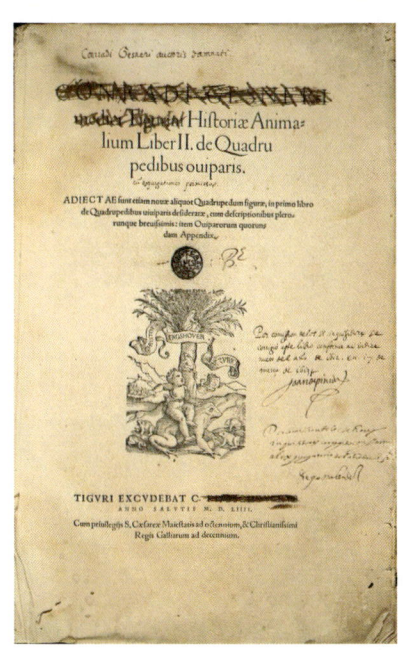

Left and Below: Conrad Gessner (1516-1565), *Conradi Gesneri Medici Tigurini Historiae Animalium…*, Tiguri: C. Froschouerus, [1554]. fQL41.G39 1554 pt. 2 Rare Crerar. The John Crerar Library.

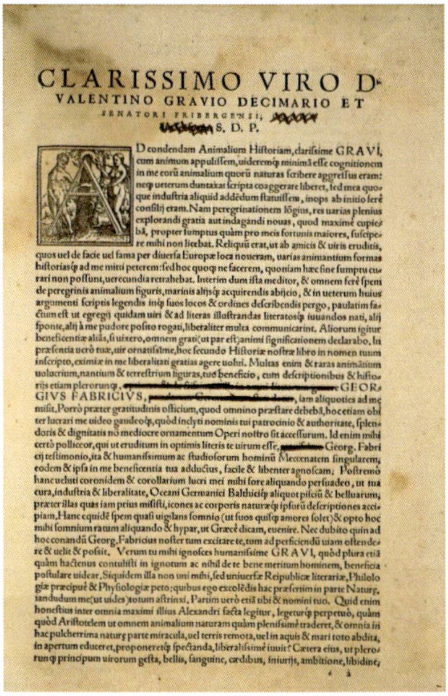

A Divided Audience: The Protestant Conrad Gessner wrote books on numerous uncontroversial topics, including this encyclopedia of animals. The makers of the *Index* decided that Catholics could own the book, but Gessner frequently thanks and praises fellow scientists who sent him drawings or observations, and the Index commanded that, while the Catholic owner could have the information and the name, praise must be crossed out if the scientist was a Protestant, since heretics are not "learned" or "excellent." In many cases like this, the Inquisition's goal was clearly not destroy or even control information, but to remind the reader on every page—through the vivid black blots—of Inquisition's presence and authority, and that reading Protestant authors brought one close to a dangerous divide.

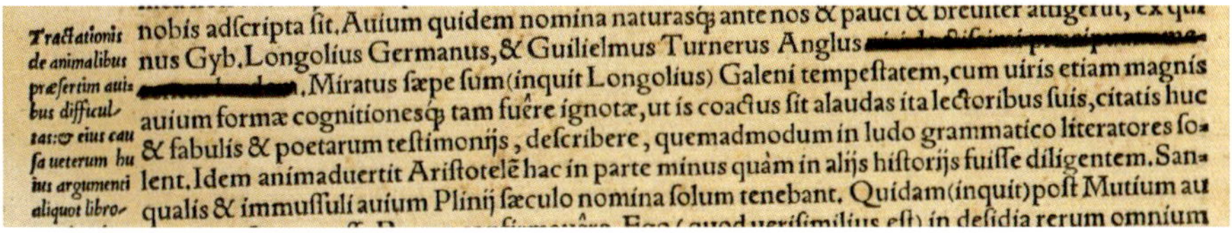

With Special Permission: German physician and botanist Leonhart Fuchs (from whom Fuchsia, the plant and color, take their names) published medical texts, especially on the medical applications of plants. A firm Protestant, his works were condemned by the Inquisition, but were invaluable to doctors. Historian of Science Hannah Marcus has uncovered hundreds of cases in the Inquisition granted doctors three-year renewable licenses to own Fuchs's works, usually with the stipulation that they destroy his name: some cut it out, some change it to a pun or nonsense word, some black it out, and some draw a thin line through, obscuring nothing.

Above and Left: Leonhart Fuchs (1501-1566), *Methodvs Sev Ratio Compendiaria Perueniendi ad Veram Solidamq*, [Venice: Per I.A. & P. de Nicolinis de Sabio, 1543]. R128.6.F92 Rare.

Conquest Through Ridicule: Sometimes inquisitors used humor to mock and belittle condemned authors. Here Dominican friar Egidius de Andrea has carried out the order to excise the author's name Balduinus, not by blacking it out, but by changing it to Babbuinus (babboon) and preceding it with insults such as ingnorantissimus (most ignorant). Balduino himself was educated at the University of Padua—a haven of heterodoxy protected by the Venetian Republic—and this controversial work, whose content the censor has left intact, outlined the weaknesses and limitations of Aristotelian logic, and influenced Galileo's science.

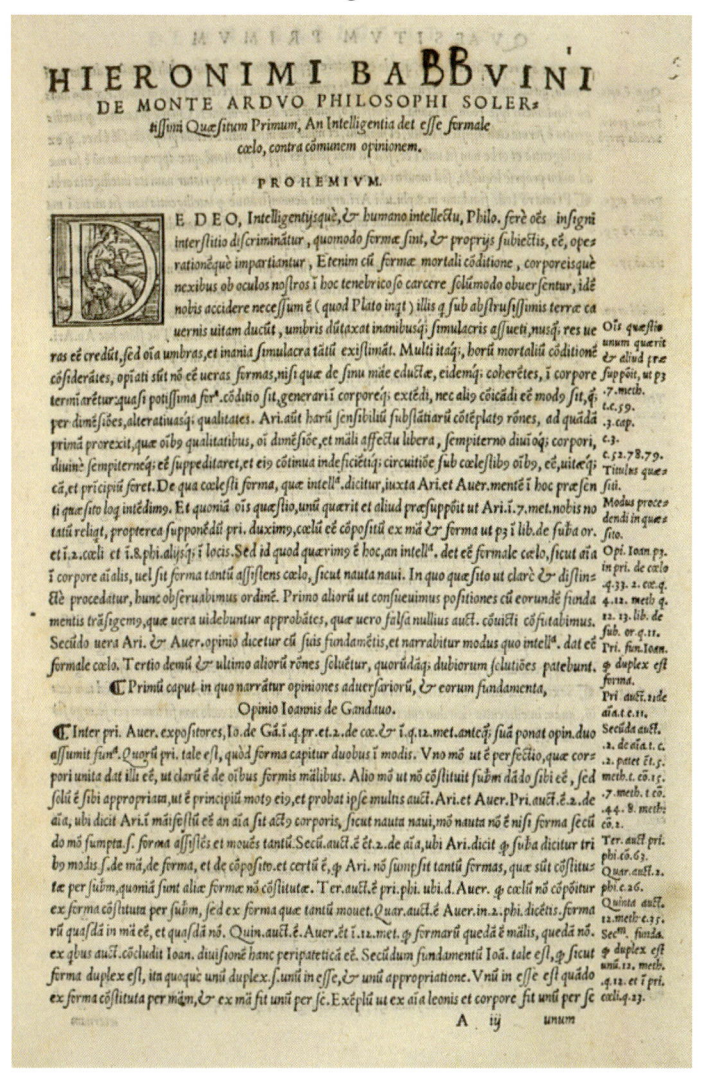

Above: Girolamo Balduini (fl. 1560-1570), *Quaesita Hieronymi Balduini*, Neap.: Matthiam Cancerem, 1550. fB485.B35 1550 Rare. *Gift of the Joseph Halle Schaffner Endowed Book Fund.*

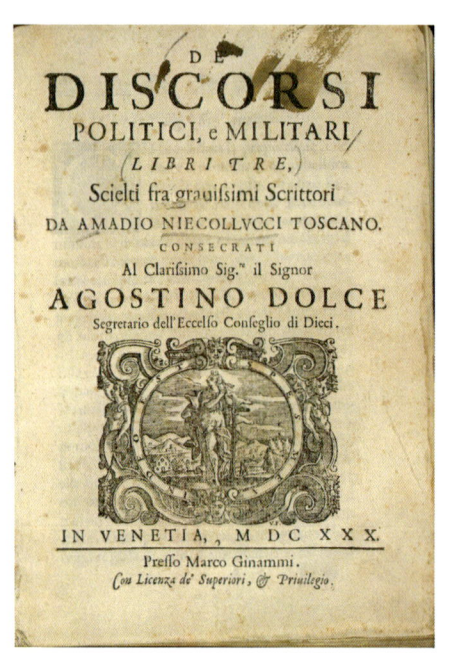

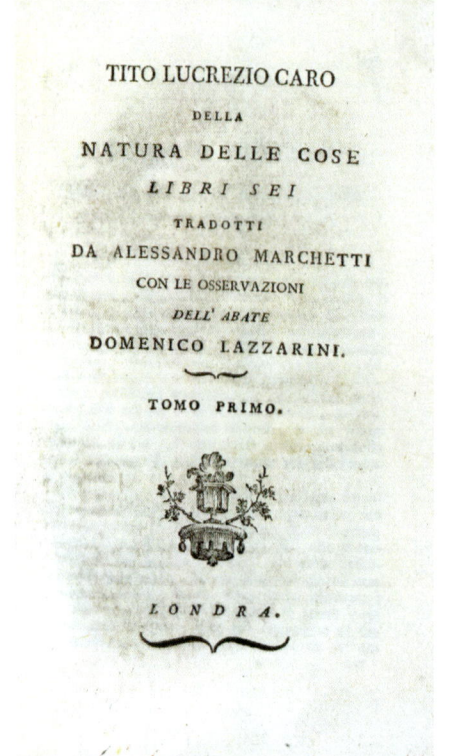

Left: Amadio Niecollvcci [Niccolò Machiavelli] (1469-1527), *De' discorsi politici, e militari libri tre scielti fra grauissimi scrittori da Amadio Niecollvcci Toscano*, Venetia, Presso Marco Ginammi, 1630.
JC143.M136 Rare.

Turning a Blind Eye: After his death, Machiavelli became a kind of mythical archetype, the wicked atheist who justifies sin and whose name "Niccolo" became a nickname for the Devil "Old Nick." Yet the Inquisition never considered him as dangerous as heretical theologians. This 1630 edition of Machiavelli's Discourses managed to be printed in Catholic Venice using the transparent pseudonym "Amadio Niecollvcci," aided, no doubt, by local censors who considered Machiavelli a minor threat, and by the impregnable Venetian Republic's comparative independence from Rome.

Left: Tito Lucrezio Caro, *Della Natura Delle Cose Libra Sei*, London: S. n., n.d. *On loan from Ada Palmer.*

Right and Below: Titus Lucretius Carus, *Della Natura della Cose*. Ms 418 MssCdx.

Policing Elites vs. Policing the Public: *De rerum natura (On the Nature of things)* by the Roman poet Lucretius explains the doctrines of Epicureanism, including denial of Providence, divine creation, the immortal soul, and atomist science. The Inquisition considered the Latin text benign since it could only be read by elite scholars too wise to be "misled" by its "errors." However, when in 1669 the mathematician Alessandro Marchetti translated it into Italian for the general public, the translation was banned, and added to the *Index*. Manuscripts of the forbidden translation, like the one displayed here, were owned by many prominent figures including Voltaire, while this early printed edition claims to be printed in "Londra" (London), but is likely an Italian product attempting to evade censors.

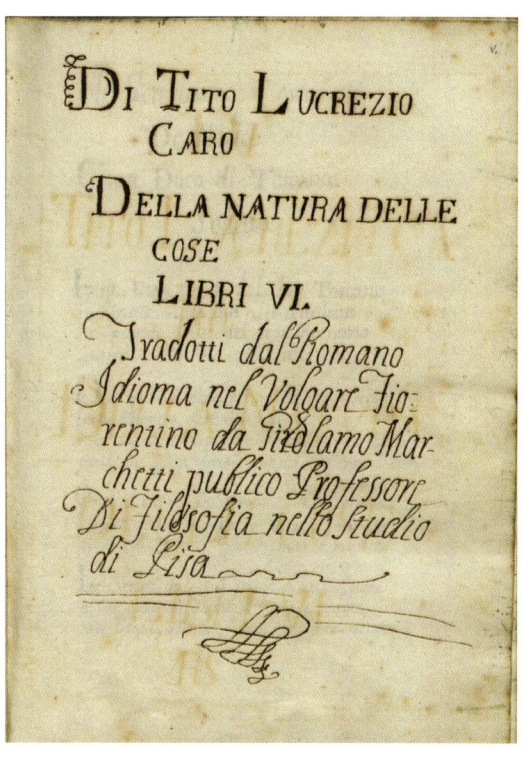

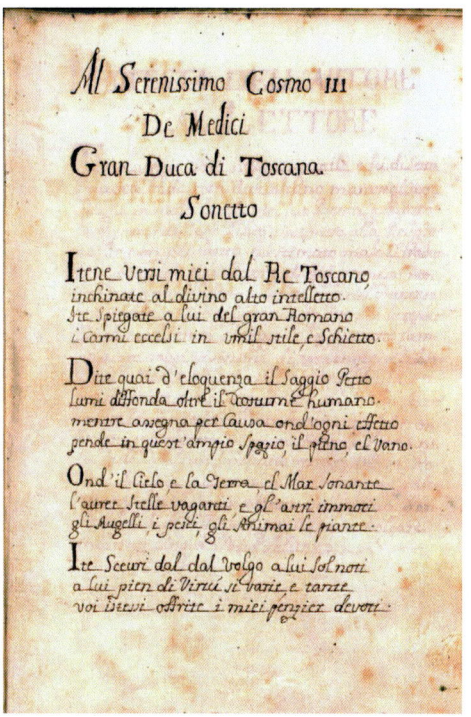

[73]

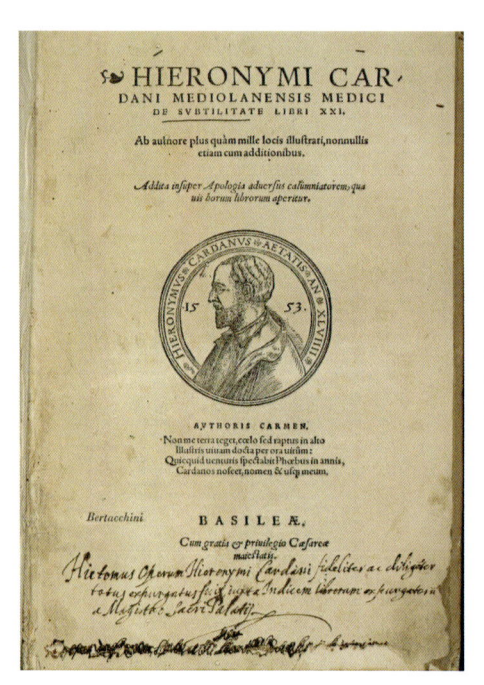

Pages 74-79: Girolamo Cardano (15011-1576), *Hieronymi Cardani Mediolanensis Medici De Subtilitate Libri XXI*, Basel: Ex officina etrina, 1560. Q155.C26 1560 Rare.

No Other Protector: Gerolamo Cardano (1501-1576) was an Italian mathematician, physician, chemist, inventor, and astrologer who taught at the University of Pavia in the north of Italy. He then moved to the University of Bologna, more renowned but located in the Papal States, which made faculty more vulnerable to Inquisition than faculty at distant universities who could seek protection from local dukes or city councils. Cardano was arrested by the Inquisition in 1570, imprisoned for several months, and forced to renounce his professorship. This work—primarily treating minerals—has been expurgated following the Inquisition's guidelines.

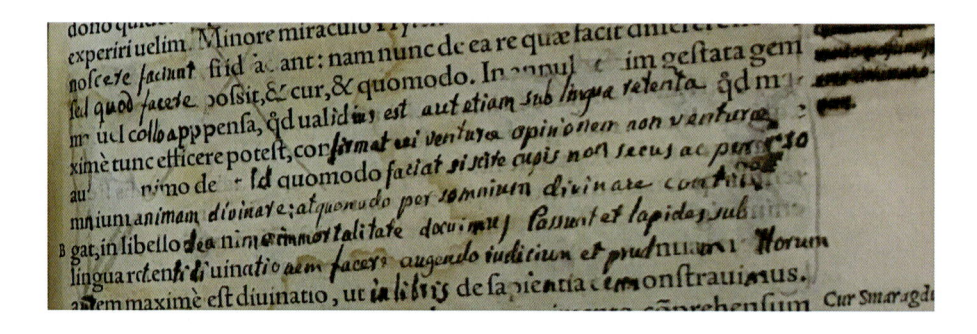

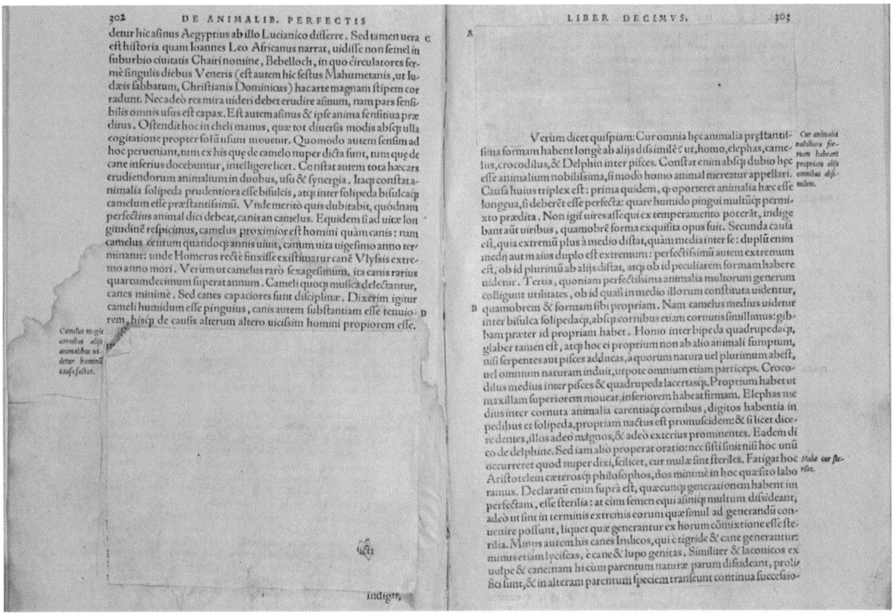

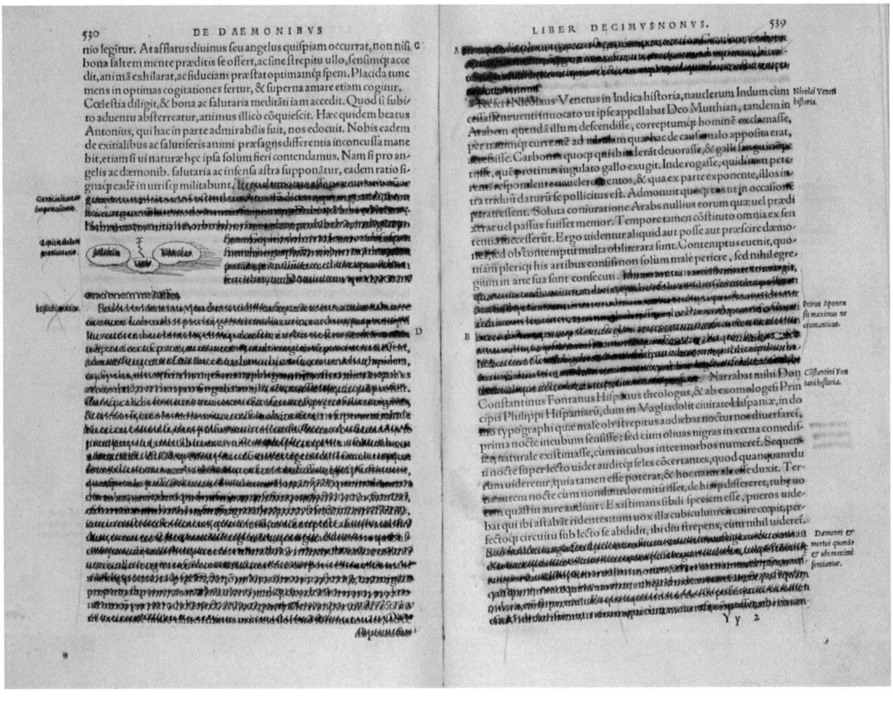

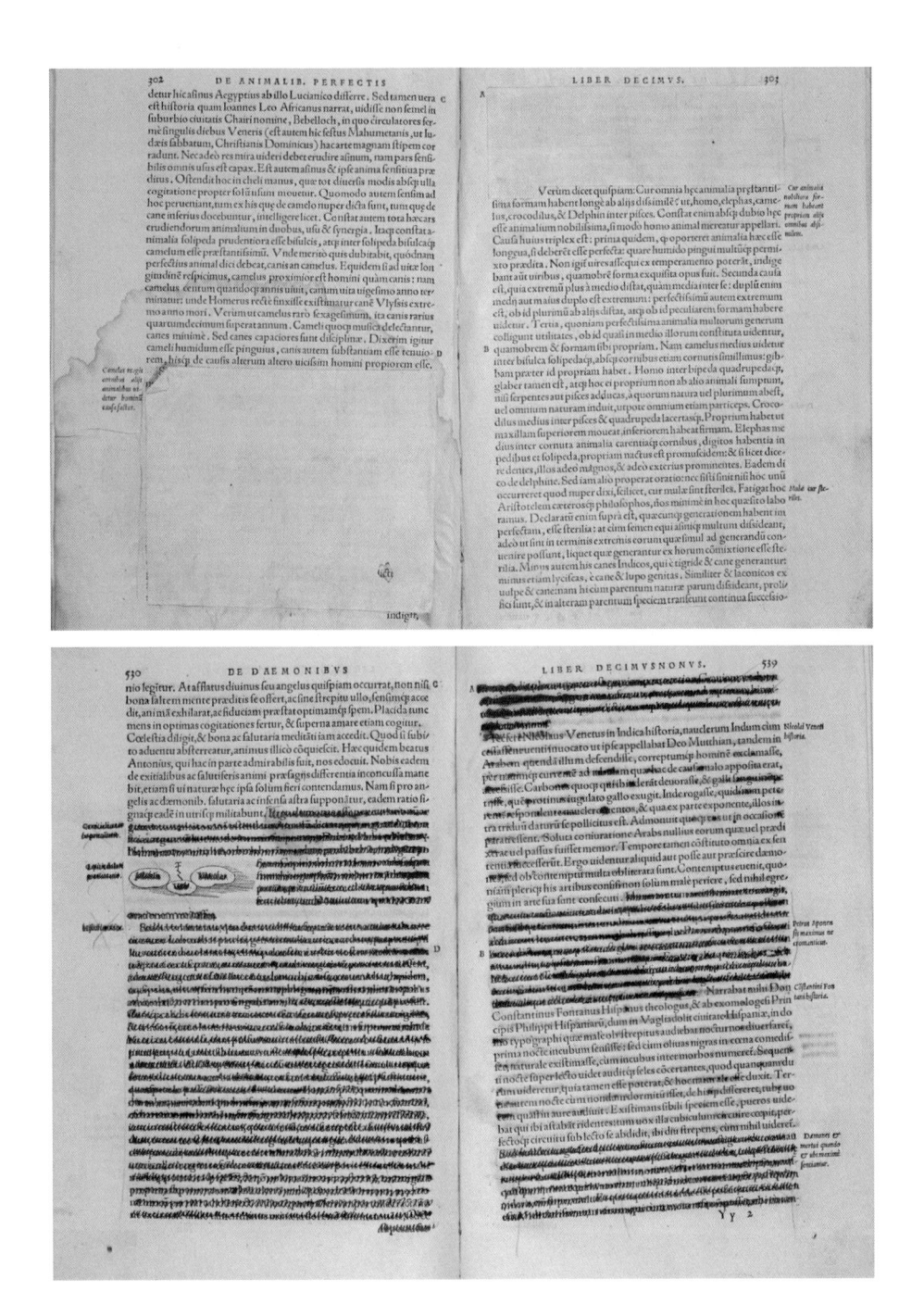

Pages 76-77: The e is nothing to see here. This text is written over, scorched through, and physically removed.

Pages 78-79: Someone pasted a blank page over this section of text but then a later reader peeled it off and then copied the the text that was peeled off back into the passage The written over text is also shown in detail in the bottom facing image.

ripitur. Sed & quædam [illegible] non est dicendum animalia plantas esse. Itaq; ad sermonem de homine transeamus.

Homo ipse propter quatuor factus est: primum, ut diuina cognosce ret: secundum, ut illis mortalia medius existens connecteret: tertium, ut mortalibus imperaret. Necesse enim erat & in hoc genere uelut & in cœlesti, aliquod esse optimum ac nobilissimum, quodq; imperitet cæ teris, h¹ic autem ui, illic uerò spontè. Quartum, ut quicquid mente exco gitari posset, id omne opifex maior ipsa cogitatione præstaret, essetq; animal fallax. Nam belluæ fallaces esse nõ poterant ob stultitiã, superi uerò

imperium obtinuerit, magnitudo incredibilis, [...]
[...]li. At in feruidis regionibus maximas ciuitates esse necesse est: pri
[...]li, q̃ soli pars aut sterilis est, si aquis careat: aut fertilissima, si abun-
[...]nitur, ob hanc inæqualitatẽ cùm locus multitudini alendæ opportunus
[...]nitur, par est amplissimam urbem condi, numerosissimumq̃ po-
[...]um in eam confluere. Alia ualidior causa est, q̃ cum procul ueniant
[...]ces, & per loca deserta periculosaq̃, necesse est ut simul plures ue-
[...]nt mercatores, ac in modum agminis, ob securitatem: quare cùm in
[...]uã urbem sedem posuerit, incõmodum nimis esset eam societatem
[...]ari, non solùm mercatorib. sed urbibus: unde melius est & longè fa-
[...]s, uicinos omnes in eum locum confluere, quod cum multis perse-
[...]tannis, cõtingit etiam è paruo pago urbem fieri populosissimam.
[...]es igitur sunt, Quinsai, Singui, Cambala & Cairum. Hãc ciuitatem
[...]noar Illyricus seruus Elcaim Mahumetanorum Pontificis in Ægy-
[...]to ædificauit securitatis causa, uocatãq̃ nomine Pontificis Elcaira,
[...]e corrupto uocabulo Cairum. Si quis obijciat Byzantium seu Con-
[...]tinopolim, tametsi cum his quæ LX. atq̃ amplius habent passuum
[...] ambitu conferri minimè debeat, causa tamen imperium est. [...]

Quatuor urbes maxima orbis. Cairi urbis or[i]go.

[heavily censored text — illegible]

dum iuxta ignem est, id est, super prunas positus, obscurior sit ac rubicundior, ab igne remotus splendescit. Verùm parum hoc genus à carbunculo nobilitate differt, rarissima, ut dixi, mediocri magnitudine. Referūt ad hoc genus uires omnes manifestè, obscurè uerò ad aureum, nullo modo ad aqueum, hic enim uilis est, & effœtarum uirium: augere præterea diuitias ac autoritatem existimant, cor uerò confirmare admodum, lætitiamq̄ nō obscurā gignere. Horū igitur causam nō tanquam uerorum, sed ut possibilium afferamus. Frigidi temperamenti est: atq̄ hoc fermè omnibus cōmune gemmis, & spiritui humano commodus, seu substantiæ similitudine, seu claritate, seu alia causa, unde illum reparans & confirmans hilarē reddit: nihil enim aliud est tristitia, quàm uel contractio spiritus, uel paucitas, uel obscuritas. Eadem igitur ratione, ut quidam se expertos retulerunt, si quid aliud cor confirmat: pestem quoq̄ arcet, quæ maximè contingit ob metū & cordis imbecillitatem, quæ duo hyacinthus abolet: ob hoc pueri, & mulieres, & timidi, peste corripiuntur celerrimè: iuu...
tum igitur iuuab... arcendo ...
tum & mansuetum redde...
ad cuius in...

Hyacinthus quomodo à fulmine hominem tueri possit. Viri clari fulmine extincti.

Re...
exigu...
tam re...
lo Th...
XXV...
quotr...
consil...
thum ferre, quos nunquam fulmen læsurum est, uel ut prohibeat ne lædatur qui fert hyacinthū, etiam si fulmine tactus fuerit. Plures excogitari modos posse non uideo. Tangi fulgure nec lædi uix est uerisimile: neque qui scribunt, non lædi, sed non tangere scripsere. Rursus prohibere etiam ne ueniat, maius miraculum erit quàm hoc: actiones enim saltem conspicuæ & magnæ contactu fieri solent. Fato uerò ita esse constitutum, proximum fabulæ esse uidetur. Illud igitur melius est dicere, ex hilaratum spiritum cordis etiam hoc commodi assequi, ut hominem eò dirigat, quò omnino à fulgure tutus sit. Dicere autem, quòd etiam si tangatur, non lędatur, medicum est ac magis naturale: quanquam miraculo euidenti proximius sit.

Diximus in his, morē Philosophi secuti, qui in tam arduis quęstionibus satis esse putat, si magis absurda deuitemus. At quòd lapides nos tueantur à casu, uelut de Erano, uocata Turchesia referunt, quæ annulo gestata, si ex equo cadat homo, excipere omnem ictum creditur, atq̄ frangi etiam in frusta seruato homine, minus difficilem habet causam, tametsi arduam: adijciunt, oportere dono esse acceptam. Lapis hic colore cœli

Turchesia.

LIBER SE[PTIMUS]

conspicuus est, nitetq́; Probatur autē, q̃ nocte [...]
[...]rs auersa & quę in imo est, nigra sit, q̃ uenas ex inferiore parte reci[...]
[...] q̃ lenis sit nec admodū frigidus, q̃ excipiat. Et cùm talis etiam fuerit,
[...]rulea uideat̃, coloremq́; gemmę excipiat. Quinetia ignibus propè ad[...]
perspicuus, nec gēma: lima enim tangit. Quinetiā ignibus propè ad[...]
[...]us efflorescit color, & solo manuum udo flaccescit, & diluit̃. Ob hoc
[...]tū est, an seplasia gemmarioū uulgata sit fama tantæ uirtutis, ut ma[...]
precij ac modicæ pulchritudinis ac caducę lapis reperiret emptores.
[...]chi apud quos nascit̃ alias ei esse putāt uires, q̃ aduersus ueneficia &
[...]phaticos. Ergo si prohibeat cadentiū damna, hoc fiet homine minus
[...]sso: nam & ob hanc causam cadentibus uiliorib. ac macilentis equis
[...]o mollis est, ut celerius equite ipso cadente lędat̃. Est mihi Erano, &
[...]periclitamur. Sed lapidē ipsū ictum excipere, supra fidē est: forsan
[...]no quidē accepta, nec experiri contigit, nec tanti est uoluisse scire ut
[...]periri uelim. Minore miraculo Hyę[ni]m & S[m]ar[ag]dū futura p[...]   *Smaragdus.*
[...]cere faciunt siid a[...]ant: nam nunc de ea re quæ facit disserere nolo,
quod facere possit, & cur, & quomodo. In [...] im gestata gem
uel collo appensa, q̃d ualid[...] est aut etiam sub lingua retenta, q̃d m[...]
nē tunc efficere potest, confirmat [...] uenturę opinionem non uenturę[...]
[...] nimo de[...] Sed quomodo faciat si scire cupis non secus ac per so[...]
[...]ium animam diuinare: atquo[mo]do per somnium diuinare contig[it]
[...]in libello de animę immortalitate docuimus. Possunt et lapides sub
[...]qua retenti diuinatio[n]em facere, augendo iudicium et prudentiam horum
[...]em maximè est diuinatio, ut in libris de sapientia demonstrauimus.   *Cur Smaragdus*
[...]angi uerò Smaragdū in coitu quandocq̃; experimento cōprehensum   *in coitu quan-*
[...]cunt. Vt utresse habeat, fragilior omnium gemmarū est Smaragdus.   *doq̃; frangatur.*
[...]um uerò abundanti tenuiq̃; humido cōcoctio accesserit, calore uexata
[...]srumpit: nam humidū concalefactū in aerem transit, maiusq̃; occupat
[...]aciū, inde disrumpit: hoc enim demonstratū est superius. Incalescere
[...]urimū corpus in Venere, & anhelitus frequētia, & sudoris aduentus
[...]iam quandocq̃; docet, caloreq̃; hic magis imprimit, quia nō quemadmo[dum]
[...]um in exercitationib. sensim dissoluitur. Venenis maximè resistit epo   *Cur Smaragdus*
[...] hæc gemma, quoniā mollitie uincitur à natura plus omni alia gemma: *præcipuè resi-*
[...]erspicuitate substantiā spiritus recreat humidi cōcocti abundantia, na   *stit uenenis.*
[...]uræ humanæ confert, & ueneni naturā retundit: quia uerò lapis, sta bi[...]
[...]es uires retinet. Eorum uerò quę uisui grata sunt, ferme nullum homini
[...]on utile est. Dico autem gēmas, aurum, argentū, sericum, purpurā, mo[...]
[...]o ars aspectū non decipiat. Itaq̃; Smaragdus cùm pulchritudine præ   *Gemmarum no-*
[...]antissima sit gemmarū, ut duritia & soliditate Adamas, gratia Sapphi[...]   *bilium propriæ*
[...]us, alacritate Carbūculus, ac splendoris uarietate Opalus, nitore Chry[...]   *laudes.*
[...]olithus, diuersitate Achates, ita etiam Smaragdus hominis salubritati
[...]plus conferet: uerum ut mollissima est, ita obnoxia omnibus maximè ca[...]
[...]ibus. Vitiatur ab igne & æstu, à contactu duriorum gemmarū, præci[...]

B

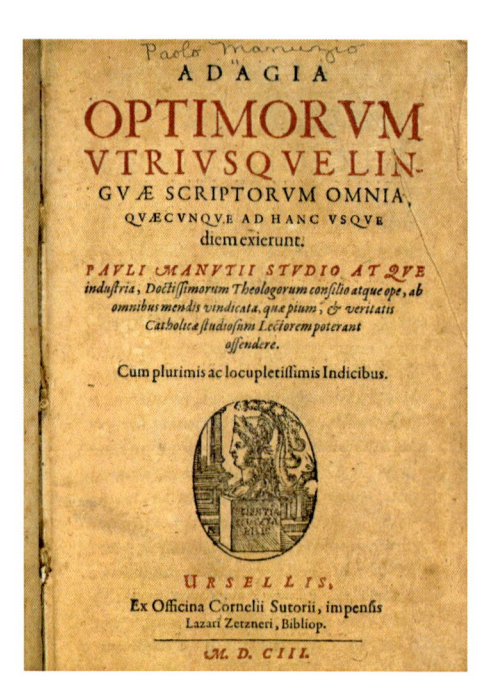

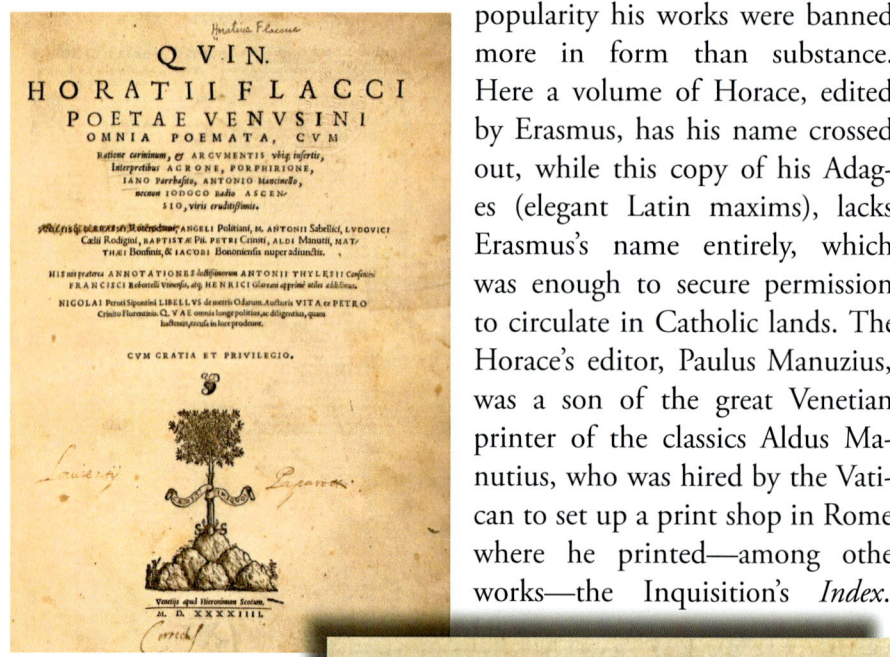

Left: Paolo Manuzio (1512-1574, *Adagia Optimorvm Vtrivsqve Lingvae Scriptorvm Omnia…*, Ursellis: L. Zetzneri, 1603. PN6413.M3 1603 Rare.

Below and Facing: Horace *Quin. Horatii Flacci Poetae Venusini…*, Venice: Hieronimum Scotum [1544]. fPA6393.A2 1544 Rare. *Gift of the Joseph Halle Schaffner Endowed Book Fund.*

Censoring a Beloved Bestseller: Dutch humanist Erasmus of Rotterdam was a masterful Latin stylist, scholar, and, for several decades, the most widely printed author in Europe. While remaining Catholic, he corresponded with Luther and endorsed a compromise between Protestants and Catholics, for which the Church criticized him fiercely. As a result of his popularity his works were banned more in form than substance. Here a volume of Horace, edited by Erasmus, has his name crossed out, while this copy of his Adages (elegant Latin maxims), lacks Erasmus's name entirely, which was enough to secure permission to circulate in Catholic lands. The Horace's editor, Paulus Manuzius, was a son of the great Venetian printer of the classics Aldus Manutius, who was hired by the Vatican to set up a print shop in Rome where he printed—among other works—the Inquisition's *Index*.

[80]

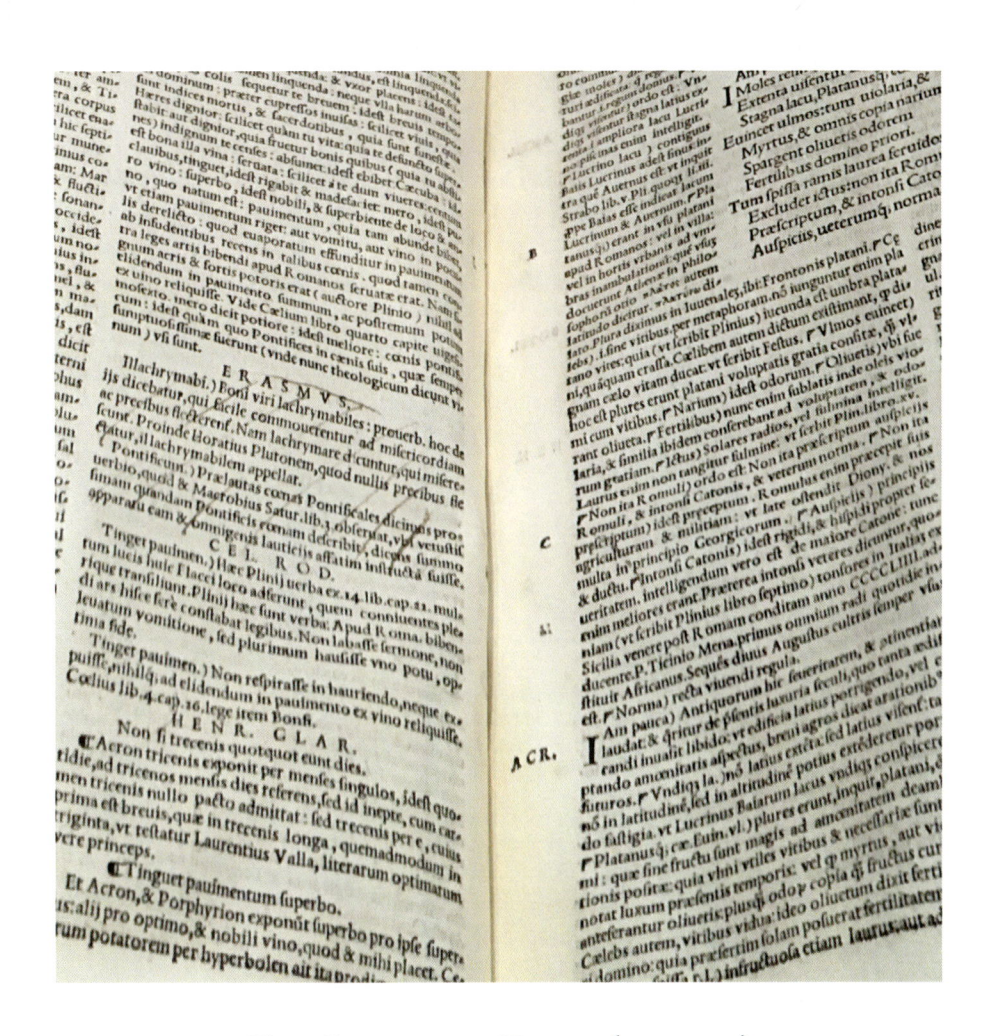

The Council of Trent (1559-1565)

Convened by the papacy to formulate a systematic response to Protestantism, the Council of Trent issued these ten rules to govern books in the period of Catholic self-reform which we now call the Counter-Reformation. The rules reflect special concerns of the period—Protestant sects, translated Bibles, astrology—but also many perennial concerns of censorship: obscenity, sexuality, presumed danger to children, the special status of the Classics, sorting true from false scientific claims, the power of translation, how to control publishers, booksellers, and readers as well as authors, the administrative necessity of keeping records or copies of banned materials, and a central body's struggles with overlapping authorities and with the challenge of policing a large region or empire containing multiple areas, peoples and cultures.

TEN RULES CONCERNING PROHIBITED BOOKS DRAWN UP BY THE FATHERS CHOSEN BY THE COUNCIL OF TRENT AND APPROVED BY POPE PIUS

I — All books which have been condemned either by the supreme pontiffs or by ecumenical councils before the year 1515 and are not contained in this list, shall be considered condemned in the same manner as they were formerly condemned.

II — The books of those heresiarchs, who after the aforesaid year originated or revived heresies, as well as of those who are or have been the heads or leaders of heretics, as Luther, Zwingli, Calvin, Balthasar Friedberg, Schwenkfeld, and others like these are absolutely forbidden. The books of other heretics, however, which deal professedly with religion are absolutely condemned. Those which do not deal with religion and have been examined and approved , are permitted .

III — The translations of writers, also ecclesiastical, which have till now been edited by condemned authors, are permitted provided they contain nothing contrary to sound doctrine. Translations of the books of the Old Testament be permitted to learned and pious men only . Translations of the New Testament made by authors of the first class of this list shall be permitted to no one, since great danger and little usefulness usually results to readers from their perusal.

IV — Since if the Sacred Books are permitted everywhere and without discrimination in the vernacular, there will by reason of the boldness of men arise therefrom more harm than good, the bishop or inquisitor, may permit the reading of the Sacred Books translated into the vernacular by Catholic authors to those who they know will derive from such reading no harm but rather an increase of faith and piety, which permission they must have in writing. . Bookdealers who sell Bibles written in the vernacular shall be subject to other penalties .

V — Those books which sometimes produce the works of heretical authors, in lexicons, concordances, apothegms, parables, tables of contents and such like, are permitted if corrected

VI — Books which deal in the vernacular with the controversies between Catholics and heretics of our time may not be permitted indiscriminately . There is no reason, however, why those should be prohibited if they contain sound doctrine, just as popular sermons are not prohibited. But if hitherto in some kingdom or province certain books have been prohi iscut, these may, if their authors are Catholic, be pe ted iscut after they have been corrected.

VII — Books which professedly deal with, narrate or teach things lascivious or obscene are absolutely prohibited, since not only the matter of faith but also that of mo , which are usually easily corrupted through the reading of such books, iscut those who possess them are to be severely punished by the bishops. Ancient books written by heathens may by reason of their elegance and quality of style be permitted, but may by no means be read to children.

VIII — Books whose chief contents are good but in which some things have incidentally been inserted which have reference to heresy, ungodliness, divination or superstition, may be permitted if they have been purged by Catholic theologians. The same decision holds good with regard to prefaces, summaries or annotations removed by condemned authors.

IX — All books and writings dealing with geomancy, hydromancy, aeromancy, pyromancy, oneiromancy, chiromancy, necromancy, or with sortilege, mixing of poisons, augury, auspices, sorcery, magic arts, are absolutely repudiated. The bishops shall diligently see to it that books, treatises, catalogues determining destiny by astrology, which in the matter of future events, consequences, or fortuitous occurrences, or of actions that depend on the human will, attempt to affirm something as certain to take place, are not read or possessed. Permitted, on the other hand, are the opinions & natural observations which have been written in the interest of navigation, agriculture or the medical art.

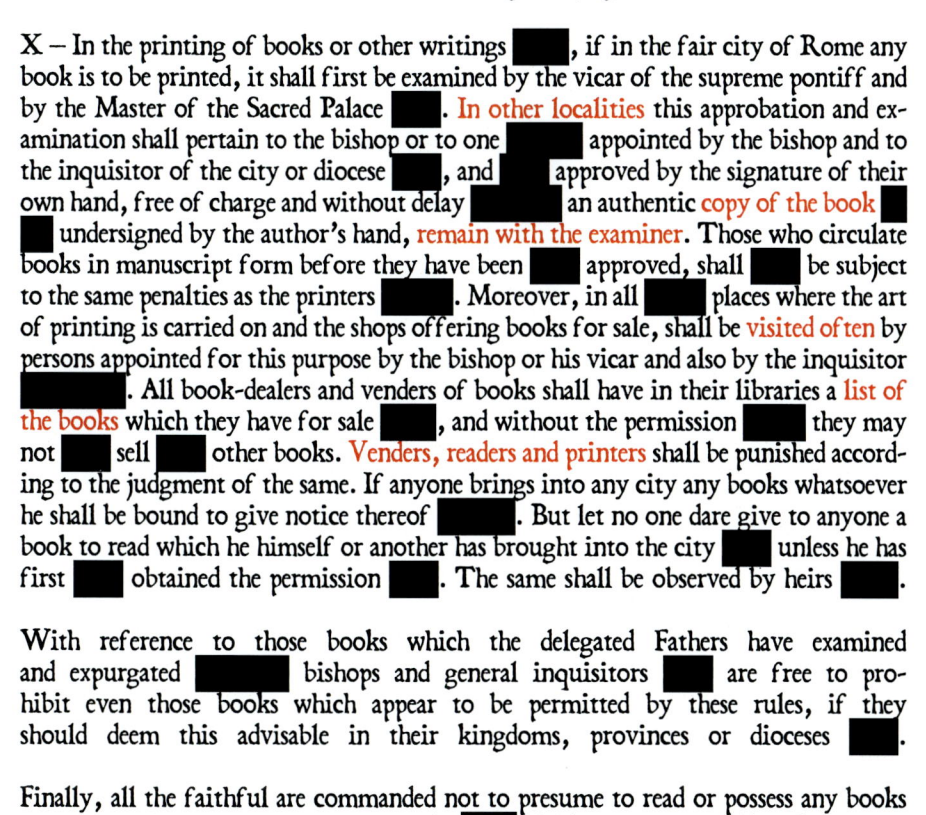

X — In the printing of books or other writings, if in the fair city of Rome any book is to be printed, it shall first be examined by the vicar of the supreme pontiff and by the Master of the Sacred Palace. In other localities this approbation and examination shall pertain to the bishop or to one appointed by the bishop and to the inquisitor of the city or diocese, and approved by the signature of their own hand, free of charge and without delay an authentic copy of the book undersigned by the author's hand, remain with the examiner. Those who circulate books in manuscript form before they have been approved, shall be subject to the same penalties as the printers. Moreover, in all places where the art of printing is carried on and the shops offering books for sale, shall be visited often by persons appointed for this purpose by the bishop or his vicar and also by the inquisitor. All book-dealers and venders of books shall have in their libraries a list of the books which they have for sale, and without the permission they may not sell other books. Venders, readers and printers shall be punished according to the judgment of the same. If anyone brings into any city any books whatsoever he shall be bound to give notice thereof. But let no one dare give to anyone a book to read which he himself or another has brought into the city unless he has first obtained the permission. The same shall be observed by heirs.

With reference to those books which the delegated Fathers have examined and expurgated bishops and general inquisitors are free to prohibit even those books which appear to be permitted by these rules, if they should deem this advisable in their kingdoms, provinces or dioceses.

Finally, all the faithful are commanded not to presume to read or possess any books contrary to the prescriptions of these rules. And if anyone should read or possess books by heretics he incurs immediately the sentence of excommunication. He who reads or possesses books prohibited under another name shall, besides incurring the guilt of mortal sin, be severely punished according to the judgment of the bishops.

Translation provided by the Modern History Sourcebook

P. seulin f.   C. Vermeulen

NO ONE EXPECTS THE PHILIPPINE INQUISITION

The largely independent Spanish and Portuguese Inquisitions were two of the most far-reaching systems of institutionalized censorship in Earth's history, affecting spaces from the Netherlands and Iberia to sub-Saharan Africa, North and South America, the Philippines, Sri Lanka, Goa in India, and affecting China and Japan. Both were unstable, with multiple overlapping authorities—Jesuits, Dominicans, local governors, indigenous elites, and officer of the distant Crown and Pope—competing to exert control while cut off from central oversight by months of travel. Sometimes different censors had authority over different people, individuals categorized as European falling under one, those classified as indigenous under another, though categorization was complex, and two siblings of mixed parentage might choose to present themselves as different categories in documents, since each offered unique legal and career opportunities. One of the greatest anxieties of both empires was to keep Protestantism out of their colonies, which extended to anxiety about any text in English or German, or printed in a Protestant capital.

Facing and Pages 86-88: Gabriel Dellon, *Relation de l'Inquisition de Goa*, Paris: Chez Daniel Horthemels, 1688, BX1733.G7D297 Rare.

With No Restraining Power Near: Portugal-ruled Goa, on the west coast of India, from 1510 to 1961. Goa's Inquisition, initiated by Jesuit leader Francis Xavier, suppressed Hindu, Buddhist, and Muslim practice, and burnt all books written in Sanskrit, Konkani, or Marathi regardless of content. This damning account by French physician Gabriel Dellon describes how he was arrested in Goa for having criticized the Inquisition and the validity of baptism, and was excommunicated, stripped of his property, and sentenced to five years in the galleys, a story which influenced Voltaire's *Candide*.

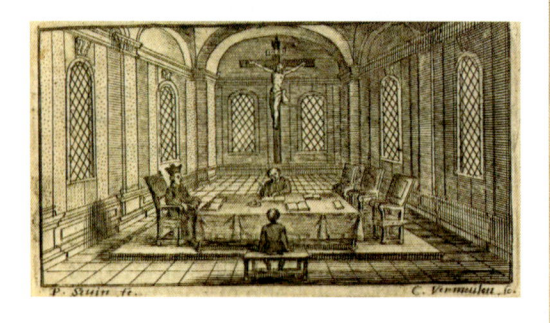

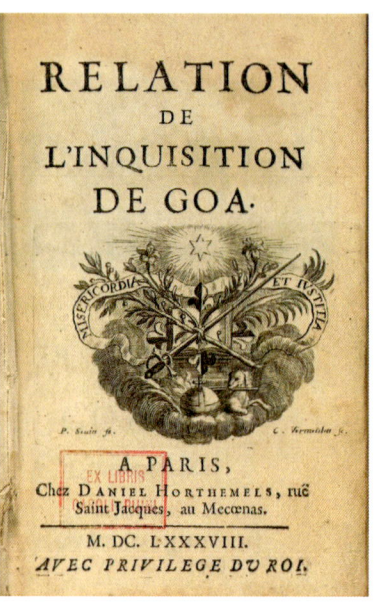

RELATION
DE
L'INQUISITION
DE GOA.

MISERICORDIA ET IUSTITIA

A PARIS,
Chez DANIEL HORTHEMELS, ruë
Saint Jacques, au Mecœnas.
M. DC. LXXXVIII.
AVEC PRIVILEGE DU ROI.

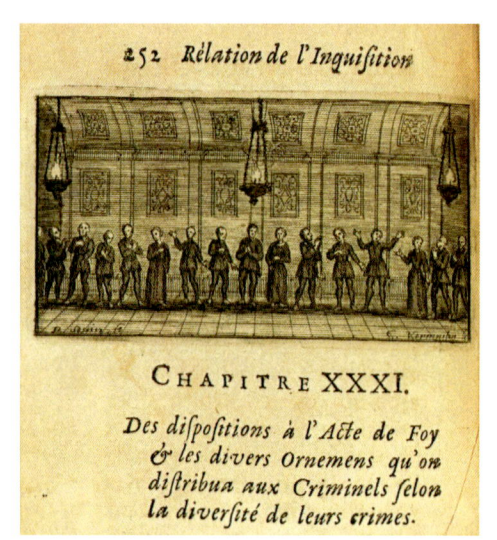

252 *Rélation de l'Inquisition*

CHAPITRE XXXI.

Des dispositions à l'Acte de Foy
& les divers Ornemens qu'on
distribua aux Criminels selon
la diversité de leurs crimes.

[86]

[87]

[88]

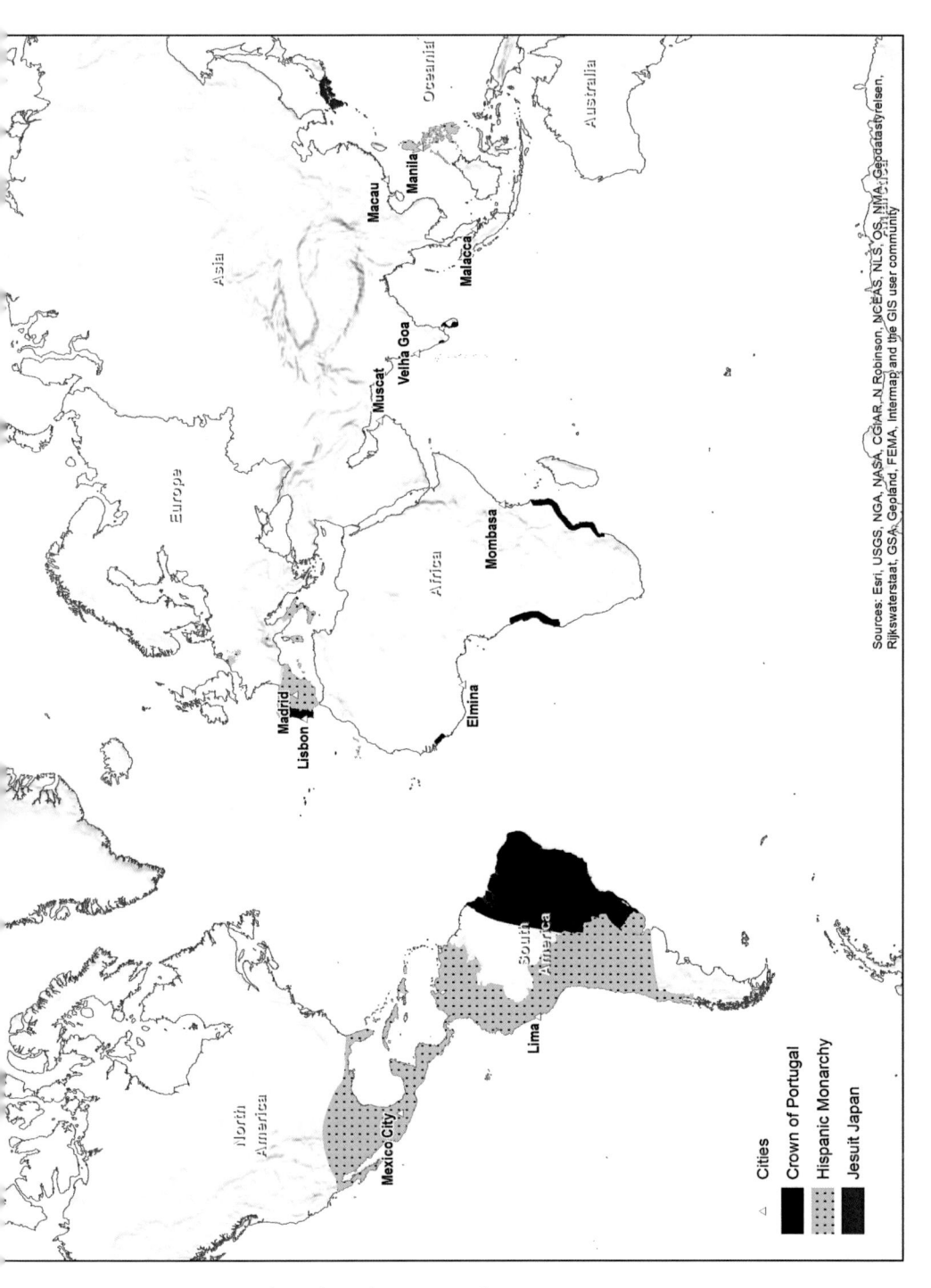

Map by Cheryl Cape and Stuart McManus.

Frontispicio.　　　　　　　　　　　　　　　　　　　　　　　Tom. 3 y 4.

EL INGENIOSO
HIDALGO
DON QUIXOTE
DE LA
MANCHA.

D. Pedro Arnal, Arquitecto, lo inventó y lo dibujó.　　　　D. Juan de la Cruz, Geografo de S.M. lo grabó.

Facing: Miguel de Cervantes Saavedra (1547-1616), *El Ignenioso Hidalgo Don Quixote de la Mancha*, Madrid: Cámara de S. M. y de la Real Academia, [1780]. alcPQ6323.A1 1780 v. 1 Rare.

Satire Survives: The Inquisition oversaw Spanish literature's Siglo de Oro ("Golden Age") including the publication of Cervantes' *Don Quixote*. In one scene, two of Quixote's friends (a barber and a priest), burn his library, fearing that he's made himself sick reading too many chivalric texts. This satirical jab at the practice of book burning was left untouched by inquisitors and even featured on the frontispiece of the 1780 edition. The only sentence in *Don Quixote* removed by inquisitors was the seemingly benign comment, "works of charity done in a luke-warm and half-hearted way are without merit and of no avail," which was read as a tacit endorsement of the Protestant doctrine of sola fide

Above: Miguel de Cervantes Saavedra (1547-1616), *El Ignenioso Hidalgo Don Quixote de la Mancha*, Madrid: Cámara de S. M. y de la Real Academia, [1780]. alcPQ6323.A1 1780 v. 2 Rare.

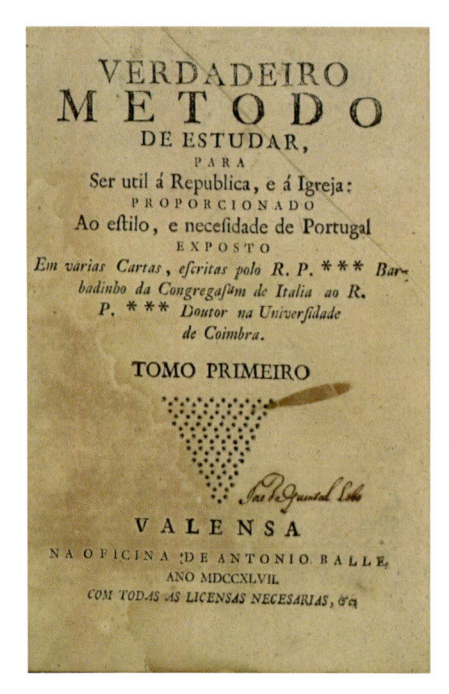

Left: Luis António Verney, *Verdadeiro Método de Estudar*, Valencia, Spain: Offic of António Balle, 1747. *On loan from Ada Palmer.*

Dissent From Within: Luis Antonio Verney, born in Portugal of French émigré parents, was a leader of Portugal's Enlightenment. This educational treatise criticized Jesuit teaching and triggered major educational reforms. The Inquisition seized and destroyed the first edition when it reached Lisbon harbor, so only a few copies survive, guarded by fake title pages. This second edition was printed in secret by Manuel de Santa Marta Teixeira, himself a preacher and office of the Inquisition, one of many Enlightenment-era censors sympathetic to progress who undermined the system from the inside.

Silencing Local Religion: Portuguese explorers reached Ceylon (modern-day Sri Lanka) in 1505. *This Account of the Happy Progresses of the Mission* in Ceylon recounts what is called a dark age in modern Sri Lankan histories, as missionaries led by Goa's Inquisition worked to suppress local religions and spread Christianity. Accustomed to Jews and Muslims as their non-Christian audiences, missionaries struggled to communicate Abrahamic metaphysics to people steeped in Buddhist and Hindu worldviews. Portugal's conquests in Sri Lanka grew until the 1630s when indigenous powers allied with the Dutch East India Company to drive Portugal out, at the cost of admitting a diffe ent colonial power.

Above and Lower Facing: Antonio Attaide, *Relazione de' felici progressi della missione de Ceylano*, Rome: Stamperia di G. Zempel, 1734. fBV3275.A8 Rare.

Hear Ye! Hear Ye! Condemnations had to be speedily communicated to readers and booksellers, often in broadsides or pamphlets like this royal decree announcing the condemnation in Portugal of Guillaume Thomas François Raynal's *Philosophical and Political History of the Two Indies*. A collaboration with others including Diderot and Baron d'Holbach, the history was spotty on its actual history but attempted to recount European conquests in East Asia and the Americas, advancing democratic ideas and decrying the atrocities of slavery. The decree states that "no person, of whatever station" may have the book, and specifies where law-abiding citizens may turn in their copies.

Left : D. José I, King of Portugal, *Edital da Real Meza Censoria*, [Portugal]: s.n., 1773
On loan from Ada Palmer.

[93]

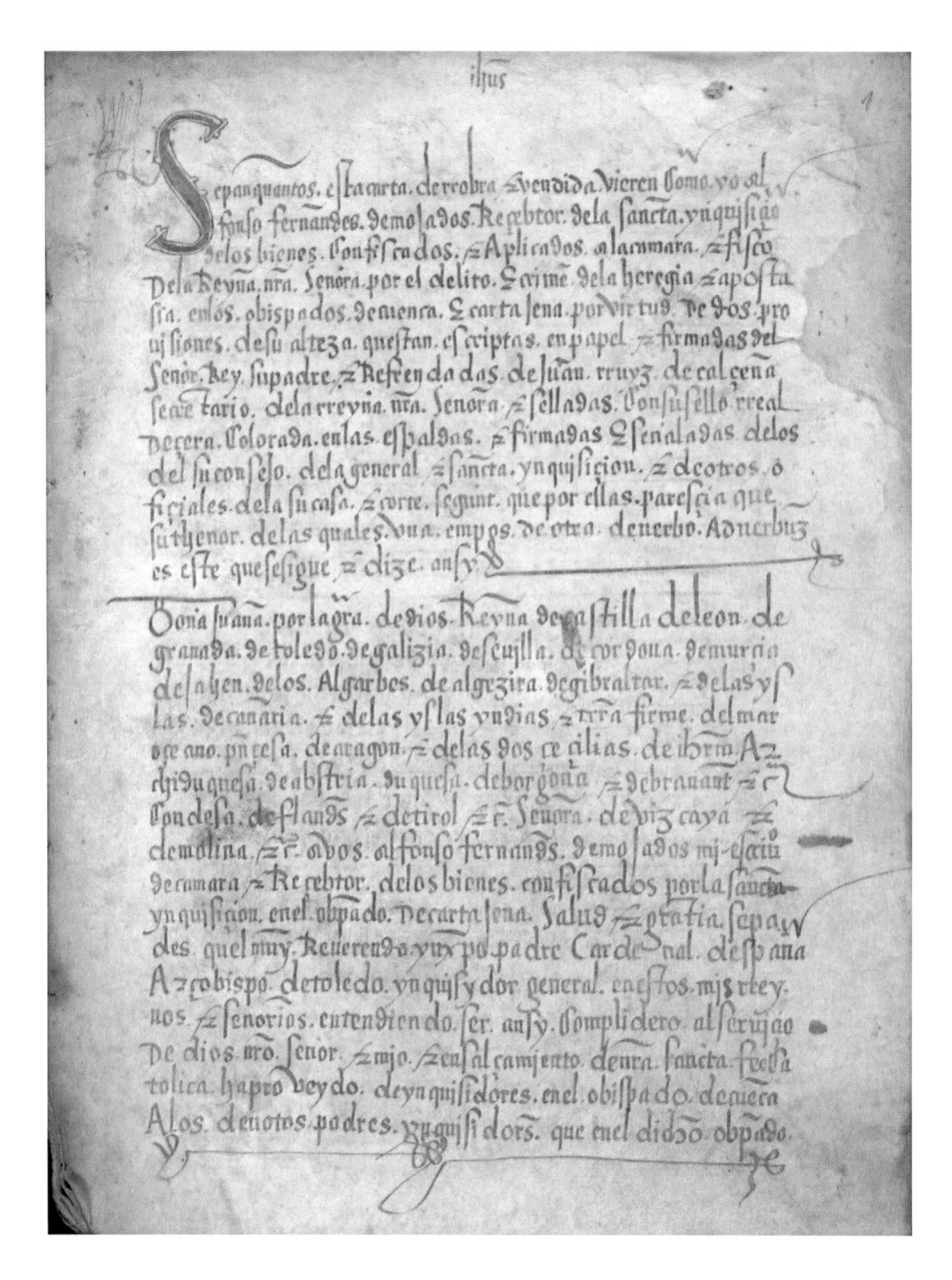

Above: [Sale Documents for Inquisition Confiscations], S.l.: 1513. Ms1181 MssCdx.

A Self-Funding System: Following administration of an *auto-da-fé* ("act of faith"), the belongings of convicted heretics were routinely collected and sold at auction, as described in this archival document. This helped fund the local Inquisition branch, making it easier for more active branches to hire more officers.

Below: *Avto Pvblico de Fee*, Seville: For Francisco de Lyra, 1648, BX1735.S268 1648 Rare. *The George Williamson Endowment Fund.*

Performing Persecution: The Spanish and Portuguese Inquisitions revived and expanded the *auto-da-fé*, a ritual of public penance. When the local Inquisition had accumulated and tried a number of prisoners, an all night public vigil and daybreak mass were followed by a parade, in which the accused marched wearing ritual garments which coded their various crimes—heresy, treason, "judaising," witchcraft etc.—as well as their sentences. At the end some were released, others tortured or burned. This document describes an *auto-da-fé* "celebrated" in southern Spain in the seventeenth century.

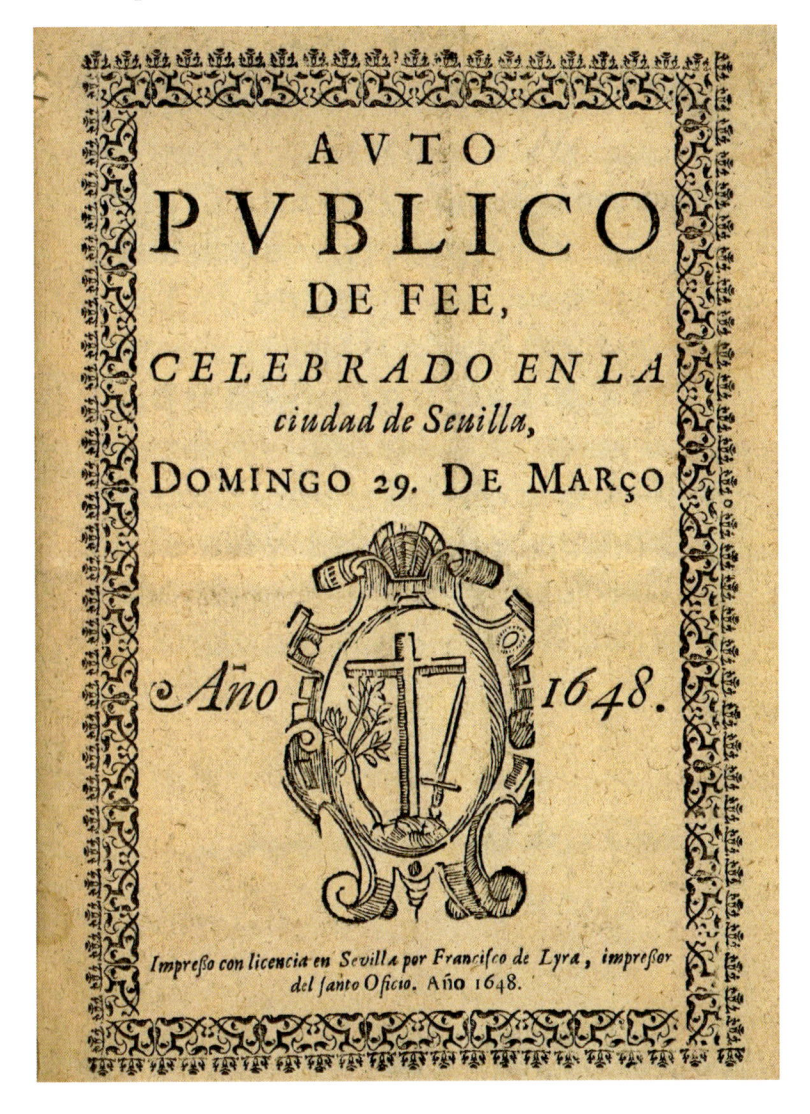

Right: Solom Ibn Verga (1460-1554), *Shevet Yehudah*, Amsterdam: Henricum Westenium, 1680. Rosenberger 42-341 Rosen.

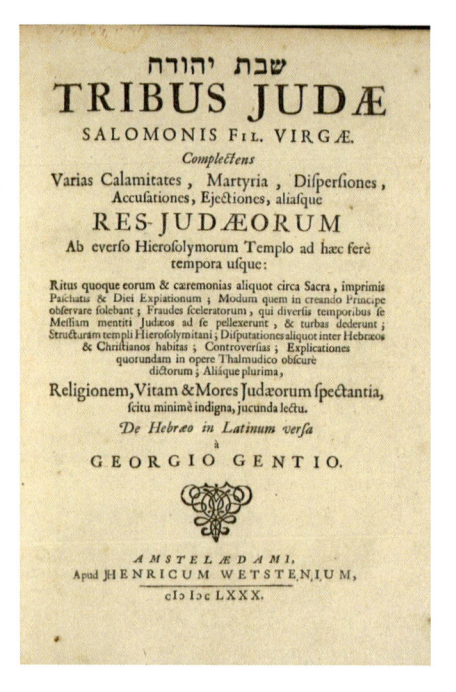

Surviving the Inquisition: This work, written in Hebrew and later translated, was authored in the early sixteenth century by Spanish historian Solomon ibn Verga (1460-1554). A Sephardic Jew, he fled the Spanish Inquisition, settling in Turkey, where he wrote this exhaustive account of the persecution of Jews in Spain and Portugal, based on eyewitness and secondhand accounts. The work was never condemned, but was not published in Spain for centuries. This Latin translation was published in Amsterdam, whose comparatively free press became a refuge for books banned elsewhere.

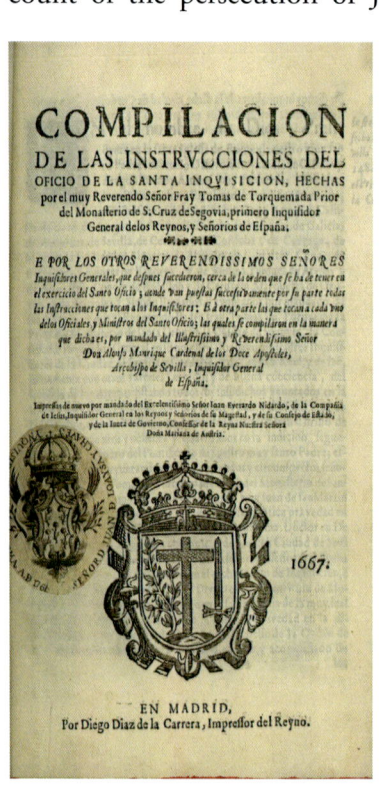

Left: *Copilacion de las instruciones del Oficio de la Santa Inquisicion, hechas por el muy Reverendo Señor Fray Tomas de Torquemada* [Compilation of the instructions of the Office of the Holy Inquisition, made by the very reverend Friar Tomas de Torquemada], Madrid: Diego Diaz de la Car-rera, 1761 III/3369, *Real Biblioteca, Patrimonio Nacional.*

The Purpose of the Inquisition: The first head of Spain's Office of the Inquisition was Dominican Friar Tomas de Torquemada. His instructions, published in 1485, sought to educate lower ranking Inquisition officer about the purpose of the Inquisition (stopping "those conversos who are Judaizing our Christian names") and to outline practices for dealing with implicated individuals.

Below; Jacopo da Trezzo (Italian c. 1515/1519-1589), *King Philip II of Spain (1527-1598) (obverse), Apollo in a Quadriga (reverse)*, 1555, Cast bronze medallion, Diameter: 2 11/16 in. (6.8 cm). 1977.114. *On loan from the David and Alfred Smart Museum of Art, University of Chicago.*

New Rigor: This coin depicts King Philip II of Spain who ruled from 1556-1598. His reign coincided with the early Counter-Reformation, a period of renewed Catholic intensity initiated in response to the Protestant Reformation. In an attempt to preserve Spain's Catholic unity, Philip reinvigorated the Spanish Inquisition, which was originally established in 1478. The newly revived Inquisition greatly expanded preexisting censorship, particularly of allegedly heretical books. In 1559 an *Index of Prohibited Books* was published by the Spanish Inquisition under Grand Inquisitor Fernando de Valdés. In a further attempt to prevent contact with heretical ideas, Philip issued a prohibition against Spanish students studying in foreign universities.

[97]

(347)

nit ut ipsarum tenore non plene et specifice, ut decebat, sed in genere et confuse nobis ab eo exposito, litteræ ipsæ contra sanctorum patrum et prædecessorum nostrorum decreta ac communem observantiam expeditæ sint. Quo factum est ut multiplices querelæ et lamentationes factæ fuerint tam contra Nos de illarum expeditione hujusmodi, quam contra majestates vestras et contra dilectos filios Michaelem de Morillo, magistrum, et Joannem de sancto Martino, beccalaureum in theologia, ordinis prædicatorum professores; quos dictarum litterarum prætextu inquisitores in vestra civitate hispalensi nominastis, pro eo quod (ut asseritur) inconsulte, et nullo juris ordine servato procedentes, multos injuste carceraverint, diris tormentis subjecerint, et hæreticos injustè declaraverint, ac bonis spoliaverint, qui ultimo supplicio affecti fuere: adeo ut quam plures alii justo timore perterriti in fugam se convertentes, hinc inde dispersi sint, plurimique ex eis se christianos et veros catholicos esse profitentes ut ab oppressionibus hujusmodi releventur, ad sedem præfatam, oppressorum ubique tutissimum refugium, confugerint; et interpositas à variis et diversis eis per dictos inquisitores illatis gravaminibus appellationes hujusmodi querelas continentes, nobis præsentaverint; earumdem appellationum causas committi, de ipsorum innocentia cognosci, cum multiplici lacrimarum effusione humiliter postulantes. Nos vero habita super his cum venerabilibus fratribus nostris sanctæ romanæ ecclesiæ cardinalibus deliberatione matura, de illorum consilio ut querelis hujusmodi in posterum obviaremus per quasdam nostras litteras in negocio hujusmodi juxta juris dispositionem per inquisitores, et locorum ordinarios in simul decrevimus esse procedendum. Et quamquam multorum judicio attentis querelis prædictis ad officium Inquisitionis hujusmodi alii quam Michael et

Left: Juan Antonio Llorente (1756-1823, *Histoire Critique de l'Inquisition d'Espagne*, Paris: Treuttel et Würz, 1817-18. BX1735. L71 v. 4 Rare.

Strife between Inquisitions: Juan Antonio Llorente (1756-1823) was a Spanish cleric and commissary of the Inquisition. Loyal to Napoleon, he fled France following the Peninsular War, where he wrote the first comprehensive history of the Inquisition. The work details letters of correspondence, shown here, between Pope Sixtus IV and the Spanish monarchy. Here Sixtus condemns Ferdinand and Isabella for their persecution of Spain's Jews. These letters show the early schism between the Spanish monarchy and the Vatican, which initially opposed this separate Inquisition.

[98]

Above: *Index Librorum Prohibitorum et Expurgandorum Novissiumus,* Madrid: Ex Typographaeo Didaci Diaz, 1667. fZ1020.I667.

Not Pictured: *Cathalogvs/Libroru,* [New York: De Vinne Press, 1896. Z1020.I896b Rare.

Standardizing Condemnation: Rome's expanded 1559 *Index* focused on Protestantism and local Italian concerns, but Spain issued its own versions continuing its anxiety about *conversos* (converted Jews). This massive *Index* of 1667 was printed in Spain but was a joint effort to standardize both Rome's and Spain's condemnations in one volume. Such guides aimed to help inquisitors across Europe keep up with the breakneck pace of Spanish condemnations. This page shows the entry for the physician Conrad Gessner, whose encyclopedia appeared on page 69.

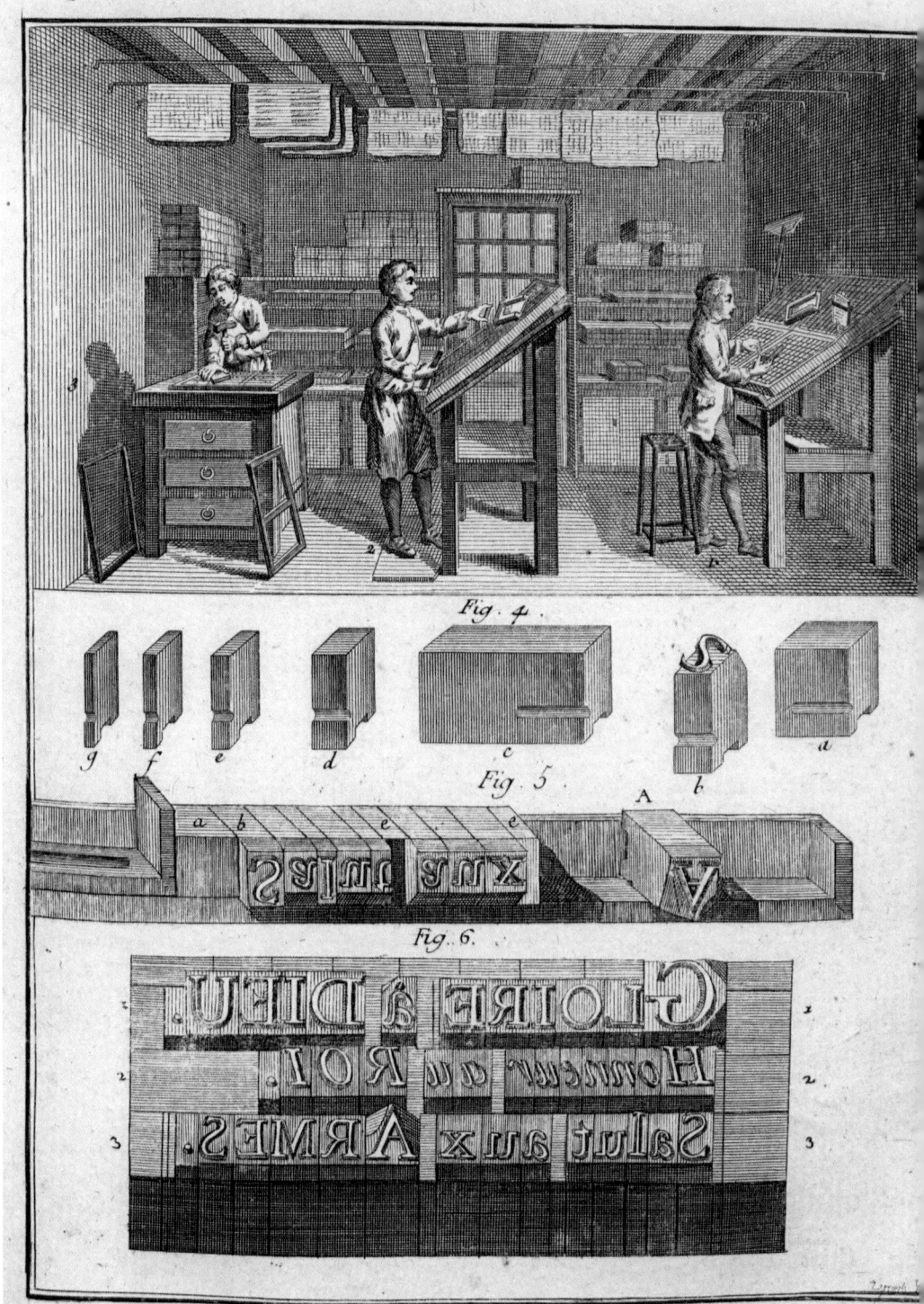

Imprimerie en Lettres, L'Opération de la Casse.

With the Approval of the King

"Avec Approbation et Privelége du Roy" (With the Approval and Privilege of the King) might be the ironic motto of the French Enlightenment, the phrase required on every title page to indicate that a work has been approved for publication. Since the Inquisition's inception local inquisitors, personally vulnerable to local politics, had been powerless to refuse when kings or dukes demanded licenses for their court scholars to possess condemned books. As kings consolidated their power, a system of royal censors took over most book licensing, but clerics could still denounce a work to the Inquisition even if it had royal approval. Since aristocrats and even kings embraced many ideas and authors of the Enlightenment, moderately radical works usually secured royal approval, especially since many scholars who paid their bills working as royal censors were themselves authors and members of the new movement. Thus, moderate works—such as the *Encyclopédie* of Diderot and d'Alambert—often received royal approval only to be later condemned by Rome, which the Catholic king was then obliged to recognize, at least official . So while Montesquieu, Voltaire, Rousseau and the *Encyclopédie* were banned and burned in public, we have numerous records of clandestine book traders facing few repercussions from carrying these authors. For other works, however—Protestant tracts, criticisms of the king, or works of the Catholic movement known as Jansenism—the consequences could be severe.

Facing: *Encyclopédie*, Yverdon, Switzerland: [F.B. de Félice], 1770-1780
AE25.E66 Plates v. 7 Rare.

Only Slightly Banned: The *Encyclopédie*—spearheaded by Diderot and d'Holbach—aimed to achieve universal education by putting fundamental knowledge at everyone's finge tips. Diderot and associates wrote to their intellectual allies asking them to tone down their radicalism (in public at least) until the *Encyclopédie* finished, to avoid rufflin the feathers of Church or State. The texts "Vive le Roi" and "Gloire a Dieu" in this illustration of printers' type are another declaration of loyalty.

The king approved the *Encylopédie's* publication, but they only got as far as 'H' before Rome cracked down. Later volumes were smuggled in from Switzerland, but sympathetic border guards let it through so consistently that smugglers began hiding more dangerous works inside the *Encyclopédie* to cross the border.

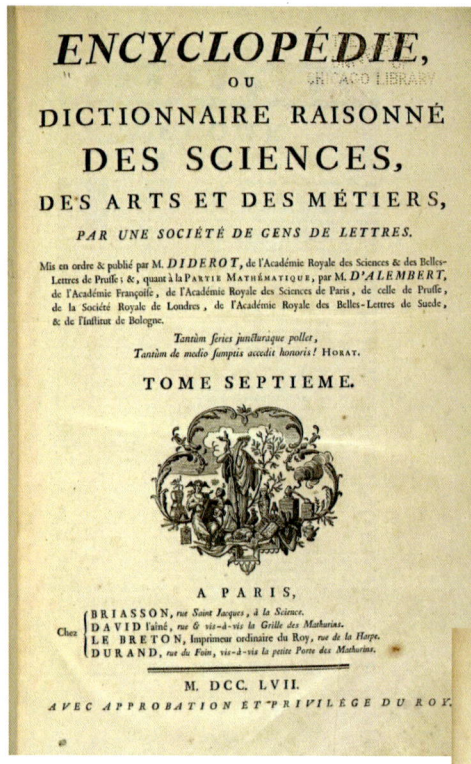

Left: Title page of the seventh volume of the *Encyclopédie*, printed in Paris with the names of its editors, the names and addresses of the four printers who teamed up to produce it in enough volume to meet demand, and "Avec Approbation et Privelége du Roy."

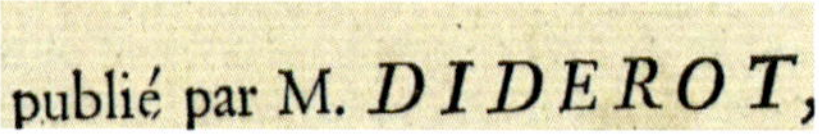

Right: Title page of the eighth volume of the *Encyclopédie*, printed after the condemnation, and vol. 8 (The first after the condemnation, printed in Neufchastel, Switzerland, by "Mr. ***"

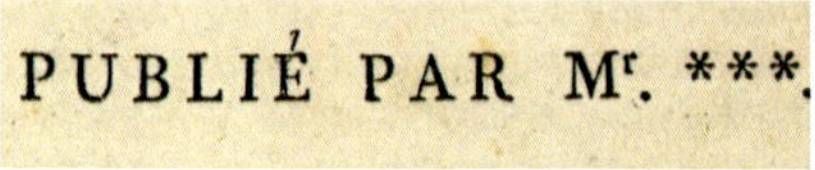

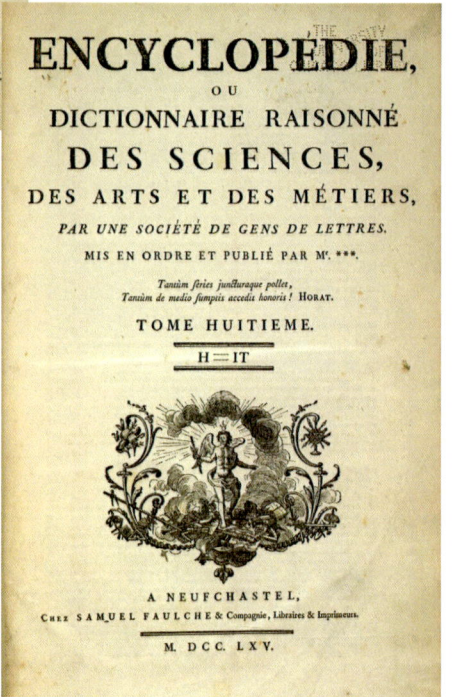

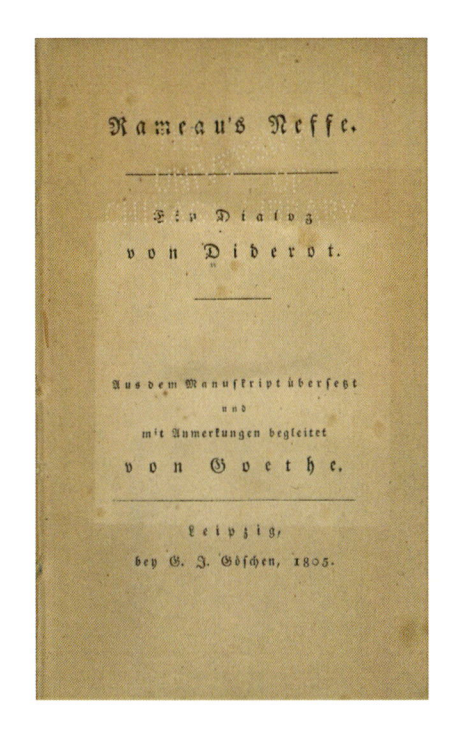

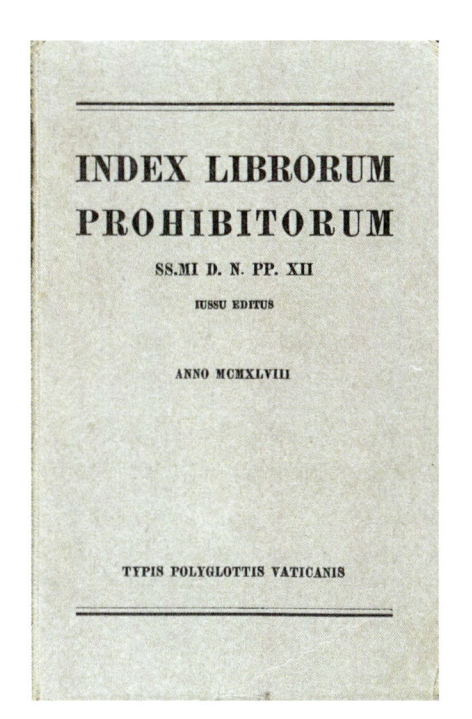

Above Left: Denis Diderot (1713-1784, *Rameau's Neff* . PQ1979.A723G54 Rare.

Above Right: *Index Librorum Prohibitorum: SS.MI D. N. PII. PP. XII*, Vatican City: Typis Polyglottis, Vaticanis, 1948. *On loan from Ada Palmer.*

Best Behavior: In the eighteenth century, atheism—still illegal—was becoming a movement, with a literature and unifying ideas. Diderot was himself an atheist, but—after three months' incarceration in 1749 for his "Letter on the Blind"—he self-censored his atheist works, circulating them only in manuscript to protect his reputation and, thereby, the *Encyclopédie*. As a result, *Rameau's Nephew*, one of the most innovative works of the century, vanished until Goethe published this 1805 German translation from a manuscript which then disappeared. Diderot's original draft turned up at a secondhand bookshop in 1890. In this 1938 *Index*, the *Encyclopédie* still appears along with some of Diderot's posthumously-published atheist works.

INDEX
Librorũ Prohibitor.
PII SEXTI P.O.M.
jussu editus

Multi eorum, qui fuerant curiosa
sectati, contulerunt Libros, et
combusserunt coram omnibus.
Act. Cap. XIX. V. 19.

An Index of Enlightenment: Once established, Rome's *Index* of banned books was constantly adapted to address new crises. This version from the eve of the French Revolution continues to focus on listing Protestant theologians and diverse Catholic heresies, but also includes figures central to the French Enlightenment, such as Voltaire, Rousseau, Diderot, D'Alambert, Thomas Hobbes, and Spinoza, and innovations of the seventeenth century.

Erasing Old Privilege: Also called the *Journal de Trévoux*, this journal reviewed mainly scientific works from 1701-1782. Written largely by Jesuits, it was conservative but moderate and cosmopolitan, opposing nationalistic discourse and offering serious and sophisticated refutations in its polemics with Voltaire, Diderot, and other leaders of the more radical Enlightenment. After the French Revolution, a censor went through this copy to efface the vestiges of the old regime, cutting out the royal coat of arms and inking over *roi* (king) in the approbation.

Facing: *Index Librorum Prohibitorum Sancrissimi Domi-ni Nostri Pii Sexti Pontificus Max*, Rome: Ex Typographia Rev. Cameraw Apostolicae, 1786. Z1020.I786 Rare.

Right: *Mémoires pour l'Histoire des Sciences & des Beaux Arts*, A Trevoux: Chez Etienne Ganeau, n.d. AS161.M456 v.1 1751 Rare.

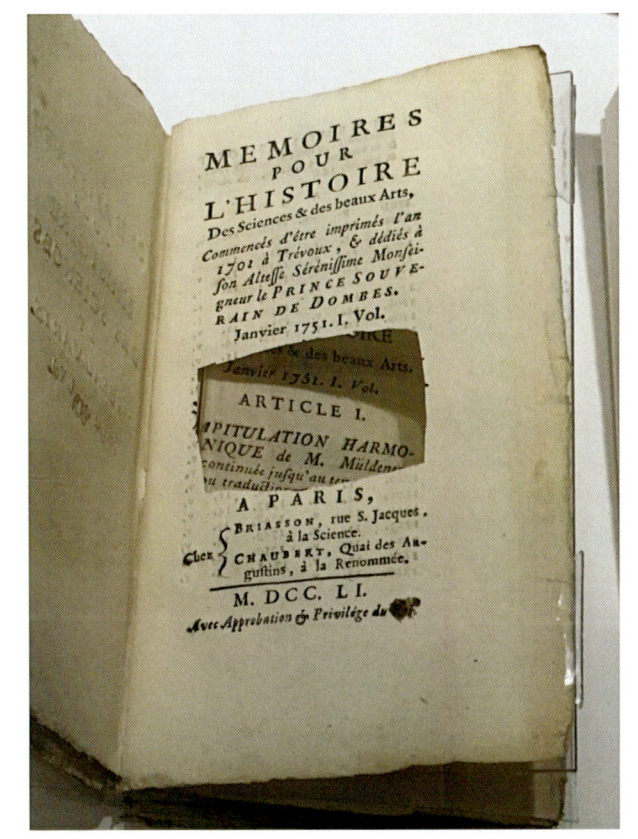

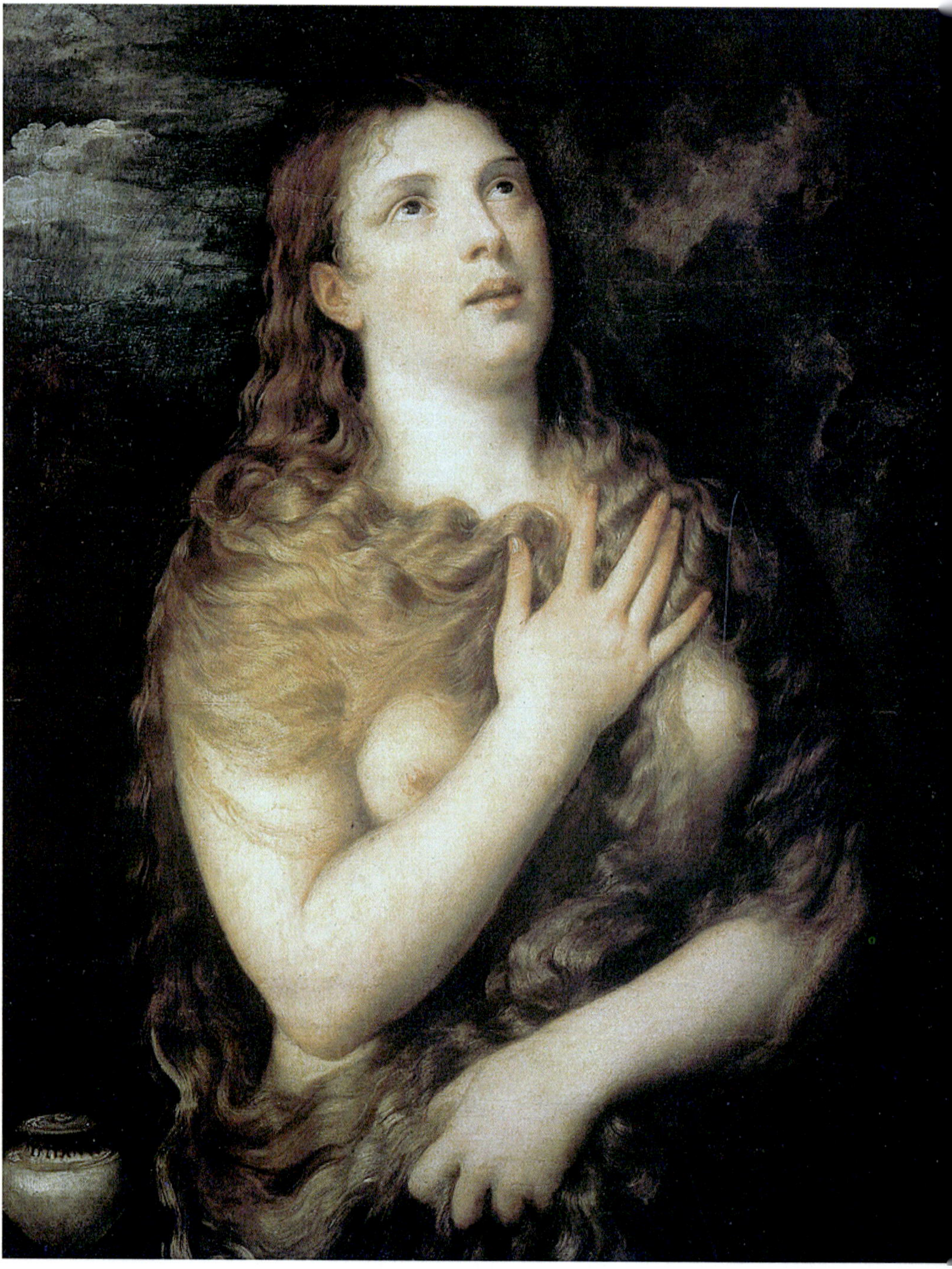

The Church and Art

> *"Even the painters, to whom as also to the poets all things are permissible, though they may have painted a naked woman, yet they cover the privy parts of the body with some sort of drapery, imitating their guide Nature, which has hidden far from sight those parts that are in some degree shameful."*
> – Poggio Bracciolini (rediscoverer of Lucretius), criticizing Antonio Panormita's 1425 *Hermaphroditus*

> *"I would not esteem the man's poem and talent any the less for his jokes being highly 0avoured. Shall we praise Apelles or Fabius or any painter the less because they have painted naked and unconcealed those details of the body which nature prefers hidden? If they have depicted worms and serpents, mice, scorpions, 0ies, and other distasteful creatures, will you not admire and praise the artist's art and skill?"*
> – Guarino da Verona (translator of Martial and Juvenal) praising Antonio Panormita's 1425 *Hermaphroditus*

In the Renaissance, new paintings and sculptures were usually commissioned by wealthy elites with too much clout for the Inquisition to touch them or the artists they protected, but art censorship still came in several forms. The Vatican attempted to restrict imagery used in religious art, fearing that viewers could be led to heresy if confused. For example, attempts were made—though inconsistent and hard to enforce—to limit which kinds of halos or coronas could surround which saints, and to specify that art could depict one or three aspects of God (Father, Son, Holy Spirit) but never two, for fear of muddling viewers' understandings of the Trinity. Nudes and neoclassical or pagan art were also attacked but inconsistently, usually when a particular local biship or influential preacher launched a campaign against nudity or paganism, which often involved the Church but rarely the Inquisition. The subject of a painting greatly affected its reception, and a Venus might draw criticism while an equally erotic nude Mary Magdalene or Saint Sebastian did not.

Facing: Titian, *Mary Magdalene*, 1533 (Palazzo Pitti, Florence).

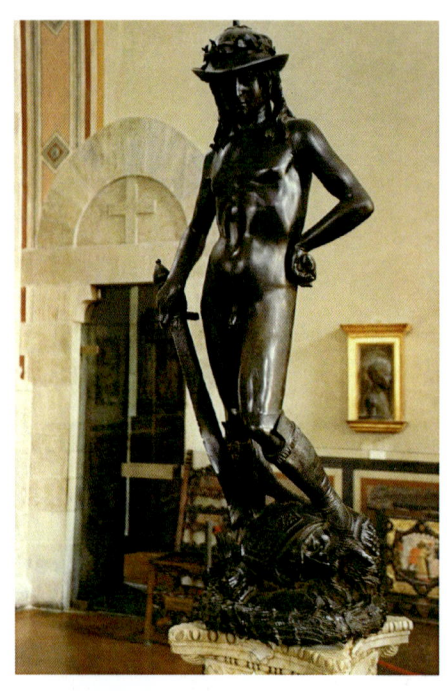

Left: Donatello, *David* (1428-32), Bargello Museum. Photograph by Patrick A. Rodgers, 2010.

Below: Donatello, plaster replica of *David* (1428-32), Victoria and Albert Museum, detail of legs and caressing wing. Photograph by Lee M, 2005.

The Nude Returns: Ancient Greek and Roman cultures had been generally comfortable with nudity, including nude athletics, public bathing, and especially nude art. Nude figures, based on classical models, proliferated in Renaissance art from the 1440s on, beginning with Donatello's bronze *David*. Such works were targets of intermittent censorship shaped by the fluctuating tastes of local powers.

[108]

❦ The Great Fig-Leafing ❦

The practice of using a fig leaf to cover genitalia began after 1530 and increased after the Council of Trent—Rome's officia response to Protestantism—largely advanced by Gian Pietro Carafa (later Pope Paul IV). Papal policies were as inconsistent as popes themselves, so isolated bursts of fig leafing took place in the Vatican's collections, particularly under Popes Innocent X (r.1644-1655) and Clement XIII (r. 1693 –1769) and then Pius IX (r. 1846-1878) who had phalluses physically broken off of ancient statues. Above, two Roman statues in the Vatican have been censored diffe ently under diffe ent popes.

Left: Roman art, *Figure with tree and lizard,* with phallus removed. Photograph by Ada Palmer, 2011.

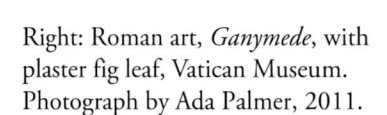

Right: Roman art, *Ganymede*, with plaster fig leaf, Vatican Museum. Photograph by Ada Palmer, 2011.

Left and Below: Roman art, *Fertility god (Liber Pater?)*, censored with plaster fig leaves, Vatican Museum. *Photographs by Ada Palmer, 2011.*

Creative Censorship: Just as most book censors were scholars and authors themselves, so those hired by the Vatican to fig-leaf their Roman collections were sculptors themselves and exercised creativity. This Roman fertility god—marked by his prominent erection—had fruit in his lap, and the censor-sculptor has wrapped leaves around to turn the phallus into a fig integrated into a bouquet.

Art's Most Famous Phallus: When first unveiled, Michelangelo's *David* was censored by Florentine authorities with a garland of copper leaves, removed later in the century. The next two centuries' of *David*'s adventures are not well documented, but a plaster fig leaf appears in the earliest photographs of the statue, removed c. 1890. When a cast of *David* was given to the Victoria and Albert Museum in London, Queen Victoria expressed distress at its nudity, and a removable plaster fig leaf was created for future visits.

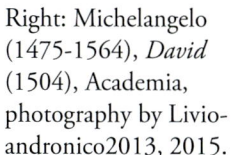

Right: Michelangelo (1475-1564), *David* (1504), Academia, photography by Livio-andronico2013, 2015.

Left: an early photograph of Michelangelo's *David* before fig leaf was removed.

[111]

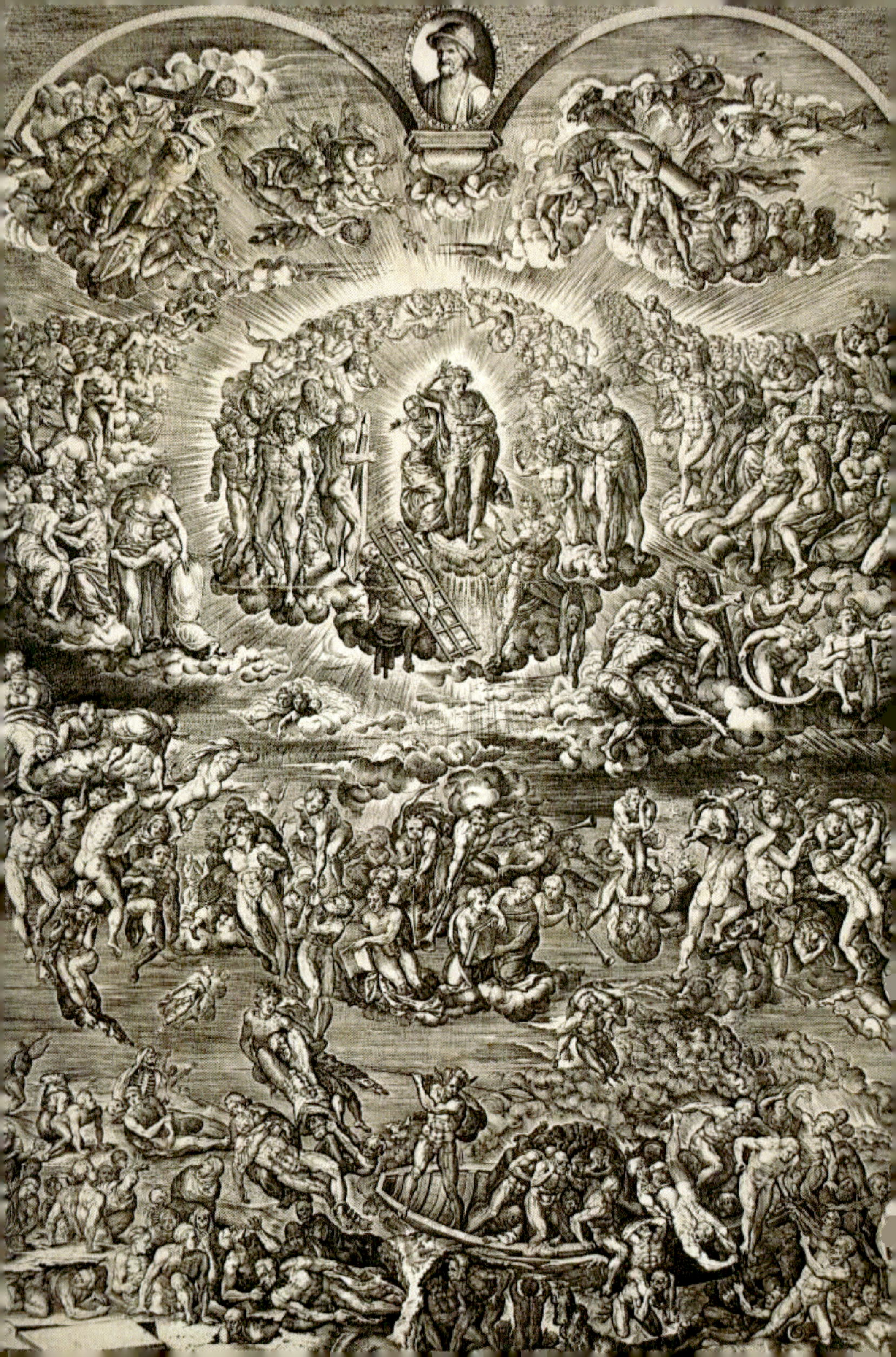

Facing: Unknown artist, *The Last Judgment (after Michelangelo Buonarroti)* n.d. engraving, 2004.104. *On loan from the David and Alfred Smart Museum of Art, University of Chicago, Gift of the Collection of Edward A. and Inge Maser.*

Original and Uncensored: Mass production of images through printed wood blocks reached Europe from Asia not long before Gutenberg developed movable type. Suddenly, popular paintings and sculptures—from fresco cycles in ducal palaces to the rediscovered *Laocoön*—were rapidly reproduced in wood blocks or etchings which spread the fame of artists and patrons and made art affordable even for poorer households. The nude figures in Michelangelo's *Last Judgment* fresco in the Sistine chapel were criticized by the pope and covered with drapes painted over figures' genitalia, yet this engraving still made the uncensored version available to the masses.

Left: Fresco detail of St. Bartholomew, showing the painted fabric drape which was added to the original to censor his genitals.

[113]

Below: Giovanni Bernardi da Castelbolognese Italian (1496-1553), *Pope Clement VII de'Medici (1478-1534) (obverse), Joseph Reveals Himself to His Brothers (reverse)*, 1529-1530, Struck gilt bronze medal, Diameter: 1 3/8 in. (3.5 cm). 1977.117. *On loan from the David and Alfred Smart Museum of Art, University of Chicago.*

A Pious Papacy: This coin depicts Pope Clement VII, who held the papacy from 1523-1534. During his papacy, Clement suppressed every edition of Sonetti Lussuriosi, an erotic work by Italian author Pietro Aretino., published in 1524, the book was accompanied by illustrations of sexual positions by artist Guilio Romano. Due to pressure from the Roman authorities, the pair were forced to flee the city. The illustrations were preserved in a series of engravings by Marcantonio Raimondi, who was subsequently also forced into exile.

[114]

Below: Arthur Pond (1705-1758), *Pope Clement IX and the Jesuit Cardinals (after Carlo Maratta)*, 1736, etching on wove paper, 1976.145.330. *On loan from the David and Alfred Smart Museum of Art, University of Chicago, University Transfer from Max Epstein Archive.*

Private Retaliation: This image is a copy of a caricature of Pope Clement IX surrounded by a group of Jesuit cardinals. The original drawing, created by Italian artist Carlo Maratta, who had also painted an official portrait of Clement IX, was intended to be an attack on the Jesuit cardinals who exposed the artist's love affair and forced his mistress to flee. Jesuits themselves have often been linked to the Inquisition, although the order was founded in 1534, 60 years after the original founding of the Inquisition. Early Jesuit missionary, St. Francis Xavier, proposed the founding of the Goan Inquisition. Between its founding in 1561 and its temporary disbanding in 1774, the Goan Inquisition brought over 16,000 people to trial. These were primarily members of the native population, targeted by the Inquisition for practicing Crypto-Judaism.

Above: *Last Supper/ Feast in the House of Levi*, Paolo Veronese, 1573, oil on canvas, 218 x 516 inches.

Subject Not Content: It was a common practice to supplement religious scenes with imagery from contemporary life: ordinary furniture in the Virgin Mary's bedroom, or shepherds chatting outside the window encouraged viewers to imagine holy scenes happening in the real world around them and let artists display their creativity and skill. But in this piece by Paolo Veronese the addition of numerous lively and secular-feeling figures to a Last Supper—which usually includes only Christ and the apostles—caused a sufficient stir to bring Veronese before the Venetian and Roman Inquisitions. This is one of few fully documented cases in which the Inquisition—as opposed to local bishops or other authorities—censored an artist. Ordered by the Inquisition to "fix" the painting, rather than painting over the extra figures, Veronese changed the painting's name, claiming it did not depict the Last Supper but the Feast in the House of Levi, which was enough to appease the censors. The trial of a Venetian artist in the name of Rome's Inquisition also reflected Rome's continuing efforts to exert authority over the largely independent republic.

Below: *Maja Desnuda* and *Maja Vestida,* Francisco de Goya (1746-1828), 1797/1797, oil on canvas, 97 x 190 cm/95 x 190 cm.

When the Patron Gets in Trouble: Even in the nineteenth century the Inquisition remained a useful tool for others to manipulate. Goya's paired paintings *The Nude Maja* and *The Clothed Maja* were in a collection of nudes belonging to Spanish Prime Minister Manuel de Godoy. In 1808, the Inquisition prosecuted Godoy and Goya, not on its own initiative but as part of larger political maneuvers to remove Godoy from power. Goya was acquitted after claiming he had simply imitated the nudes of Titian and Velásquez, artists admired even by kings of Spain.

Below: Francisco de Goya (1746-1828), *Page from the Disaster of Wars – Plate 71 – Against Common Good,* 1810, etching, 9 ¾ x 13 ⅛ inches 2008.222bq, *David and Alfred Smart Museum of Art, University of Chicago, The Paul and Miriam Kirkley Fund for Acquisitions.*

Still a Live Issue: Goya's *Disaster of Wars* print series was a reaction to the immense suffering caused by the Peninsular War in early nineteenth-century Spain. *Against Common Good* is part of the "Emphatic Caprices" section in which Goya allegorically criticizes the postwar politics in Spain, including Inquisitorial practices that still continued. Here, a winged devil writes in a book, much like a judge taking notes at an Inquisitorial trial?

Upper Facing: Francisco de Goya (1746-1828), *Trials (Ensayos),* 1797-98, etching, aquatint, and burin, 2003.22. *On loan from the David and Alfred Smart Museum of Art, University of Chicago, Gift of Brenda F. and Joseph V. Smith.*

A Thousand Words: A series first published in 1799, Goya's *Los Caprichos* highlights the follies and caprices of contemporary Spanish society. The 80 etchings and aquatints were largely inspired by the artist's interest in the French Revolution, particularly the taboo writings of Jean-Jacques Rousseau. Goya was aware of the politically contentious nature of the series—an awareness which is reflected in his evasive captions and allegorical imagery. However, the images themselves openly presented both political and anticlerical themes, including those leveled against the Spanish Inquisition. Pressure from the Inquisition led Goya to suspend sales of the series soon after publication. The unsold works were purchased in 1803 by King Charles IV, who effectively shielded Goya from the Inquisition.

Left: Francisco de Goya (1746-1828), *There is Much to Suck (Mucho hay que chupar)*, 1797-98, etching and aquatint, 2003.13. *On loan from the David and Alfred Smart Museum of Art, University of Chicago, Gift of Brenda F. and Joseph V. Smith* .

[119]

War on Images: This woodcut depicts Saint Luke (right) displaying a portrait of the Virgin Mary and infant Christ. Luke is traditionally believed to have been the first painter of religious icons and is the patron saint of artists. According to legend, Luke painted the *Virgin and Child* from life. Since the eleventh century, numerous images have been identified and subsequently venerated as this original icon. Despite this association, debates about the theological validity of visual images have been waged throughout the history of the Christian Church. Periods of iconoclasm, the destruction of religious images, have arisen in both the Eastern and Western Churches.

Above: Ludolph Büsing (1599/1602-1669), *Saints Mark and Luke (after Georges Lallemand)*, c. 1623-1625, three-color chiaroscuro woodcut on laid paper, 1967.116.100. *On loan from the David and Alfred Smart Museum of Art, University of Chicago, University Transfer from Max Epstein Archive, Purchase, 1949.*

Left: Unknown Artist (German, Rhenish), *Madonna and Child*, late 16th-century stoneware, painted and gilded, Height: 24-5/8 in. (62.6 cm) 1967.32. *On loan from the David and Alfred Smart Museum of Art, University of Chicago.*

Iconic: Following the beginning of the Protestant Reformation in 1517, waves of iconoclasm swept throughout Northern Europe. This controversy surrounding religious icons stemmed from the Ten Commandments, which forbid the creation and worship of images. While some theologians argued that images were a beneficial teaching tool, others saw their existence as a dangerous source of idolatry. Statues, such as this figure of the Virgin Mary and Child, were a particular point of concern and were destroyed in large numbers in the mid- to late-sixteenth century.

ANTICOPERNICVS
CATHOLICVS,
SEV
DE TERRAE STATIONE, ET DE SOLIS MOTV,
contra systema Copernicanum, Catholicæ Assertiones.
AVCTORE
GIORGIO POLACCO VENETO.

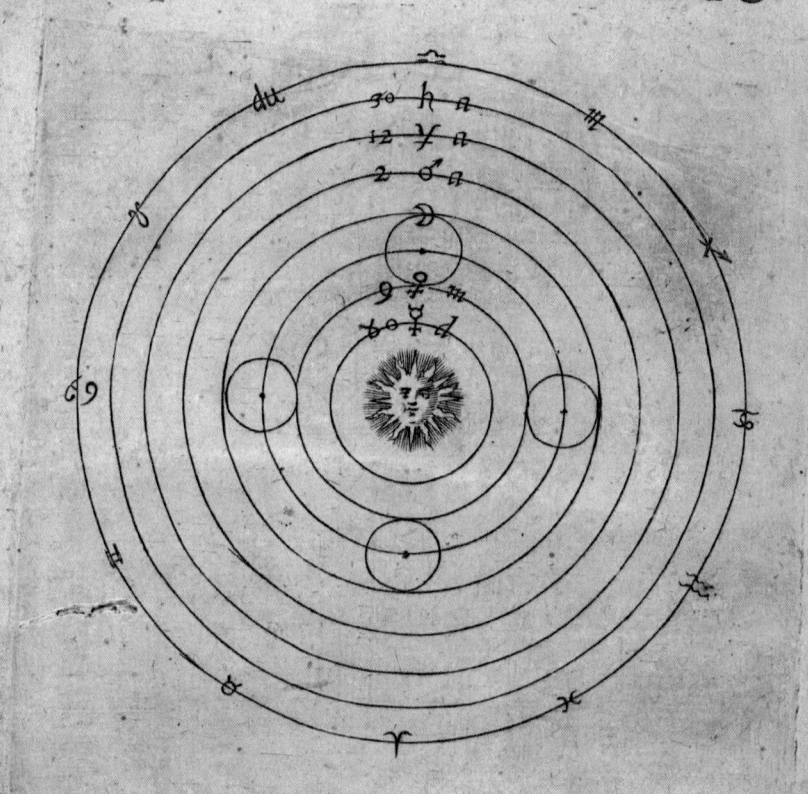

VENETIIS, Apud Guerilios. M DC XLIV.

SVPERIORVM PERMISSV, ET PRIVILEGIO.

Universal Acids/Toxic Ideas

> "What progress we are making. In the Middle Ages they would have burned me. Now they are content with burning my books."
> —Freud, *Letter to Ernest Jones*, 1933

> "I deny not, but that it is of greatest concernment in the Church and Commonwealth, to have a vigilant eye how Bookes demeane themselves as well as men; and thereafter to confine, imprison, and do sharpest justice on them as malefactors: For Books are not absolutely dead things, but doecontain a potencie of life in them to be as active as that soule was whose progeny they are ▬▬▬ as lively, and as vigorously productive, as those fabulous Dragons teeth; and being sown up and down, may chance to spring up armed men."
> – Milton, *Areopagitica*, 1644

In trying to explain Darwin's the full impact, Daniel Dennett describes the theory of evolution as a "universal acid"—something that cannot be contained because it can burn through any container. This case showcases universal acids of the intellectual world, ideas that might not be controversial today, but once seemed to threaten the very glue that held society together. Before Darwin, figures including Machiavelli, Luther, Hobbes, and Spinoza sparked such widespread efforts to contain or destroy their "toxic" ideas that new techniques or even new laws or institutions developed to oppose them. Most of these volumes are 'anti-theses' attacking infamous works, but such published refutations disseminated and advertised the very ideas they sought to combat. Consequently the most sensational cases of intellectual censorship tended, not to destroy ideas, but to guarantee their fame and survival, while most lost works are those which faded into the silence of obscurity.

Facing: Giorgio Polacco (fl. 1644), *Anticopernicus Catholicus…*, Venice: Guerilios, 1644. QB36.C8P76 1644 Rare.

Giorgio Polacco's Anti-Copernicus Catholicus attacks heliocentrism, not only on theological grounds, but with mathematical and observational rebuttals which require thoroughly explaining the Copernican original.

Information through Infamy: These texts—like many in this section—attack controversial authors, but consequently increase the fame of the very authors they seek to silence. Below, the anti-Lucretius poem by Cardinal de Polignac imitates the Roman Lucretius' poetic style while attacking his Epicurean depiction of a self-ordering nature with no need for gods. This refutation helped spread Lucretius' ideas to Enlightenment scientists and radicals. On the opposite page, Edward Earl of Clarendon's *Brief View and Survey* is one of numerous efforts to refute the grim depictions of God, nature, and humanity advanced by "the beast of Malmesbury" as contemporaries called the infamous Thomas Hobbes.

Below: Melchior de Polignac (1661-1742?, *L'anti-Lucrece, poëme sur la religion naturelle*, Paris: Jean-Baptiste Coignard & Antoine Boudet: 1749. PA8557.P7A63B7 v. 1 Rare.

Facing: Edward Hyde Earl of Clarendon (1609-1674 *A Brief View and Survey of the Dangerous and Pernicious Errors to Church and State, in Mr. Hobbes's Book, Entitled Leviathan*, Oxon., [England]: Printed at the Theater, 1676. JC153.H66C6.

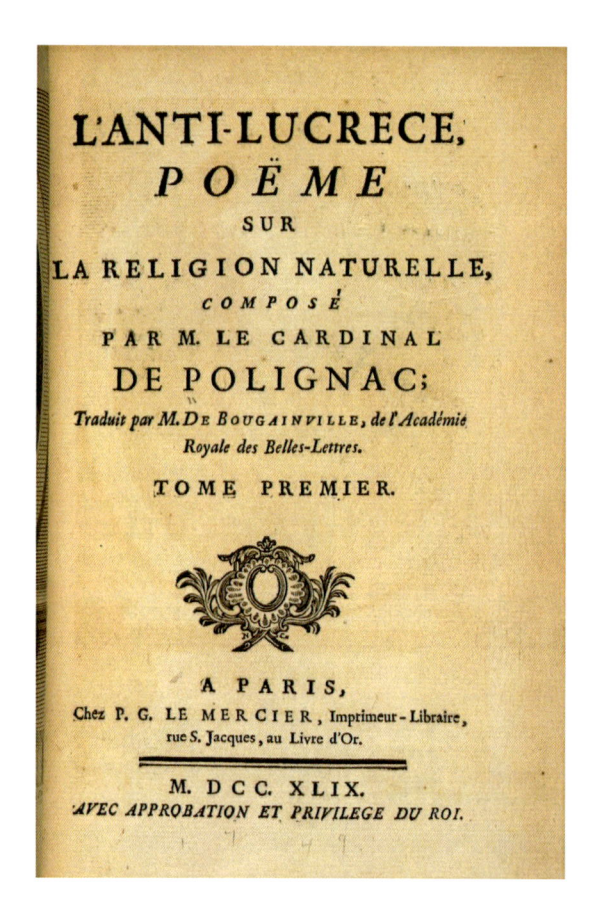

A BRIEF VIEW and SURVEY OF THE Dangerous and pernicious ERRORS TO CHURCH and STATE, In Mr. *HOBBES*'S BOOK, Entitled LEVIATHAN.

By *EDWARD* Earl of *Clarendon*.

The second Impression.

OXON: Printed at the *THEATER*. 1676.

Anti-Machiavell:

OR,

HONESTY

AGAINST

POLJCY.

An anfwer to that vaine difcourfe, *The cafe of the Kingdome ftated,* according to the proper intrrefts of the feverall Parties ingaged.

By a Lover of Truth, Peace, and Honefty.

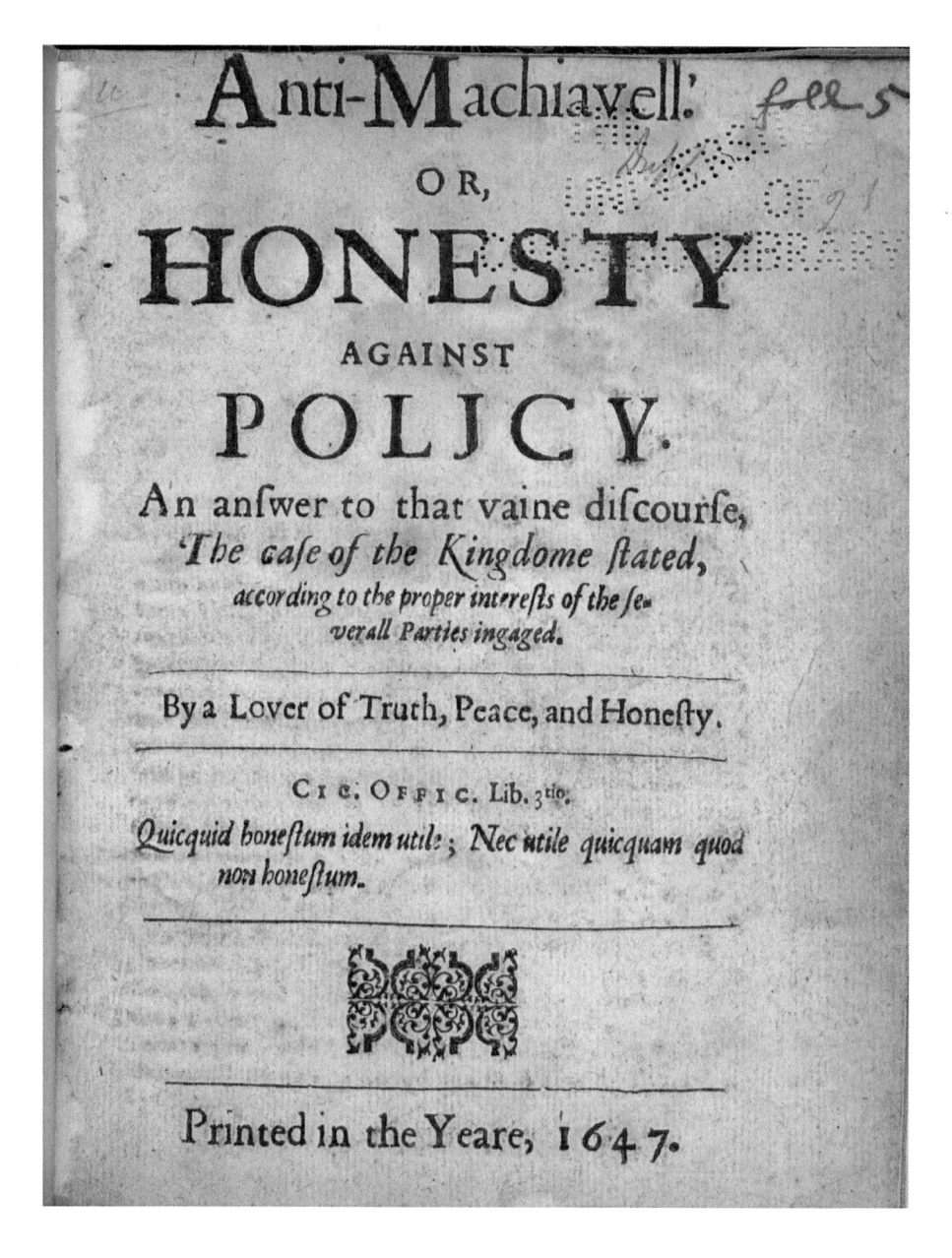

Cic. Offic. Lib. 3tio.
Quicquid honeftum idem util?; Nec utile quicquam quod non honeftum.

Printed in the Yeare, 1647.

Above: A Lover of Truth, *Peace, and Honesty Anti-Machiavell: Or, Honesty against Policy* [London: s.n.], 1647. DA412.A1 no. 234 Rare.

Facing: King of Prussia Frederick II (1712-1786), *Examen du Prince de Machiavel: Avec des Notes Historiques & Politiques...*, A La Haie, France: Au dépens de la Compagnie, 1743. JC143.M4F9 1743 Rare.

"The Murderous Machiavel": Machiavelli's infamy increased, rather than decreasing, over the three centuries after his death, as he was mythologized as the archetype of wicked intelligence. Innocent Gentillet, a French Protestant, published the first *Anti-Machiavelli* in 1576, blaming many of France's ills on Machiavelli's influence on France's Florentine-born queen Catherine de Medici. The 1647 *Anti-Machiavelli* displayed here, authored by "a Lover of Truth, Peace and Honesty," was the last major attack before Machiavelli's reception was transformed by the suggestion that he was a source for Hobbes's 1651 *Leviathan*, an accusation which enormously increased Machiavelli's readership as Hobbes' opponents sought to hone weapons against the younger monster by practicing on the elder. Frederick the Great's *L'Anti-Machiavel*, with a preface by Voltaire, fashions Frederick as a moral prince by showing his opposition to Machiavelli.

Arch-Heretics: While the earlier *Index* reserved the title "Arch-Heretic" for Protestant leaders, later popular literature applied it to the most menacing intellectuals: Machiavelli, Hobbes, the Marquis de Sade, and the radical Jewish philosopher Spinoza. A pillar of the early Enlightenment, Spinoza's extreme views on God and Nature, and his expulsion from his own Jewish community for heterodoxy, earned him a reputation for atheism even though his writings are deeply pious. He was also a famously good person, and the myth of Spinoza the good atheist, like that of the "Murderous Machiavel," was a powerful presence in discourse separate Spinoza's own ideas. This book attacking Spinoza's *Tractatus Theologico- oliticus* was published by a Dutch follower of Descartes.

Right: Regnerus van Mansvelt (1639-1671), *Adversus anonymum theologo-politicum liber singularis...*, Amsterdam: Abrahamum Wolfgang, 1674. B3985.M3 Rare.

Facing: Pierre Bayle (1647-1706), *Dictionaire Historique et Critique, Vol. 4*, Amsterdam: Chez P. Brunel, 1730. fCT142. B365 v.4 Rare.

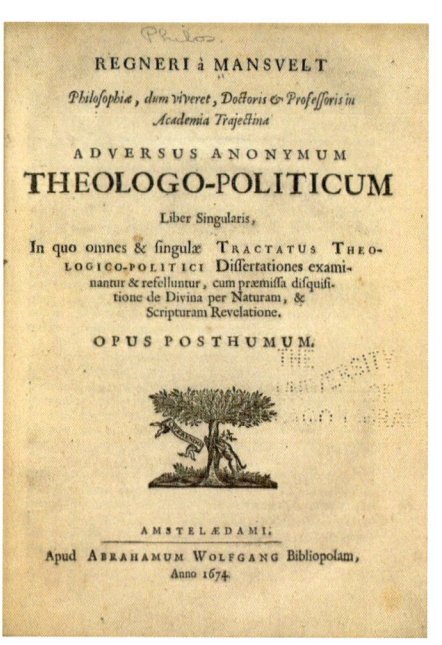

Evading in Plain Sight: Pierre Bayle's extremely influential *Historical and Critical Dictionary* contains a secret: its massive footnotes—each many times longer than the entry—hide radical ideas which evaded pre-publication censors who did not bother to thoroughly cross-reference what seemed like esoteric notes. Bayle's comments on the infamous Spinoza contain the first instance in the western tradition of any author claiming that an atheist could be a good person, against the common assumption that atheists—who did not fear God—would be wanton criminals and thus that religion must be mandatory for society to function. Bayle's radical claim slipped past censors, but when it came to light, Bayle—despite his own avowed piety—was accused of being an atheist, and his *Dictionary* placed on the *Index*.

ses idées. Il mourut, dit-on, bien persuadé de son Athéïsme, & il prit des précautions pour empêcher qu'en cas de besoin son inconstance ne fût reconue (*S*). S'il eût raisonné conséquemment, il n'eût pas traité de chimérique la peur des Enfers (*T*). Ses Amis prétendent que par modestie il souhaita de ne pas donner son nom à une Secte (*U*). Il n'est pas vrai que ses Secteurs soient en grand nombre. Très-peu de personnes sont soupçonnées d'adhérer à sa Doctrine: & parmi ceux que l'on en soupçonne; il y en a peu qui l'aient étudiée; & entre ceux-ci, il y en a peu qui l'aient comprise, & qui n'aient été rebutez des embarras & des abstractions impénétrables qui s'y rencontrent (*m*). Mais voici ce que c'est: à vue de païs on apelle Spinozistes tous ceux qui n'ont guere de Religion, & qui ne s'en cachent pas beaucoup. C'est ainsi qu'en France on apelle Sociniens tous ceux qui passent pour incrédules sur les mystères de l'Evangile, quoi que la plupart de ces gens-là n'aient jamais lu ni Socin, ni ses Disciples. Au reste, il est arrivé

(*m*) Ce pour cela qu'il y a des gens qui croient qu'il ne faut pas le réfuter. Voiez les Nouvelles de la Rép. des Lettres, Juin 1684, Art. VI, pag. m. 388, 389.

(*S*) *Il prit des précautions pour empêcher qu'en cas de besoin son inconstance ne fût reconue.*] Je veux dire qu'il donna bon ordre, qu'en cas que l'aproche de la mort, ou les effets de la maladie, le fissent parler contre son Systême, aucune personne suspecte ne fût témoin. Voici le fait; ou du moins voici ce qu'on en a dit dans un Ouvrage imprimé (137): ,, C'est peut-être ici les Athées ,, ne desirent ,, la loüange que foiblement? Mais que pouvoit-on faire de ,, plus que ce qui fut fait par Spinoza, un peu avant que ,, de mourir? La chose est de fraiche date (138), & je ,, la tiens d'un grand homme, qui la sait de bonne part. ,, C'étoit le plus grand Athée qui ait jamais été, & qui ,, s'étoit tellement infatué de certains principes de Philosophie, que pour les mieux mediter, il se mit comme en ,, retraite, renonçant à tout ce qu'on apelle plaisirs & vanitez du monde, & ne s'occupant que des abstruses ,, meditations. Se sentant près de sa fin, il fit venir son hôtesse, & la pria d'empêcher qu'aucun Ministre ne le vint ,, voir en cet état. Sa raison étoit, comme on l'a seu de ses ,, amis, qu'il vouloit mourir sans dispute, & qu'il craignoit ,, de tomber dans quelque foiblesse de sens, ou luy fit dire ,, quelque chose dont on tirast avantage contre ses Principes. C'est-à-dire qu'il craignoit que l'on ne debitast ,, dans le monde, qu'à la veuë de la mort, sa conscience ,, s'étant reveillée, l'avoit fait démentir de sa bravoure, & ,, renoncer à ses sentimens. Peut-on voir une vanité ,, plus ridicule & plus outrée que celle-là, & une plus ,, folle passion pour la fausse idée qu'on s'est faite de la ,, constance? ,,
Une Préface que j'ai citée ci-dessus (139), & qui contient quelques circonstances de la mort de cet Athée, n'en parle point de cela. Elle m'aprend qu'il dit à son hôte qui s'en alloit à l'Eglise, quand le Sermon sera fini, vous reviendrez, Dieu aidant, parler à moi (140). Mais il mourut tranquillement avant que son hôte fût de retour, & il n'y eut qu'un Médecin d'Amsterdam qui le vit mourir (141). On avoue quant au reste qu'il avoit eu un désir extrême d'immortaliser son nom, & qu'il eût sacrifié très-volontiers à cette gloire la vie présente, eût-il falu être mis en pièces par un peuple mutiné. *Amro plane non inhabiat, alioqui delata sibi Professoris munera aliquoties non respuisset homo gloriæ avidior & nimis ambitiosus, qui vel cum Wittiis amicis suis crudeliter dilacerari sublatius optavit, modo vita brevi gloria cursus foret sempiternus* (142).

(*T*) *S'il eût raisonné conséquemment, il n'eût pas traité de chimérique la peur des Enfers.*] Qu'on croie tant qu'on voudra que cet Univers est l'ouvrage de Dieu, & qu'il n'est point dirigé par une Nature simple, spirituelle, & distincte de tous les corps; il faut pour le moins que l'on avoue qu'il y a certaines choses qui ont de l'intelligence, & des volontez, & qui sont jalouses de leur pouvoir, qui exercent l'autorité sur les autres, qui leur commandent ceci ou cela, qui les châtient, qui les maltraitent, qui se vengent sévérement. La terre n'est-elle pas pleine de ces sortes de choses? Chaque homme ne le sait-il pas par expérience? De s'imaginer que tous les êtres de cette nature se soient trouvez précisément sur la terre , qui n'est qu'un point en comparaison du monde, c'est assurément une pensée tout-à-fait déraisonnable. La raison, l'esprit, l'ambition, la haine, la cruauté, seroient plutôt sur la terre que par tout ailleurs? Pourquoi cela? En pourroit-on bien donner une cause bonne ou mauvaise? Je ne le croi point. Nos yeux nous portent à être persuadez que ces espaces immenses que nous apellons le ciel, ou il se fait des mouvemens si rapides & si actifs , sont aussi capables que la terre de former des hommes, & aussi dignes que la terre d'être partagez en plusieurs dominations. Nous ne savons pas ce qui s'y passe; mais il nous faudra croire qu'il est plus-probable , ou du moins possible , qu'il y se trouve des êtres pensans qui étendent leur empire, aussi bien que leur lumière, sur notre monde. Ce que nous ne les voions pas, n'est point une preuve que nous leur soions inconus ou indifférens; nous sommes peut-être une portion de leur

menter éternellement son propre ouvrage. Il est le pere de tous les hommes, disent-ils; il châtie donc paternellement ceux qui lui désobéissent, & après leur avoir fait sentir leur faute, il les remet en grace auprès de lui. C'est de la sorte qu'Origene raisonnoit. D'autres suposent que Dieu ôtera l'existence aux créatures rebelles , & qu'aiant un *quem das finem Rex Magne laborum* (143), on l'apaisera, on l'atendra. Ils poussent si avant leurs illusions, qu'ils s'imaginent que les peines éternelles dont il est parlé dans l'Ecriture ne sont que comminatoires. Si de telles gens ignoroient ou n'eût un Dieu, & qu'en raisonnant sur ce qui se passe dans notre monde, ils se persuadassent qu'ailleurs il y a des êtres qui s'intéressent au genre humain, ils ne pourroient s'empêcher de délivrer d'inquiétude, qu'au cas qu'ils crussent la mortalité de l'ame : car s'ils la croioient immortelle, ils pourroient craindre de tomber sous le pouvoir de quelque maître farouche, qui auroit conçu du chagrin contre eux à cause de leurs actions ; c'est en vain qu'ils espéreroient d'en être quittes pour quelques années de tourment. Une nature bornée peut n'avoir aucune sorte de perfection morale : elle peut fort bien ressembler à nos Phalaris & à nos Nerons, gens capables de laisser leur ennemi dans un cachot éternellement, s'ils avoient pu posséder une autorité éternelle. Espérera-t-on que les êtres malfaisans ne dureront pas toujours: mais combien y a-t-il d'Athées qui prétendent que le soleil n'a jamais eu de commencement, & qu'il n'aura point de fin? Voilà ce que j'entendois, lors que j'ai dit qu'il y a des êtres qui pourroient paroître plus redoutables que Dieu lui-même. On se peut flater en jettant la vue sur un Dieu qui est infiniment bon, & infiniment parfait, & on peut tout craindre d'une nature imparfaite ; on ne sait si sa colere ne durera point toujours. Personne n'ignore le choix du Prophete David (144).
Pour apliquer tout ceci à un Spinoziste, souvenons-nous qu'il est obligé par son principe à reconoître l'immortalité de l'ame ; car il se regarde comme la modalité d'un être essentiellement pensant. Souvenons - nous qu'il ne peut nier qu'il n'y ait des modalitez qui se fâchent contre les autres, qui les mettent à la gêne, & à la question, qui font durer leurs tourmens autant qu'elles peuvent, qui les envoient aux galeres pour toute leur vie, & qui feroient durer de suplice éternellement, si la mort n'y mettoit ordre de part ou d'autre. Tibere , Caligula, cent autres personnes sont des exemples de ces sortes de modalitez. Souvenons - nous qu'un Spinoziste se rend ridicule, s'il n'avoue que tout l'Univers est rempli de modalitez ambitieuses, chagrines, jalouses, cruelles; car puis que la terre en est pleine, il n'y a nulle raison de s'imaginer que l'air & les cieux n'en soient pas pleins. Souvenons-nous enfin que l'essence des modalitez humaines ne consiste pas à porter de grosses pieces de chair. Socrate étoit Socrate le jour de sa conception, ou peu après (145); tout ce qu'il avoit en ce tems - là peut subsister en son entier , après qu'une maladie mortelle aura fait cesser la circulation du sang, & le mouvement du cœur dans la maniere dont il s'étoit agrandi : il est donc après sa mort le même modalité qu'il étoit pendant sa vie , & ne peut considérer que l'essentiel de sa personne : il n'échapa donc point par la mort à la justice, ou au caprice de ses persécuteurs invisibles. Ils peuvent le suivre par tout où il ira, & le maltraiter sous toutes les formes visibles qu'il pourra acquérir.
On pourroit se servir de ces considérations, pour porter à la pratique de la vertu ceux mêmes qui croupiroient dans les Impiétez de semblables Sectes ; car la Raison veut qu'ils craignent principalement d'avoir violé des Loix révélées à leur conscience. C'est à la punition de ces fautes qu'il seroit plus aparent que ces êtres invisibles s'intéresseroient.

(*U*) *Ses amis prétendent que par modestie il souhaita de ne pas donner son nom à une Secte.*] Raportons les termes de la Préface de ses *Opera posthuma*, & n'en retranchons rien.

(137) Pensées diverses sur les Cometes, num. 181, pag. 565, & 566. Voiez "Histoire des Ouvrages des Savans, Mars 1689, pag. 82.

(138) Les Pensées sur les Cometes furent imprimées en 1683.

(139) Dans la Remarque (H).

(140) *Ad audiendum sacratorem sacrum horis pomeridianis*, inquit, *EO volente, ad sermonem redibis.* Bortholtus, ref. Libri tribus impostoribus, pag. 6.

(141) *Idem, ibidem.*

(142) *Idem, ibidem.*

(143) Virgil. Æneid. Libr. I. Vers. 245.

(144) Aiant à choisir entre d'être vaincu par ses ennemis, ou d'être afligé de quelque fleau envoié de Dieu, il répondit au Prophete Gad, Je te prie que nous ne tombions entre les mains de l'Eternel: car ses compassions sont en grand nombre: & que je ne tombe point entre les mains des hommes. II Livre de Samuel, Chap. XXIV, Vers. 14.

(145) Spinoza, faiseur de Microscopes, devoit croire que l'homme est engendré & animé successivement, & qu'aussi Socrate étoit Socrate avant que sa mere l'eût conçu.

Upper Facing and Below: William Jennings Bryan (1860-1925, *The Menace of Darwinism*, New York: Fleming H. Revell Company, [1922]. QH367.B9 Sci. The John Crerar Library.

Moral Facts: Charles Darwin's work was immediately deemed controversial because the evidence he mounts for his own theory of evolution is counterfactual to biblical narrative, as well as the Bible's morals. Many years after his death, this controversy would bubble into the famous Scopes Trial against the teaching of evolutionary theory in schools. William Jennings Bryan, fundamentalist hero with a long history of protesting Darwinism in America, volunteered to help the prosecution. Published before the trial, which would make Bryan and his views famous, *The Menace of Darwinism* captures the extent to which evolutionary theory represented more than a biological fact. Bryan blamed Darwin for World War I and the degeneration of morality, the family, and civic virtue in America. The 'survival of the fittest' at the micro-level led to the destruction of social bonds, while at the macro-level it could be seen to contradict the Bible's chronology, leading to the loss of faith.

> 62   THE ORIGIN OF MAN
>
> inanimate matter and with its myriads of living things, all obedient to the will of the great Law Giver.
>
> Darwin concerns himself with only that part of man's existence which is spent on earth—while the Bible's teachings cover all of life, both here and hereafter.
>
> Darwin begins by assuming life upon the earth; the Bible reveals the source of life and chronicles its creation.
>
> Darwin devotes nearly all his time to man's body and to the points at which the human frame approaches in structure—though vastly different from—the brute; the Bible emphasizes man's godlike qualities and the virtues which reflect the goodness of the Heavenly Father.
>
> Darwinism ends in self-destruction. As heretofore shown, its progress is suspended, and even defeated, by the very genius which it is supposed to develop; the Bible invites us to enter fields of inexhaustible opportunity wherein each achievement can be made a stepping-stone to greater achievements still.
>
> Darwin's doctrine is so brutal that it shocks the moral sense—the heart recoils from it and refuses to apply the "hard reason" upon which it rests; the Bible points us to the path that grows brighter with the years.
>
> Darwin's doctrine leads logically to war and to the worship of Nietzsche's "Superman"; the Bible tells us of the Prince of Peace and heralds the coming of the glad day when swords shall be beaten into ploughshares and when nations shall learn war no more.
>
> THE ORIGIN OF MAN   63
>
> Darwin's teachings drag industry down to the brute level and excite a savage struggle for selfish advantage; the Bible presents the claims of an universal brotherhood in which men will unite their efforts in the spirit of friendship.
>
> As hope deferred maketh the heart sick, so the doctrine of Darwin benumbs altruistic effort by prolonging indefinitely the time needed for reforms; the Bible assures us of the triumph of every righteous cause, reveals to the eye of faith the invisible hosts that fight on the side of Jehovah and proclaims the swift fulfillment of God's decrees.
>
> Darwinism puts God far away; the Bible brings God near and establishes the prayer-line of communication between the Heavenly Father and His children.
>
> Darwinism enthrones selfishness; the Bible crowns love as the greatest force in the world.
>
> Darwinism offers no reason for existence and presents no philosophy of life; the Bible explains why man is here and gives us a code of morals that fits into every human need.
>
> The great need of the world to-day is to get back to God—back to a real belief in a living God—to a belief in God as Creator, Preserver and loving Heavenly Father. When one believes in a personal God and considers himself a part of God's plan he will be anxious to know God's will and to do it, seeking direction through prayer and made obedient through faith.
>
> Man was made in the Father's image; he enters

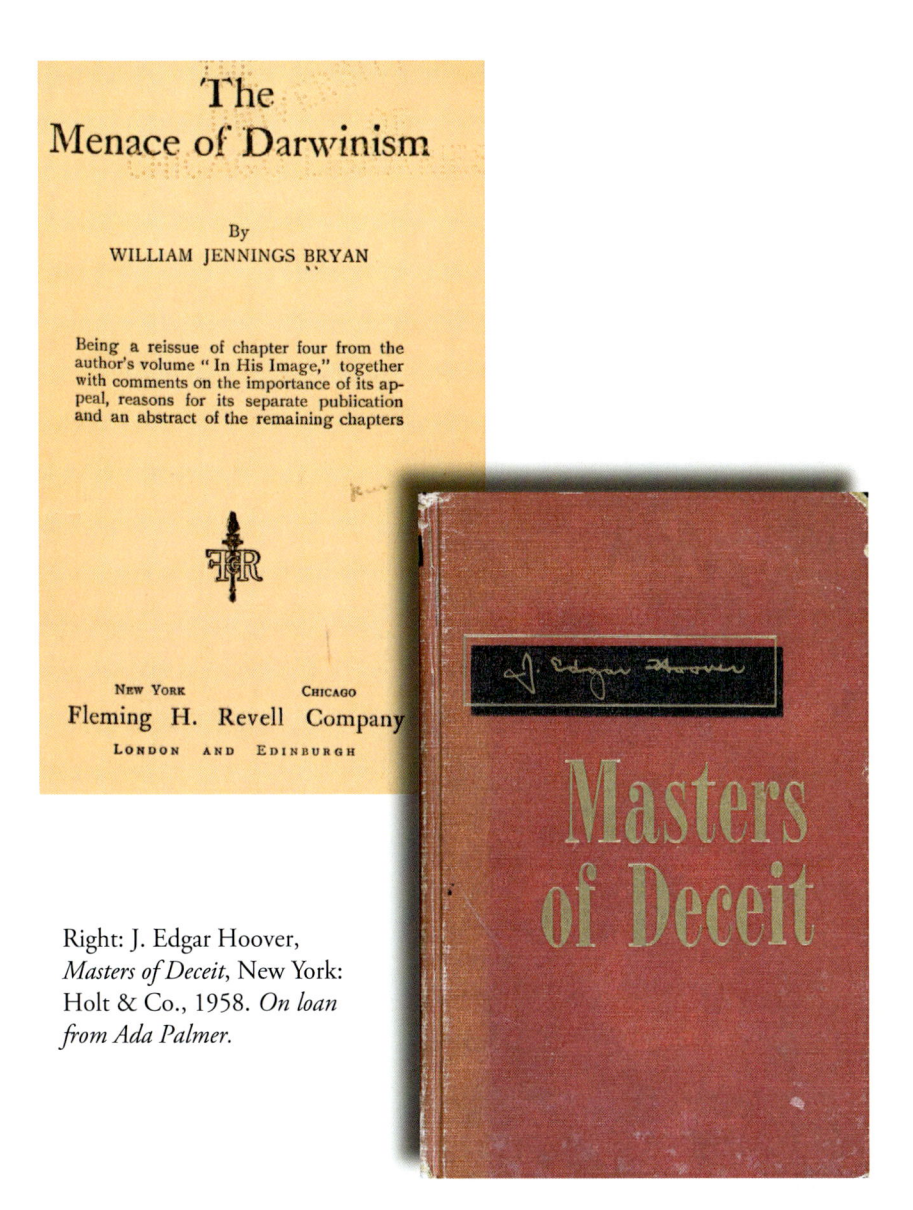

Right: J. Edgar Hoover, *Masters of Deceit*, New York: Holt & Co., 1958. *On loan from Ada Palmer.*

Modern Acids: This anti-communist book dates from the Second Red Scare, when America was fired by fear of a Soviet-engineered communist uprising. As head of the FBI, J. Edgar Hoover oversaw the examination and dismissal of thousands of government employees and a secret program to distribute anonymous documents about the communist affiliations of private citizens, especially teachers, lawyers, and labor leaders. While Hoover's institutional activities resembled the Inquisition in many ways, this counterfactual and ahistorical book engages with the ideas of Karl Marx in some depth, much as earlier 'anti-theses' engaged with Hobbes, Copernicus, or Luther.

GANIMEDIS·IVVENIS·TROIANVS·RAPTVS·A·IOVE

Censorship of the Classics

> "Any incident, passage, or even word which might be thought exceptionable by the strictest delicacy, is entirely omitted, and on no occasion has the fair purity of the youthful mind been for one moment forgot, in offering, and in selecting these pages for their perusal."
> – Caroline Maxwell, *The Juvenile Edition of Shakespeare, Adapted to the Capacities of Youth*, 1828.

> "Wherever then in his books I have found a statement concerning the Trinity contrary to those which in other places he has faithfully made on the same subject, I have either omitted the passage as garbled or misleading, or have substituted that view of the matter"
> – St. Jerome on censoring Origen as he translates, *letter LXXX to Rufinius*

Classical literature has long occupied a privileged position in Western culture, yet the classics have been dogged by censorship, targeting pagan or philosophical content, or erotic content. While we might expect Medieval Europe and the Inquisition to be the classics' primary adversaries, veneration for the golden age largely protected the classics in these periods, and those which were destroyed were more often victims of neglect or fi e than intentional destruction, though neglect too can be a form of censorship. It was the Victorian period that saw the most extensive censorship of the Classics, which were repeatedly sanitized through selective publication, inexact translation, or distorting paraphrase. While intending to protect young readers or suit the tastes of older ones, editors and translators who modified the original language and spirit of classics were in effect censors.

Facing: Speculum Romanae Magnificentiae (A151), *The Abduction of Ganymede*, Engraving, Michelangelo Buonarroti, Philippe Thomassin (engraver), [1618].

An Enormous Audience: The engraving on the previous page shows Zeus, in the form of an eagle, abducting Ganymede, a beautiful young mortal, to serve as his cupbearer and lover on Mount Olympus. As a mythological example of a sexual relationship between an older man and a teenaged boy, Ganymede is emblematic of Greek pederasty, and a popular subject of homoerotic art. This engraving reproduces a popular drawing created by Michelangelo for his beloved Tommaso dei Cavalieri, a handsome youth to whom the artist addressed numerous erotic letters and poems. The engraving, evidence of a large demand for copies of the powerfully homoerotic image, was printed by Philippe Thoassin, a French printer living in Rome, who was previously arrested for printing an engraving of Protestant King Henry IV of France.

Vertuno et Pomona

La falce dammi, el capo mi trasforma   Cosi si uolge in tutto, et si conforma
Et dir potrai ch'io nacqui in mezzo a' capi   Mia faccia, et sempre il uer par che ti sapi
Di marte istesso rubaro la forma   Ma più cercar no so forme si noue
S'io uesto darme chiari et ueri lampi.   Che per Pomona amor non mi ritroui

Facing: Speculum Romanae Magnificentiae *(C632)*, *Love Stories of the Gods*, Engraving, [1535?]

Salacious Scenes: The Speculum Romanae Magnificentiae is a collection of Renaissance prints of Roman scenes and themes, produced for popular consumption by a variety of artists and printers. Many of the prints reproduce popular paintings and statues, both ancient and contemporary. The print on the previous page depicts Vertumnus, the Roman god of seasons, seducing Pomona, the goddess of fruit trees. It is part of a set of fifteen to twenty engravings depicting Greek myths of seduction, and illustrates the kind of erotic classical content that was frequently censored in Medieval and post-Renaissance Europe, but enjoyed a Renaissance revival.

Left: Speculum Romanae Magnificentiae (C857), *Satyr Teaching a Young Boy,* engraving, Rome, [1614].

A satyr, armed with his characteristic pan flutes and erection, teaches a young man how to play music. This scene represents both pederastic relationships and the erotic themes of myth.

Below: Speculum Romanae Magnificentiae. (C629, *Cupid Handing a Drinking Bowl to Bacchus.*

Here, Bacchus, the Roman god of wine and madness, is garlanded in grapevines. Cupid, the god of sexual desire, offers him wine, and completes this scene of Classical debauchery.

Right: Speculum Romanae Magnificentiae. (C655), *Lasciviousness*, s.a.

This print depicts a personified Lasciviousness, bare-breasted, holding a lobster in one hand and clutching the horn of a goat with the other. The lobster and goat symbolize gluttony and virility, respectively. With her laurel wreath and statuesque pose, *Lasciviousness* is a classicized image of pagan vice.

Left: Speculum Romanae Magnificentiae (C848), *Venus*, Ca. 1614.

Venus, Roman goddess of love, holds Cupid's bow and arrows, which he uses to incite desire. She points into the distance, as though directing him to his next target.

Left: *Standing Female (Aphrodite?) Holding a Pomegranate.* Molded and modeled earthenware statue with slip- and cold-painted decoration. Height: 8 15/16 in. (22.7 cm). II BCE. 1967.115.62. *David and Alfred Smart Museum of Art, University of Chicago, The F.B. Tarbell Collection, Gift of E.P. Warren, 1902.*

This statue likely represents Aphrodite, the Greek goddess of love and sexuality. Her bare breasts and suggestive contrapposto pose are ubiquitous in classical sculpture. The pomegranate in her hand symbolizes fertility and loss of virginity. In her depiction and domain, she represents the erotic themes that pervade the classics, many of which are ascribed to her influence

Right: *Candlestick and Inkwell (or Sandbox) Depicting a Kneeling Statue,* cast bronze statue, with base: 9 3/4 in. (24.8 cm) Height of satyr: 8 1/8 in. (20.6 cm). c. 1500-1509. 1973.58. *David and Alfred Smart Museum of Art, University of Chicago, Gift of the Samuel H. Kress Foundation.*

Satyrs are lusty, half-male creatures from classical myth. Consistently depicted with erections, they were often associated with the Greek cult of Dionysios, the god of wine and madness. The early modern viewer of this piece of decorative art would likely see a symbol of classical licentiousness and indulgence.

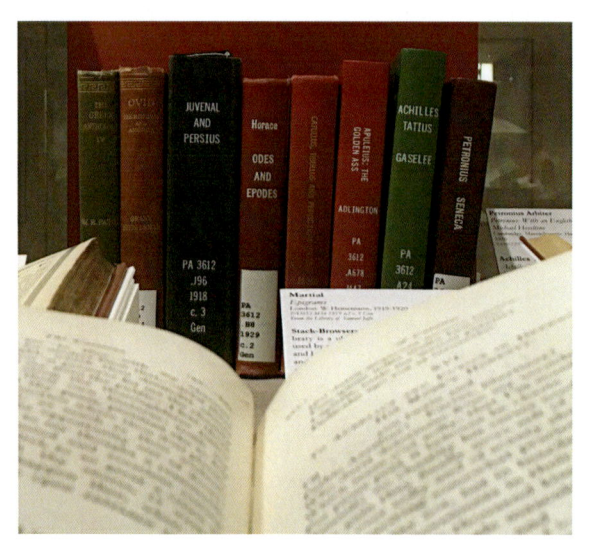

Left:

(Open)
Martial, *Epigrams*, London: W. Heinemann, 1919-1920. PA3612.M34 1919 v.2 c. 5. Gen. From the Library of Samuel Jaffe.

(Standing, from left to right)
The Greek Anthology, Cambridge, Massachusetts: Harvard University Press, [1916-1918], PA3611.A24 v.4 c.5 Gen.

Ovid, *Heroides and Amores*, London: W. Heinemann, 1914. PA3612.O9 1914 Gen.

Juvenal, *Juvenal and Persius*, London: W. Heinemann, 1918. PA3612.J96 1918 c. 3 Gen.

Horace, *Horace: The Odes and Epodes*, London: W. Heinemann, 1929. PA3612.H8 1929 c. 2 Gen.

Gaius Valerius Catullus, *Catullus, Tibullus, and Pervigilium Veneris*, Cambridge: Harvard University Press [1950]. PA3612.C44 1950 Gen.

Apuleius, *The Golden Ass*, London: W. Heinemann, 1915. PA3612.A678M47 1915 c.2 Gen.

Achilles Tatius, *Achilles Tatius: With and English Translation by S. Gaselee*, London: G.P. Putnam's Sons, 1917. PA3612.A24 1917 Gen.

Petronius Arbiter, *Petronius: With an English Translation by Michael Heseltine*, Cambridge, Massachusetts: Harvard University Press, 1930. PA3612.P5 1930 Gen.

Stack-Browsers Beware: The Loeb Classical Library is a ubiquitous collection of classical works, used by many scholars and students, with the Greek and Latin texts facing an English translation. Editors and translators bowdlerized many early Loeb editions, including those here, removing objectionable material through excision or euphemistic translation. In this translation of Martial's *Epigrams*, translator Walter Ker has removed sexually explicit terms from Epigram XLV, and has provided Italian, instead of English, for the entirely obscene Epigram XLVI. These censored editions remain in the stacks of this and many other libraries, where patrons have no way to realize they are censored.

[138]

Taming a Wild Poet: Catullus, a first-century BCE Roman poet, wrote numerous poems about himself and his contemporaries, many of which are obscene, explicit, or mention homosexuality. Over the centuries, editors and translators have censored Catullus in a variety of ways. For example, in the poems in which Catullus jokes about a prominent Roman whose name means "penis," a 1990 translation by Guy Lee, done for an Oxford classroom edition, rendered the name as "TOOL" in all caps, intentionally bringing the student reader's attention to the presence of censorship. Catullus 16 is a particular challenge for bowdlerizers, repeatedly mentioning sex acts. The version below, from 1894, is one of many efforts to render the poem both clean and comprehensible at the same time. A student has provided an alternate translation in pencil.

Catullus 16:
Pedicabo ego vos et irrumabo,
Aureli pathice et cinaede Furi,
qui me ex versiculis meis putastis,
quod sunt molliculi, parum pudicum.
Nam castum esse decet pium poetam
ipsum, versiculos nihil necesse est;
qui tum denique habent salem ac
   leporem,
si sunt molliculi ac parum pudici
et quod pruriat incitare possunt,
non dico pueris, sed his pilosis
qui duros nequeunt movere lumbos.
Vos, quod milia multa basiorum
legistis, male me marem putatis?
Pedicabo ego vos et irrumabo.

Literal prose translation: **"I will assault you anally and orally, submissive Aurelius and catamite Furius—you who think, from my verses, which are effeminate, that I'm too immodest. For it is appropriate for a dutiful poet to himself be chaste, but it is not at all necessary that his poems be, which indeed have cunning and wit, if they are tender and a little shameless and can incite an itch—I'm not talking about in boys, but in those hairy men, who can't move their stiff limbs. Because you have read my many thousands of kisses, do you think I am barely a man? I will assault you anally and orally."**

Below: Gaius Valerius Catullus, *The Carmina of Caius Valerius Catullus*, London: Printed for the translators, 1894. PA6274.A2 Rare.

XVI.]   *of Catullus*   31

Qui duros nequeunt movere lumbos.
Vos, quom milia multa basiorum
Legistis, male me marem putatis?
Pedicabo ego vos et inrumabo.

XVI.

TO AURELIUS AND FURIUS IN DEFENCE OF
HIS MUSE'S HONESTY.

I'll · · · you twain and · · ·
Pathic Aurélius! Fúrius, libertines!
Who durst determine from my versicles
Which seem o'er softy, that I'm scant of shame.
For pious poet it behoves be chaste   5
Himself; no chastity his verses need;
Nay, gain they finally more salt of wit
When over softy and of scanty shame,
Apt for exciting somewhat prurient,
In boys, I say not, but in bearded men   10
Who fail of movements in their hardened loins.
Ye who so many thousand kisses sung
Have read, deny male masculant I be?
You twain I'll · · · and · · ·
              butt-fuck   blow
I will paedicate and irrumate you, Aurelius the bardache and Furius the cinaede, who judge me from my verses rich in love-liesse, to be their equal in modesty. For it behoves your devout poet to be chaste himself; his verses—not of necessity. Which verses, in a word, may have a spice and volupty, may have passion's cling and such like decency, so that

butt-fuck   blow
I will paedicate and irrumate you,

[139]

Below: Battista Guarini (1538-1612), *Alexandri Guarini Ferrariensis in C. V. Catullum Veronensem per Baptistam Patrem Emendatum Expositiones cum Indice*, Venice: Per Georgium de Rusconibus, 1521. PA6274.A25 1521 Rare.

Trusted Elites: Approved by the authority of both the Pope and the Doge of Venice, Guarini's commentary on Catullus prints his lewdest poems in full and analyzes every part. This work was likely permitted publication because it is entirely in Latin—the Inquisition trusted that those educated enough to read Latin were too wise to be corrupted by licentious content.

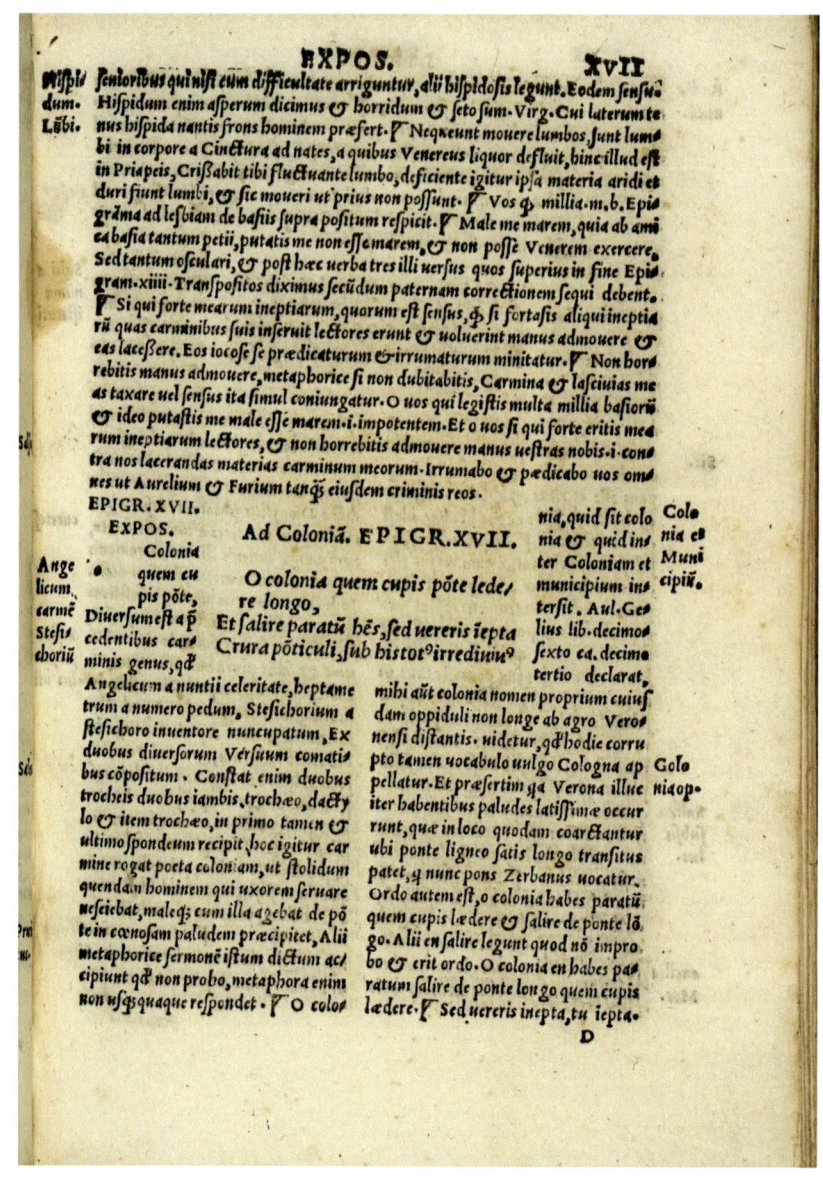

Right: Martial, *Select Epigrams of Martial*, London: R. and J. Dodsley, 1755. PA6501. A3H4 Rare.

Picking and Choosing: Selectively publishing only parts of an author's corpus was a common method of suppressing controversial material. Hay, as translator and editor, states in the preface of this volume that he has intentionally excluded some of Martial's work, largely because of obscenity, leaving only "generally moral or instructive" epigrams.

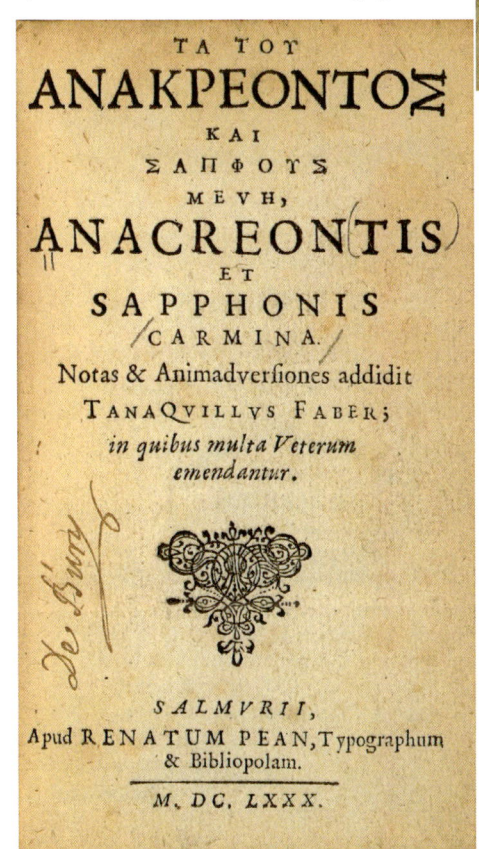

PREFACE.

SOME years ago, the following performance was undertaken for amusement; and it is hoped, the revisal and publication will not be thought entirely vanity. If it may sometimes excite mirth in the reader; that is not the principal aim and intention: which is to make him wiser, by exhibiting a picture of life by a masterly hand. What shall I call it? It is a translation or imitation of Martial; or both. Not of all his epigrams; that would be unpardonable. Many are full of obscenity, beneath a man: others of adulation, unbecoming a Roman: and great numbers concerning his own writings are omitted, for fear of cloying the reader. Some few will not admit of a translation: and not a few are too trifling to deserve it: and of this last sort, perhaps I might have been forgiven, if I had retrenched more. What I have selected are generally moral or instructive; in which a great variety of characters

Left: Anacreon, *Ta tou Anakreontos kai Sapphous Mēlē*, Salmvrii: R. Pean, 1680. PA3865.A1L5 1680 Rare.

Censorship Victorious: Sappho was a sixth century BCE female lyric poet from the Greek island of Lesbos. In the eleventh century, the infamous Pope Gregory VII burned her work because of its prominent homoerotic themes, so only fragments survive today. This 1680 book claims to contain the poetry of Sappho and Anacreon, but in fact only Anacreon appears—evidence of Gregory's success. Such cases, where an entire work was successfully destroyed after circulating, are remarkably rare in the historical record.

[141]

Below: Mary E. Burt, *Stories from Plato and Other Classic Writers.* Boston: Ginn & Co., 1895. PZ8.1.B9 Historic Children's Book Collection.

Erasing Past Mores: These stories for children, collected from classical works, omit salacious content. Many stories suggest further reading, but this tale from Catullus ends without reference to his other works, presenting only this moralizing Victorian parable which gives a deeply false impression of a poet famous for his crude and explicit poems. Collections like this helped propagate the distorting illusion that great authors in all periods never discussed sex, and that prudish Victorian mores were a historical universal.

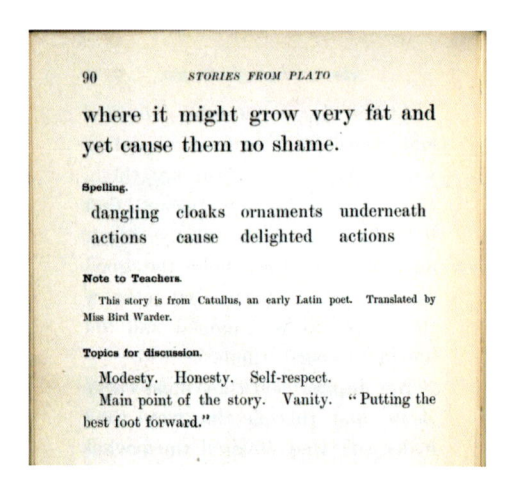

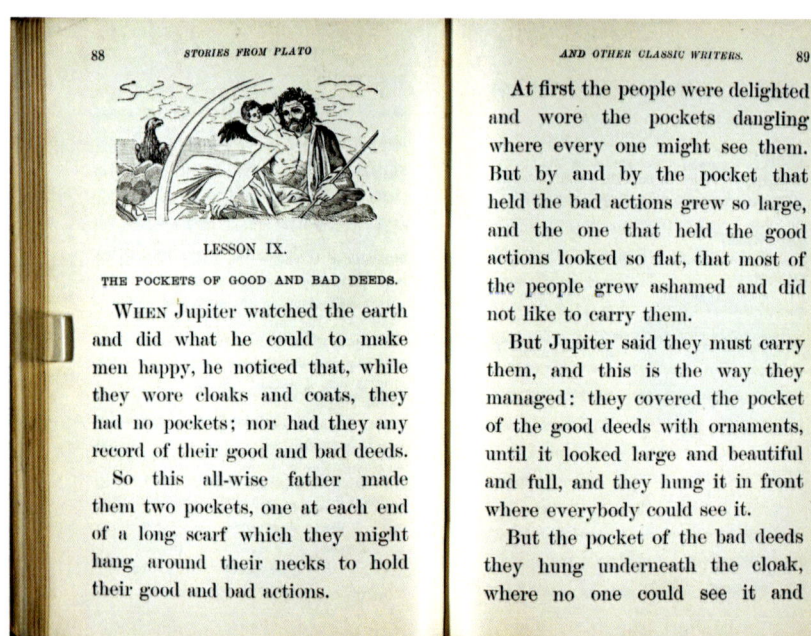

[142]

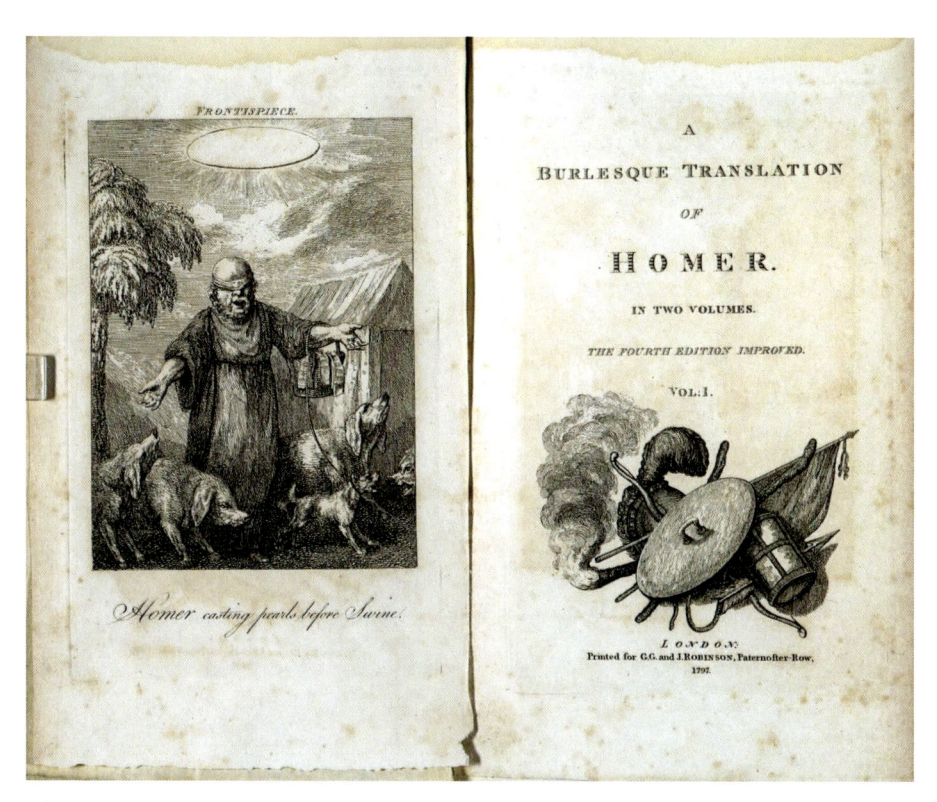

Above and Below: Thomas Bridges, *A Burlesque Translation of Homer*, London: Printed for S. Hooper, 1772. PR3326.B34H8 1772 Rare.

Making it More Dirty: This "literal translation" of Homer promises to restore the bard's "original design" but is in fact a burlesque rendition, filled with added lewd and suggestive humor. Thomas Bridges alleges that Alexander Pope's *Iliad* "has too much dignified the poem by omitting Homer's depiction of rowdy and bawdy gods and heroes." Bridges's extremely loose translation pushes in the other direction, distorting the original sense of the poem it jokingly purports to debowdlerize.

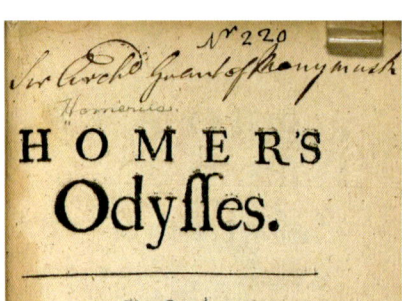

Hiding Within the Lines: After the controversy around *Leviathan*, Hobbes was blocked from publishing his own work, but he had begun his career as a Greek translator, so he turned to Homer in his final years, packing Hobbesean politics in among the verses. For example in the *Iliad*, book 4 line 465, he describes an illegitimate son of Priam as: "A lawful son where Nature is the Law."

Right and Above: Homer, *Homer's Odyssey*, London: Printed by J.C. for W. Crook, 1675. PA4025.A5H7.

Homer's Odysses. Translated By THO. HOBBES of Malmsbury. With a Large PREFACE Concerning the VERTUES OF AN HEROIQUE POE[M] Written by the Translator. LONDON: Printed by J.C. for W. Crook, at the [Green] Dragon without Temple-Bar, 1675.

To the Reader.

port, or by inference, is below the dignity not only of a Heroe but of a Man. For neither a Poet nor an Historian ought to make himself an absolute Master of any mans good name. None of the Emperors of *Rome* whom *Tacitus* or any other Writer hath condemned, was ever subject to the Judgment of any of them, nor were they ever heard to plead for themselves, which are things that ought to be antecedent to condemnation. Nor was (I think) *Epicurus* the Philosopher (who is transmitted to us by the Stoicks for a man of evil and voluptuous life) ever called, convented, and lawfully convicted, as all men ought to be before they be defamed. Therefore 'tis a very great fault in a Poet to speak evil of any man in their Writings Historical.

A sixth Vertue consists in the perfection and curiosity of Descriptions, which the ancient Writers of Eloquence call *Icones*, that is *Images*. And an Image is always a part, or rather

[144]

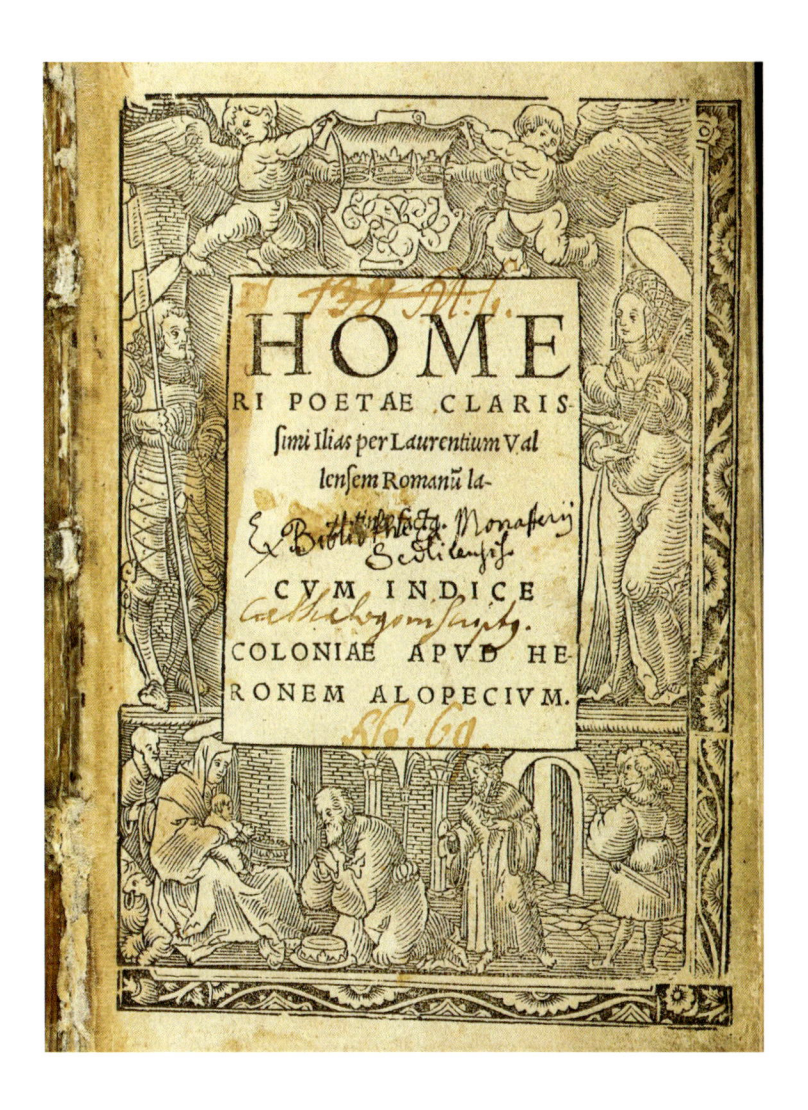

Above: Homer, *Iliad*, Coloniae: Heronum Alopecium, [1522]. PA4024.A3 1522 Rare.

Pleasing the Reader: In one of the earliest translations of Homer, Valla was accused of paraphrasing rather than translating, yet his changes may have encouraged more people to read. Renaissance scholars were eager to recover the long lost *Iliad*, but were dismayed on reading it to discover that—unlike their beloved pro-imperial Aeneid—the *Iliad* foregrounded antiwar messages and miserable heroes. Renaissance translators like Valla tweaked the *Iliad* to make it more comfortable for Renaissance readers accustomed to depictions of glorious war, increasing the book's circulation while distorting its message. Valla himself was the author of the infamous *On the Donation of Constantine*, which undermined papal claims to imperial power.

Above: Eugène Delacroix (1798-1863), *Hamlet,* Act III, Scene 2: Hamlet and Guildenstern, c. 1834, Lithography on heavy wove paper. 1967.116.84. *On loan from the David and Alfred Smart Museum of Art, University of Chicago, University Transfer from Max Epstein Archive, Gift of the Carnegie Corporation, 1927.*

Censorship in Translation

> "Censorship is the mother of metaphor. ▮▮▮▮▮ I am in favor of censorship. When there is censorship, literature becomes more virile, subtler, more composed... Without censorship we would note have Gibbon's or Voltaire's irony."
> – Jorge Luis Borges, to his friend Bioy Cesares, July 26, 1967

> "Is there any censorship in your country's media? Then you are definitely living in a fascist country! Censorship is the tool of the coward governments. Criminals are always afraid of the truths."
> – Mehmet Murat ildan, Turkish playwright, 2013

We tend to judge translations on their accuracy or elegance, but any translation adds new actors to the chain of a text's creation. As translators and new local editors and publishers move texts across linguistic and geographic barriers, they must navigate political and ideological diffe ences, and often local censorship. These objects show how intentional changes made during translation have been used used to censor, distort, silence, or propagandize, but also to advance new ideas, express forbidden dissent by hiding it in the words of another, and even to protect authors. You can find more intersections between censorship and translation—especially translation between elite or imperial languages and vernacular or indigenous ones—in the cases on Colonial Censorship and the Plural Inquisitions.

New Associations: Voltaire's famous *Letters on the English* (1733) praise England's liberal policies on religion, politics, and culture compared to France. The book was burned in France and a warrant issued for Voltaire's arrest. In the 'Letter on Tragedy' Voltaire translates Hamlet's 'To Be or Not to Be'—the first partial translation of *Hamlet* into French—but increases the role of religion in the speech, making fear of damnation the reason men "bless the hypocrisy of our lying priests" and "grovel under a minister, worshiping his haughtiness." After this, Hamlet retained an association with dissent with France, and Eugène Delacroix—who painted the famous "Liberty Leading the People," celebrating the 1830 July Revolution—produced this series of lithographs illustrating *Hamlet*.

Below: Voltaire (1694-1778), *Lettres Escrites de Londres*, (i.e. *Letters on the English*) [Basel: Jean Brandmuller & fils: 1737]. PQ2086.L4 1737 Rare.

Not Pictured: William Shakespeare (1564-1616), *Tian chou ji--Hamlet. Chinese*, Shanghai: Shang wu yin shu guan, [1930]. 5988 4421 Harvard Yenching/CJK.

Borrowed Revenge: This 1920s prose translation of *Hamlet* by Shao Ting reframed its protagonist as a righteous filial avenger angered by the state abuse. With allusions to classical Chinese tragedy, including a new title, *Tale [of] Heaven's Hatred*, Shao's translation reflected his grief at his father's assassination under Sun Yat-sen.

Not Pictured: William Shakespeare (1564-1616), *Hamlet*, Moscow: Gos. Izdvo Detskoĭlitry, 1956. PR2807.A6R9P3 Gen.

Sneaking In Dissent: Poet and novelist Boris Pasternak refused to endorse Stalin's purges or write to the party line. Forbidden to publish original work, in 1941 he published a translation of *Hamlet*, modernizing the text and seeding it with contemporary commentary by substituting politically relevant phrases like "red tape" for "the law's delay."

Right: Boris Pasternak, *Doktor Zhivago*, Moscow: "Azbukovnik", 2013. PG3476. P27D6 2013 Gen. *The Leo Endowed Book Fund.*

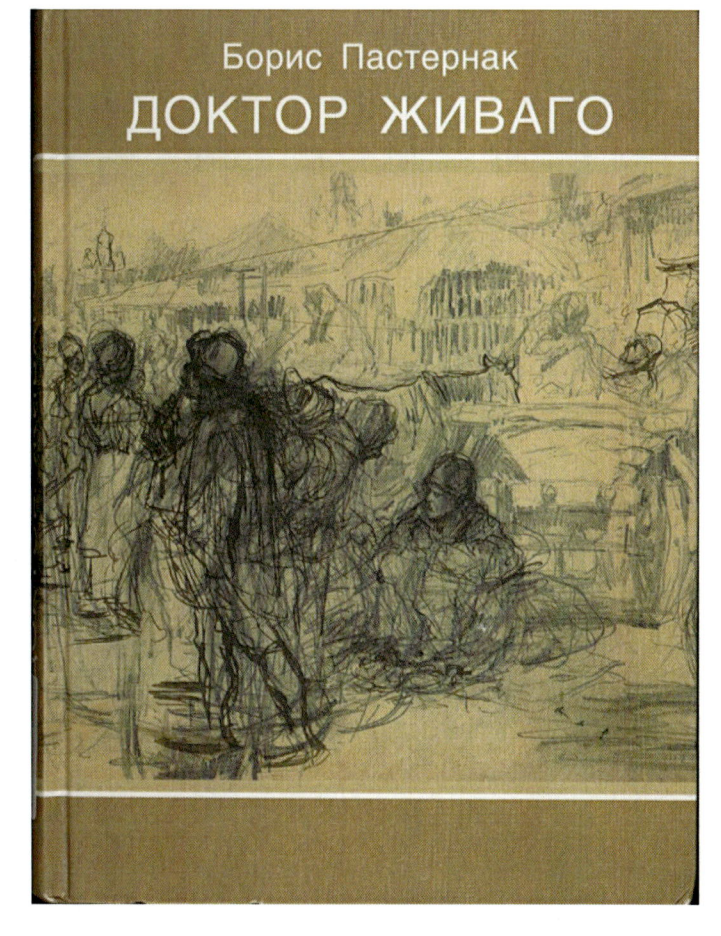

Weaponizing Translation: Banned under Stalin, Pasternak's *Dr. Zhivago* was printed clandestinely and rapidly translated into other languages. It became a pan-European bestseller and received the 1958 Nobel Prize, bringing the wrath of the Communist Party down on the author. Pasternak's name reportedly appeared on a list of those to be purged but was crossed off by Stalin. In fact everything—the Russian edition, translations, high sales, and Nobel prize—was engineered by the CIA to stir anti-Soviet feeling.

Below: Henry Kissinger (1923-), *Lun Zhongguo - On China*, Beijing: Zhong xin chu ban she, 2012. DS775.8.K4712 2012 Gen.

Removing Criticism: American Secretary of State Henry Kissinger's On China largely offe ed a positive portrayal, but the Chinese edition was censored to remove criticisms of China's human rights violations, including a depiction of the tragedy of Tiananmen. Political conversations between then-president Deng Xiaoping and Kissinger were also removed, as well as references to protesters such as Fang Lizhi who had fled China seeking US asylum. The Chinese publishers stated that it was better to have "90 percent of the book than 0."

Not Pictured: *Cha jin tu shu mu lu*, Taiwan: Taiwan jing bei zong si ling bu, [1966]. 9564 4391 Harvard Yenching/CJK.

Fearing the Translator: When Japan surrendered in 1945, Taiwan passed into the control of the fie cely anti-Communist Republic of China, which put Taiwan under martial law from 1949-1987, the longest period of martial law anywhere in world history. This index, produced by the Taiwan Garrison Command, banned mainly communist writings, but even books merely translated by communist writers, like Hawthorne's *The Scarlet Letter* or Bronte's *Jane Eyre*, were deemed harmful and forbidden.

Below: Chu Teh-chun (1920-2014), *Gouache No. 4*, c. 1960, gouache on heavy wove paper, 1980.65. *On loan from the David and Alfred Smart Museum of Art, University of Chicago, Gift of the Estate of Mandeliene Franks Ricketts.*

Artistic Freedom: *Gouache No. 4* shows the integration of traditional Chinese brushwork with gouache, a European water-based medium with a consistency similar to brush ink. This work reflects the nuances of calligraphy, showing the coexistence between Chinese and Western values. In China, Chu studied both classical Chinese painting and Western art at the National School for Fine Arts. In 1949 Chu's career in China was cut short after the Communist victory. Under Mao, all artists had to adhere to the 'party line' and during the Cultural Revolution, artists were forced to work within the style of "revolutionary romanticism." Chu fled to Taiwan, and eventually moved to France where he became the first Chinese member of the Académie des Beaux-Arts.

Right: Johannes Scherr (1817-1886), *Blücher: Seine Zeit und Sein Leben*, Leipzig: Otto Wigand, c. 1862-63 PT1105. L565 no. 3426 v.1 Lincke.

Welcome There, Unwelcome Here: This German biography treats Prussian General Gebhard Leberecht von Blücher who fought Napoleon in 1813. It asserts that, throughout Russian history, when a leader wanted to change royal dynasties, he or she hatched a plot similar to creating a modern business firm. Because this implied Catherine the Great was involved in the overthrow and murder of her husband, the Russian Foreign Censorship Committee blacked it out in all copies imported to Russia.

Not Pictured: Kwame Hkrumah (1909-1972), *I Speak of Freedom: A Statement of African Ideology*, New York: Praeger, [1961]. DT512.N73 c.2 Law.

Bottom Facing: Kwame Hkrumah (1909-1972), *Â govorû o svobode: izloženie afrikanskoj ideologii*, Moscow: Izdatel'stvo inostrannoj literatury, 1962. *On loan from Ada Palmer.*

Inserting Criticism: This autobiography of Nkrumah, President of Ghana during the Cold War, appeared in English in 1961, then in Russian translation in the USSR in 1962. The Russian version includes excisions but also additions, mainly inserting or exaggerating criticisms of the USA. The open passage recounts an interview in which Nkrumah was asked about the racial relations in the United States. The original English reads, "the racial question in the United States has often been exaggerated." This was replaced in the Russian with: "Racialism, I said, wherever it existed, obviously should be abolished."

[152]

Below: Yevgeny Zamyatin (1884-1937), *My: Roman,* New York: Mezhdunarodnoe Liter-atunoe Sodruzhestvo, 1967. PG3476.Z34M8 1967 Gen.

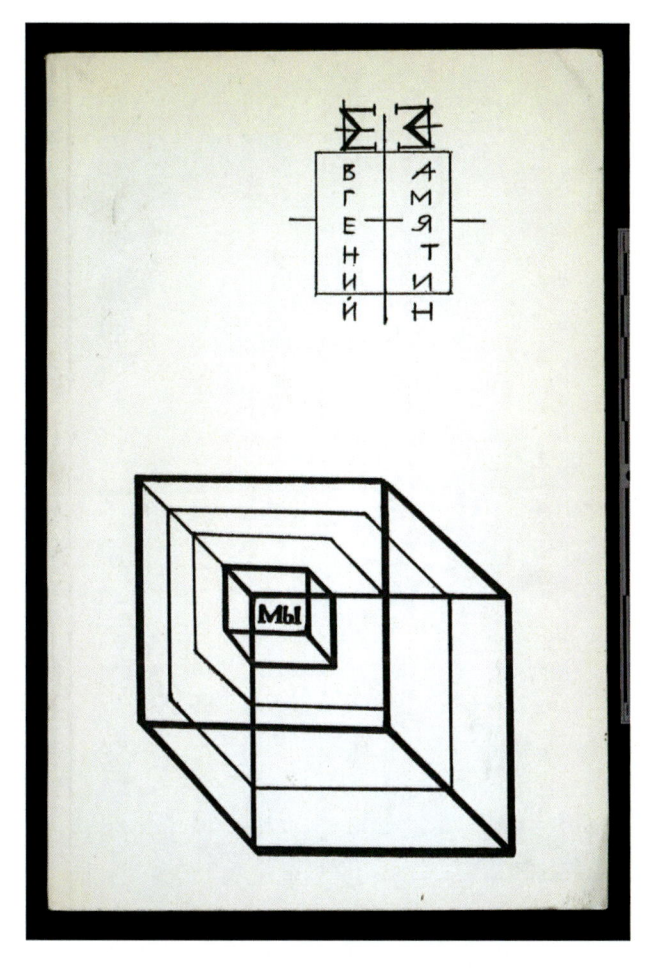

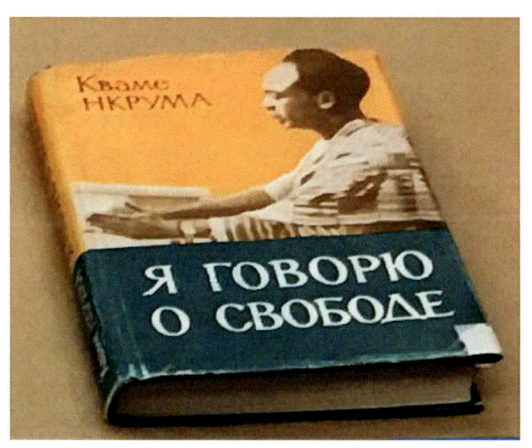

Protecting the Author: Zamyatin's novel *We* established the dystopian genre and influenced Orwell's *1984*. Banned in the USSR, it appeared in English in 1924. A Czech translation appeared in 1927, and Marc Slonim then published excerpts of the Russian original in his émigré journal *Volya Rossi (Russia's Will)*, but, to protect the author from Soviet backlash, Rossi claimed the text was retranslated into Russian from the Czech, and he even garbled some sections to make it plausible that the author was uninvolved.

[153]

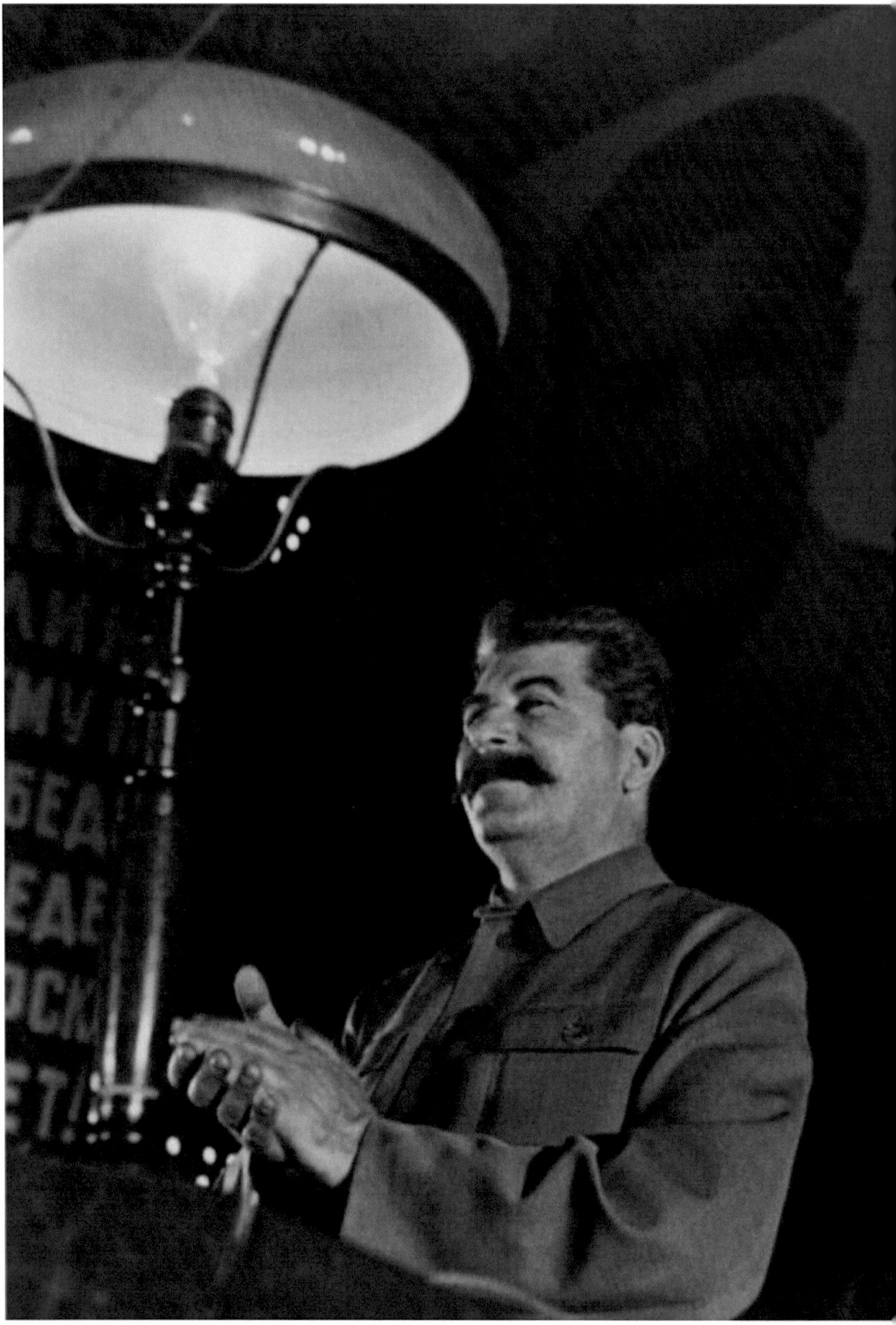

Soviet Censorship

> "The world is kept alive only by heretics: the heretic Christ, the heretic Copernicus, the heretic Tolstoy. Our symbol of faith is heresy: tomorrow is inevitably heresy to today, which has turned into a pillar of salt, and to yesterday, which has scattered to dust. Today denies yesterday, but is a denial of denial tomorrow. This is the constant dialectic path which, in a grandiose parabola, sweeps the world into infinity. The only weapon worthy of man—of tomorrow's man—is the word."
> – Yevgeni Zamyatin, *"Tomorrow,"* 1919-20

> "To me as a writer, being deprived of the opportunity to write is nothing less than a death sentence. Yet the situation that has come about is such that I cannot continue my work, because no creative activity is possible in an atmosphere of systematic persecution that increases in intensity from year to year."
> – Yevgeny Zamyatin, *"Letter to Stalin,"* 1931

The main aim of Soviet censorship, according to both Lenin and Stalin, was to promote the spirit of socialism, in order to control the masses, suppress dissent, and embed Soviet culture in public consciousness. Soon after seizing power in 1917, the Bolsheviks passed a Decree on the Press, banning authors who challenged the legitimacy of their power. Censorship reached its peak under Stalin. In 1922, the government established Glavlit, or the General Directorate for the Protection of State Secrets in the Press, which became the centralized enforcer of censorship with absolute power. It produced and updated an index of prohibited books called the Perechen Svedenii ne Podlezhashchikh Opublikovaniyu v Otkritoy Pecha-

---

Facing: Georgy Zelma (1906-1984), *Stalin*, 1935 (negative, 1992-1996 edition), gelatin silver print, printed from original negative. 1999.81w.
On loan from the David and Alfred Smart Museum of Art, University of Chicago, Gift of Linda H. and John B. Hillman.

Cold War Freeze: Born in Uzbekistan in 1906, photographer Georgy Zelma documented the USSR's political world, including Stalin's regime. Only after Stalin's death in 1952 did the USSR gradually lessen censorship, a move called the "Khrushchev Thaw."

ti ("List of Information not Suitable for Open Publication") focused on idealizing the Soviet life by removing reports of disasters, crime statistics, income fluctuations, price increases, and controversial identities. It also established Goskino (State Film Committee), censoring film and cinema, and Goskomizdat (State Committee for Publishing), overseeing literary publications. Unlike the Roman Inquisition, which had to give enormous independence to distant branches such as the Portuguese-run Goan Inquisition, the modern USSR could aspire to centralization, although movement of records and information was far from perfect, and its system—like the Inquisition's—remained vulnerable to circumvention from within by individual censors and officials sympathetic to dissenting voices.

GOSKINO: THINGS YOU MAY NOT SEE

Soviet authorities applied harsh restrictions to cinema. Among the most prominent instances was Andrey Tarkovsky's 1966 film *Andrei Rublev*, which directly addressed issues of artistic freedom, politics, religion, and autodidacticism. After its first and only screening it was harshly suppressed and ridiculed by the committee—a fate shared by his other films such as *Ivan's Childhood*, which were accused of criticizing Soviet foreign policy. These films received international awards and are often invoked as as a examples of artistic talent stifled under totalitarianism.

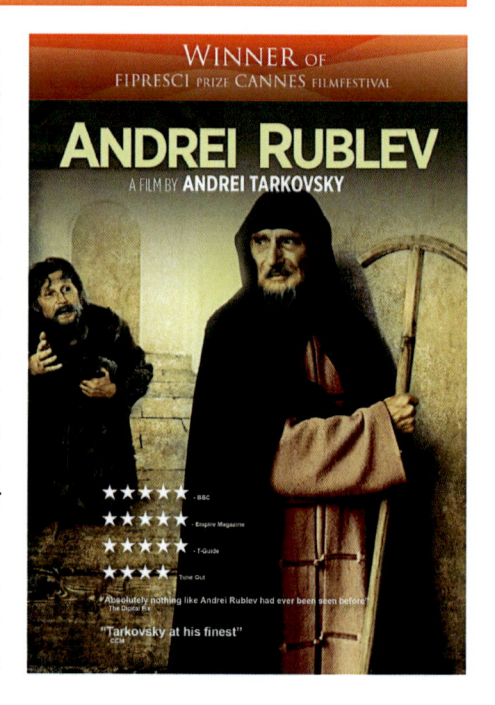

GOSKOMIZDAT: THE DEMISE OF LITERATURE

Soviet citizens had limited exposure to authors now among the classics of Eastern European thought, such as Mikhail Bulgakov, Alexander Solzhenitsyn, Ivan Bunin, Vladimir Nabokov, Leonid Tolstoy, and—featured in our exhibit—Boris Pasternak. Many authors who were initially fervent supporters of the revolution—such as Yevgeny Zamyatin whose *We* so strongly influenced Orwell, found themselves silenced, or worse. Foreign works were also censored, notably Orwell's *1984*, which Stalin realized satirized his regime as well as England's. In 1923, the infamous Soviet censor Proskuriakova spelled out qualities of 'harmful' books, which included promotion of religion, tsarist ideals, failure to portray class consciousness and the proletariat's drive to work hard, and any opposition to the narrative or project of revolutionary class struggle. The same year a book purge led by Lenin's wife Krupskaia cleansed Soviet libraries of the vast majority of the Western intellectual tradition, including such authors as Plato, Descartes, Kant, Thomas Carlyle, Henry James, the Gospels, the Talmud, and the Koran. Another purge in 1927 eliminated over sixty percent of Soviet libraries, followed by more in 1929, 1930, and 1932 which rid the libraries of another sixty percent of what remained. Opposition brought punishments varying from prison sentences to death.

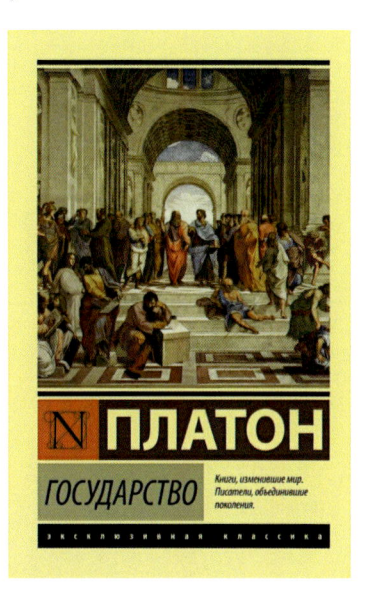

IN DEFIANCE OF CENSORSHIP

Evading Soviet censorship was not easy, yet authors and readers found ways. In opposition to Goskomizdat, an underground Samizdat ("self-produced") movement took root in 1953, after the death of Stalin. Its leaders focused on replicating and disseminating prohibited novels, poetry, speeches, political tracts, religious texts, and music before it was captured by the secret police. Although its circulation was limited, its audience included cultural leaders and even figures in Soviet power. Much circulated underground that we would not think of as high literature or political speech, such as popular American music—Judy Garland or Frank Sinatra—which was banned and associated with Western capitalism. Possessing banned pop culture—such as bootleg records reproduced on X-Ray films—was a personal micro-protest, much like what Orwell's Winston and Julia cling to in *1984*.

DID SOVIET CENSORSHIP SUCCEED?

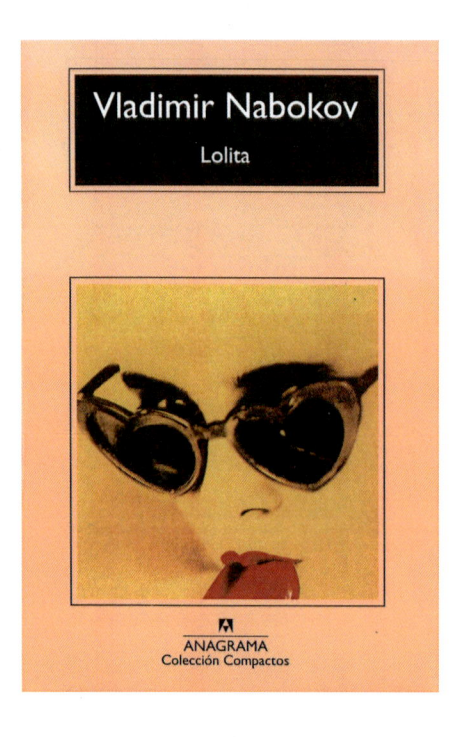

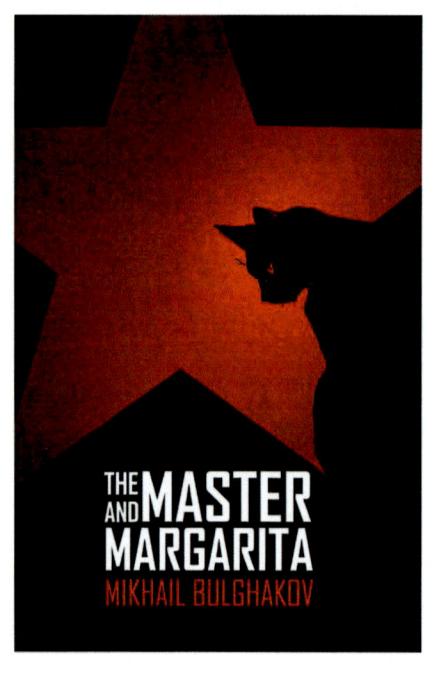

The USSR never entirely rooted out banned materials or voices of dissent, nor could it achieve the absolute surveillance Orwell imagined, with a camera in every room—that technology has only come into existence very recently. But if we remember how many of the Inquisition's activities aimed more to remind people of its presence and power, the USSR certainly succeeded in making all its citizens, and people around the world, constantly conscious of its program of control. It also dominated the fate of art and literature produced under its influence, not by eradicating dissent, but by making it circulate differently: in exile, in back alleys, in coded phrases, in private homes. Comparing the Inquisition and USSR makes abundantly clear how, as we evaluate the impact of censorship, we must look beyond the destruction of information to censorship's other objectives, such as cultivating fear, projecting power, and encouraging self-censorship. Understanding censorship's perennial goals is more important now than ever as we enter an era when it is at last genuinely possible—via the microphones in personal electronics—for a state to listen to every conversation.

[158]

The Great Firewall of China

Referred to by scholars as the most extensive effort to selectively censor human expression ever implemented, China's internet censorship is the most advanced on Earth, with more than sixty regulations and technology in place to monitor individual internet use.

New Medium, Old Methods

China's internet censorship is the most advanced on Earth, with more than sixty regulations and technology in place to monitor individual internet use. Many infrastructural elements parallel steps we see in premodern censorship. Chinese law requires all internet traffic to pass through one of several state-owned networks, and mandates state licensing of internet service providers, much like the Inquisition and Milton's England. In this system, some websites—such as the *New York Times*—are blocked entirely, but many appear with white spaces where content has been removed, constant reminders of censorship's presence, much like the Inquisition's blacked-out words. In addition to targeting political speech, Chinese policy targets slander, sexually suggestive material, and the names of specific dissidents or issues, such as Tiananmen Square.

Does Censorship Still Need Human Censors?

China uses automated keyword blocking to prevent internet users from discussing forbidden topics, but such automated filters are often circumvented using homonyms; for example, the phrase 敏感瓷 "sensitive porcelain") is used to talk about "sensitive words," or censored language, because "word" and "porcelain" are phonetically similar in Chinese. Because these filters are so easily fooled, the Chinese government still relies heavily on human censors. Some human agents assemble daily blacklists of words connected to new hot topics, while others judge which words to add to

China's permanent word blacklist. Recent research suggests that Chinese censors often allow some posts on Chinese social media which are critical of the Communist Party and its officials but focus on removing posts referencing specific events with high "collective action potential." Attempting to curate and shape social action, rather than focusing on ideas, is a new focus of censorship enabled by modern political and social science.

Above: Earth at night, with lights revealing population centers. Below: World Facebook connections. Notice areas in China, Russia, and the Middle East, bright above but invisible below. Taiwan and Hong Kong are clearly visible.

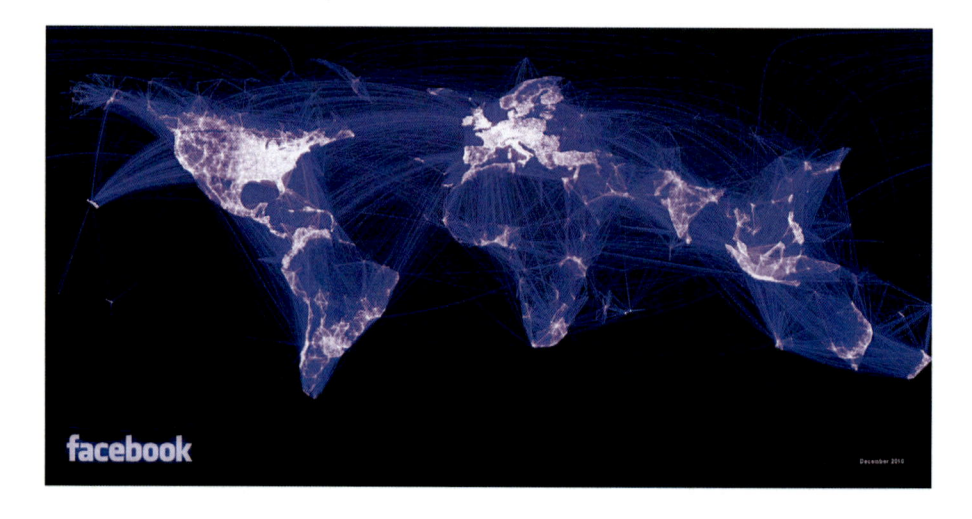

Cultivating Caution

Incarceration of cyber-dissidents in China is the most widespread in the world but difficult to fully document. While some arrests target activists or pro-democracy bloggers, broadly worded bans on anything which might throw bad light on China's government enable cases such as teacher Liu Shaokun sentenced in 2008 to a year of "re-education through labor" for sharing photographs of negligently constructed Sishuan schools which collapsed and killed children during an earthquake. Again, like the Inquisition and USSR—much of China's system focuses on encouraging self-censorship. ISP companies are held legally responsible for users' content, treated effectively as publishers and incentivized by the threat of fines or arrests to police their own customers. This farms out much of the manpower cost of surveillance to private companies, though the government also hires censors to read social media posts, and programmers to design automated filters. It is not difficult for Chinese citizens to obtain a foreign IP address to bypass internet blocks, but intermittent arrests for such activities create a chilling effect or climate of fear, making those who use such methods constantly conscious of surveillance, and more likely to rein in their own speech.

Mundane Incentives

While perhaps more Orwellian than any other real system Earth has seen, China's censorship is still inconsistent, subjective, and often far more mundane in action than Orwell's Ministries. American reporter Liz Tung, who reported for *The Atlantic* the Beijing Olympics, experienced censorship as "a humdrum series of last-minute deletions and substitutions based on the political whim of an editor or a dictate from the Propaganda Department." Works published in China are run past in-house censors before publication, but government censors have final authority, and can confiscate and destroy material. Subjective and unpredictable censorship further encourages self-censorship, since the less political content a work has, the less likely it is to face interference, expensive confiscations, or unexpected missed deadlines, which can be devastating in fast-paced publication markets such as journalism or comics. China's cultivation of self-censorship also affects the international world, as media creators, such as the Hollywood studios behind *Skyfall* and *Doctor Strange*, hope to tap lucrative Chinese markets, so remove scenes or plot points they think might offend Chinese censors.

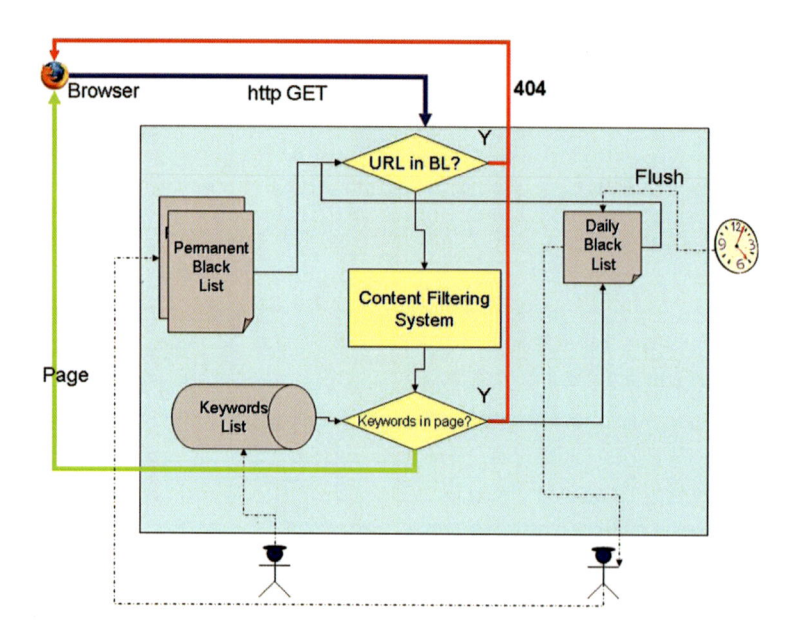

Above: An attempt to model Chinese internet censorship, showing the automated and human agents.

Below, map of world internet censorship and surveillance, 2017. Compare the pink areas to the areas which appear dark on the Facebook map.

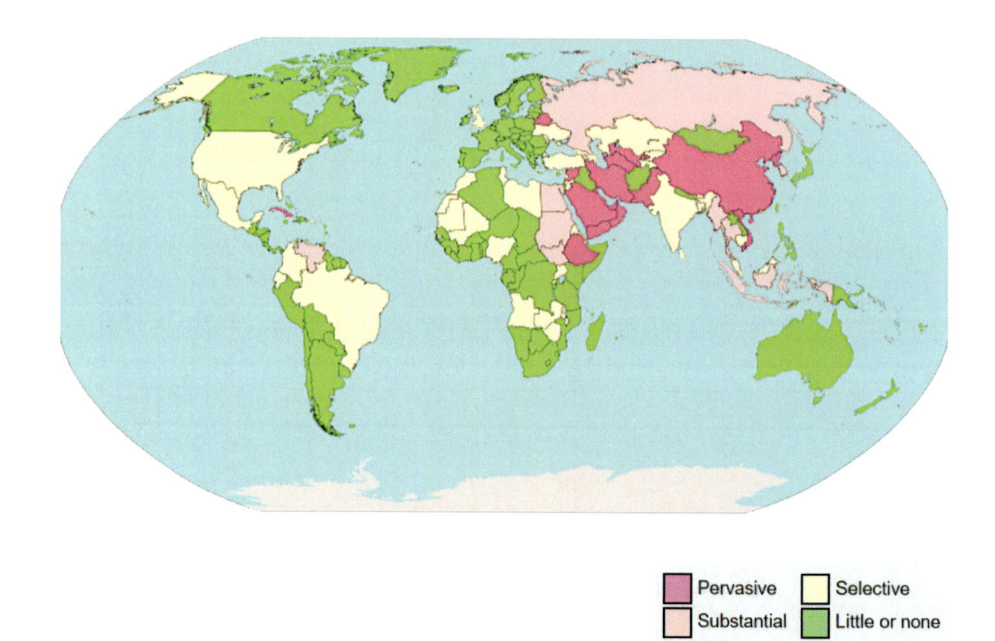

[162]

Censorship in New Zealand: What Does the First Amendment Really Do?

OFFICE OF FILM & LITERATURE CLASSIFICATION
Te Tari Whakarōpū Tukuata, Tuhituhinga

As former British colonies, New Zealand shares much culture, history, and law with the USA, so its censorship system offers a glimpse of what American censorship might be like without the American First Amendment's restriction that "Congress shall make no law ▮▮▮▮ abridging the freedom of speech, or of the press ▮▮▮▮."

How a Modern Democracy Censors

Today, New Zealand's Office of Film and Literature Classification works "to make sure that New Zealand's censorship legislation is enforced, and so help protect people from material that is injurious to the public good." Material can be restricted if it deals with "sex, horror, crime, cruelty or violence, and if its unrestricted availability would be harmful to society," while policy completely bans works which "support or promote" sexual violence, sexual exploitation of children, torture or extreme violence, bestiality, necrophilia or "the use of urine or excrement in association with degrading or sexual conduct." Citizens can use an online complaint form to report objectionable material, while the OFLC blog offers ratings guides for parents and children and posts regularly about its decisions in high-profile cases such as *Thirteen Reasons Why* and *Deadpool*. The offic also conducts research, such as studies of the effects of depictions of sex and violence on young viewers. New Zealanders may face prison sentences of up to 14 years for␣traffickin prohibited material, or 10 years for possessing it.

Evolving Over Time

Historically, most of New Zealand's censorship has been moral, born from public alarm about "indecency" in low media (pornography, advertisements, magazines, film). egulations have alternately broadened and narrowed, broadening when a new technology (such as the advent of talkies) or perceived crisis (such as the 1950s comics craze) triggered new public outcry, but narrowing as activists worked to demonstrate that the language of extant law could also impact legal activities, or respected works. Segregation has been a common alternative to bans: older laws mandated that suggestive films could only be shown to all male or all female audiences, while today's movies and games are age restricted. While early regulations were vague, banning "indecent" material in general, regulations have evolved to define more precisely what can and cannot be censored, and what actions censors and police may take. In contrast with moral censorship, New Zealand's political censorship has usually been justified as a special wartime measure, but such precedents can be reused during domestic crises.

> The timeline that follows reviews New Zealand's censorship history. Many crises—the World Wars, the comics craze, the Red Scare, the growth of film—also happened in the USA, and as New Zealand used state censorship, America created extra-governmental bodies such as the Comics Code Authority, McCarthyism's blacklisting, and the Motion Picture Association of America. Thus the First Amendment did not prevent censorship, but changed who enforced it: government or public. On the macro-scale the same movements attacked the same material, but on the micro-scale the difference between an artist facing bankruptcy under the US Comics Code or prison in New Zealand was life-changing.

1858 – Customs regulations prohibit importing "indecent" and "obscene" material.
1892 – Offensive Publications Act restricts "indecency" in advertisements.
1893 – Amendment to the Post Office Act allows post office to intercept, open and destroy mail suspected of being indecent.
1900 – Ban on sending indecent material by mail.
1906 – Offensive Publications Act amended to allow search of homes and businesses.
1908 – Lawyer takes Shakespeare to court, to make the point that New Zealand's regulations could also harm worthwhile material.
1910 – New Indecent Publication Act attempts to define "smut" and "indecency" specifically, while protecting "art" and "worthwhile" material.
1914 – Increased wartime political censorship introduced for World War I.
1916 – Popular demand for restrictions on pornographic films leads to the firs Cinematograph Film Censorship Act requiring that a government censor preview all films. The title "Chief Censor" is created for the officer in charge.
1921 – Wartime political censorship introduced for WWI is extended, justified by the Red Scare.
1930s – The invention of Talkies (films with sound) leads to new wave of bannings related to language instead of visuals.
1939 – Ministers of Customs and Education convene to discuss regulation of imported American comics and magazines.
1939 – Increased wartime censorship introduced for WWII; Boccaccio's *Decameron* banned but then permitted on appeal.
1949 – Public concern over comic books begins to grow, but the Education Department recommends no censorship.

Above: Douglas Tempest, Bamforth & Co. Ltd, England, 1918; "Witty Comic" Series no. 329.

1951 – The infamous Waterfront Strike. Dock workers had accepted 15 hour working days during the wartime labor shortage but at the war's end they were not allowed to stop. During their strike, Prime Minister Sidney Holland declares a state of emergency, using the residual wartime censorship apparatus to ban pro-union speech, and to make possession of "seditious" literature (i.e. criticism of the government) an imprisonable offence.

1952-1956 – Growing concern over comic books lead to a series of committees and regulations to examine and ban comics. Strong restrictions are also placed on reporting and discussing suicide, justified by the idea that depictions inspire imitation.

1961 – Crimes Act outlaws "indecent" performances and formalizes a ban on "blasphemous libel"; Broadcasting Act regulates TV and radio.

1963 – Indecent Publications Act sets up a tribunal and defines "indecent" more specifically.

1968 – Indecent Publications Act refined with further specifics about nudity in magazines.

1970 – 49,000 New Zealanders (out of a population of 2.5 million) sign a petition calling for stricter censorship, focused on film.

1972 – Indecent Publications Act made stricter, amid controversies involving works including the film *Clockwork Orange*, and the musical *Hair*.

1976 – Cinematograph Films Act aims to liberalize censorship policy, mandating that censors consider "injury to the public good" the main criterion for bans; Internal Affairs Minister Alan Highet argues this will "modernize" New Zealand by reducing censorship of material for adults to focus on censoring material for children. As in the USA, works accused of obscenity must prove their "artistic or other merits."

Above: *Blotting the Book*, by Neville Colvin (Standard, 1951), representing Prime Minister Holland during the Waterfront Strike.

1977 – Amendment to the 1971 Race Relations Act restricts discusions of race in public statements, while the Contraception, Sterilisation and Abortion Act limits discussion of contraceptives.
1982-84 – Controversies include the banning of magazines such as *Penthouse*; feminists push for greater sexual openness; police raid retailers.
1985 – Film censor allows explicit sex films to be released for the first time triggering opposition from the Labor Party.
1986 – Homosexual Law Reform Act legalizes male homosexuality, rendering much of New Zealand's censorship case law obsolete since it depended on homosexuality being criminal; LGBT groups spearhead pushes to relax and clarify censorship, triggering a substantial overhaul of the extant system.
1987 – Video Recordings Authority established, mandating ratings on all VHS material.
1988 – Ministerial Committee of Inquiry into Pornography begins to operate.
1993 – Films, Videos, and Publications Classification Act supplants earlier regulations.
2003 – *Manhunt* becomes the first video game banned in New Zealand. 2005
2005– Films, Videos, and Publications Classification Act updated.
2015 – Penalties for violating the restrictions on objectionable publications increased.

Main Source: *Censored: a Short History of Censorship in New Zealand,* Paul Christoffel, 1989. Learn more at www.classificationoffice.govt.nz

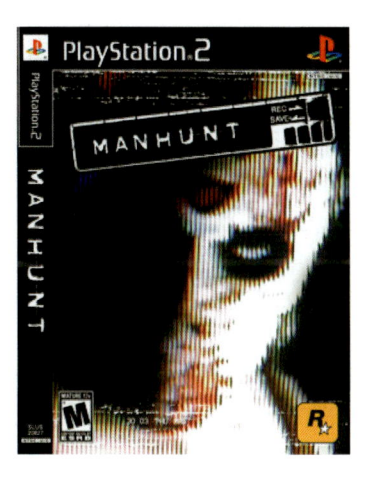

Left: Cover of *Manhunt.* Playstation2 version, Rockstar Games, 2004.

Rgiht: Poster for Stanley Kubrick's *Clockwork Orange*, Warner Bros., 1971.

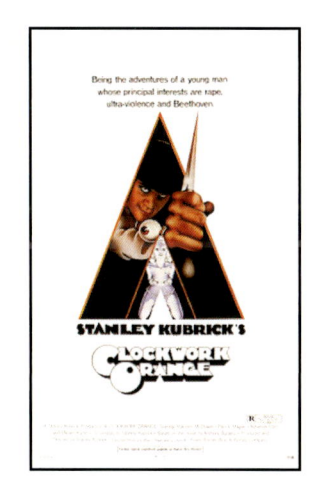

SELLING BOOKS IN UGANDA.

COLONIAL CENSORSHIP

Empires often seek to control the culture, religion, and economies of their colonial possessions to maintain power and to expand their influence. To this end, colonial powers often censor indigenous cultural and religious practices, language, and literature. In some cases empires used assimilatory educational policies or missionary work. In others banned texts, or attempted to eliminate or manipulate of native languages. Colonizing powers usually present this censorship as necessary for maintaining authority and often for "bettering" or "civilizing" colonized peoples; colonized peoples responded to control effo ts with varying degrees of compliance, resistance, and artistic innovation. See more imperial materials in the "Plural Inquisitions" case.

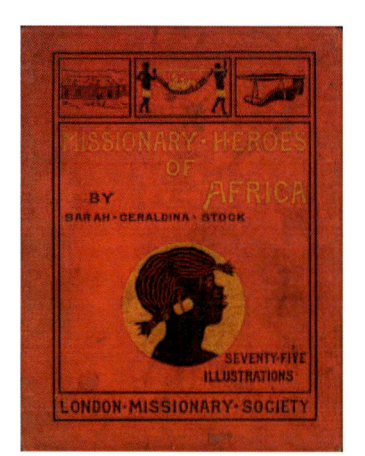

Facing, Left, Below, and Following: Sarah Geraldina Stock (1839-1898), *Missionary Heroes of Africa*, London: London Missionary Society, 1897. DT18.S7 1897 Historical Children's Book Collection.

Another Era's Heroes: This book—deeply uncomfortable to most readers today—was meant to give children an engaging and positive overview of missionary work in Africa. Through adventure narratives and illustrations, it glorifies the men and women who traveled there to spread Christianity. The book describes how missionaries changed the dress, religious beliefs, and forms of labor of African peoples, making them give up their "heathen" practices for Christian ones.

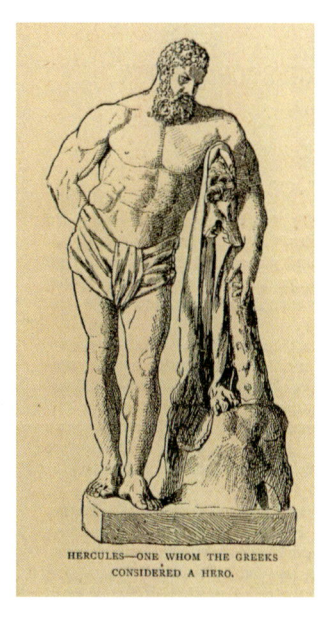

TRAVELLING IN CENTRAL AFRICA.

WOMEN OF UGANDA—CANDIDATES FOR BAPTISM.

Below: Henry Albert Willem van Coenen Torchiana (1867-1940), *Tropical Holland, Java and Other Islands,* Chicago: University of Chicago Press, 1923. DS634.T71 UC-Press.

The Language of the Rulers: Henry Torchiana was born in Java but later moved to California where he became Consul General for the Netherlands in 1913. In this treatise, he notes that "a native was not allowed to address a Dutch official or merchant in the Dutch language" (Torchiana 195). The Western nature and relative difficulty of Dutch was used to justify the restriction of the language, which reinforced the separate and unequal status of colonists and colonized.

Not Pictured: Sajjad Zahir (1905-1973), *Angaaray*, New Delhi: Penguin Books, India, 2014, PK2199.S25A5413 2014 Gen.

Indigenous Requests for Censorship: Colonized peoples also took advantage of the presence of colonial censorship to advance their own agendas. This book of stories strongly critical of Muslim culture in India was banned by the British colonial government in 1933 at the request of members of India's Muslim community. All but five copies were destroyed. The banning of *Angaaray* helped catalyze the formation of the All India Progressive Writers' Association, which stood against censorship by the colonial government.

Protect and Proselytize: As part of their efforts to spread Christianity across the world, Christian missionaries codified and applied local languages in the Americas and elsewhere. These were often the subject of intense scrutiny by censors, and in some cases the Inquisition, as it was essential that native neophytes not be exposed to heretical doctrines. The example here, printed in 1759 on the press founded by the famous Mexican polymath Juan José Eguiara y Eguren (1696-1763), contains sermons and moral lectures (pláticas) in Nahuatl, an indigenous language still spoken in some parts of Mexico and Central America.

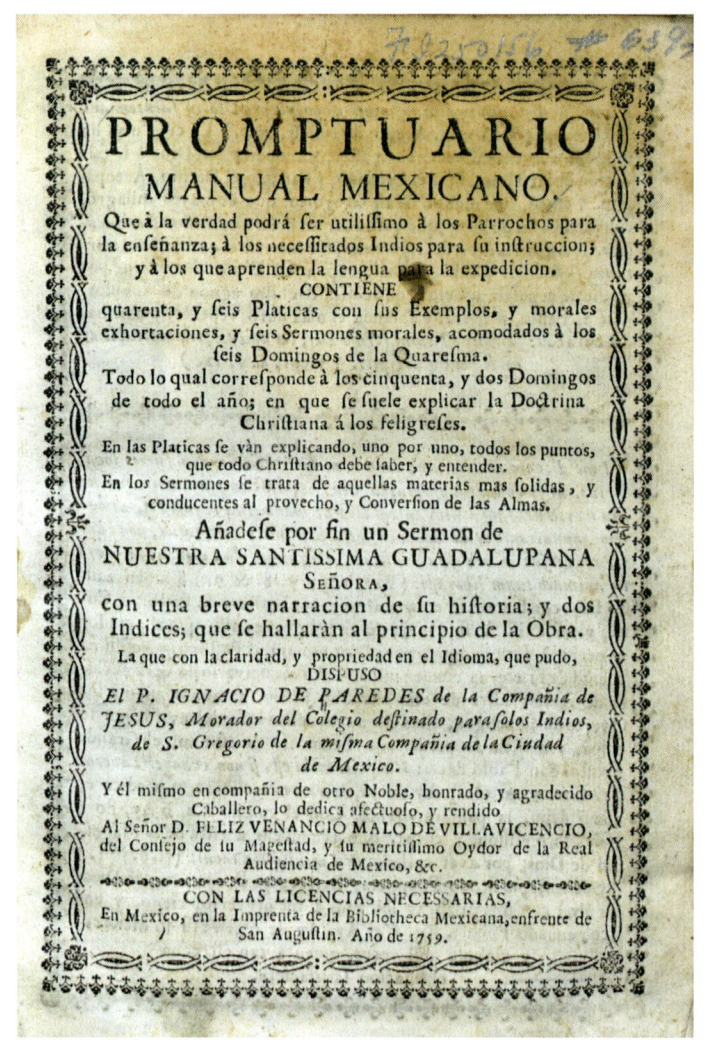

Above: Ignacio de Paredes, *Promptuario Manual Mexicano*, Mexico: Imprint of the Mexican Library, 1759. PM4068.1.P3 Rare.

Below: John Bartholomew & Co., *The British Empire: Showing Degree of Self-Government*, Edinburgh: John Bartholomew & Co., [1889], G3201.F33 1889.J6 Map Collection.

Plural Imperial Policies: Just as the Inquisitions were decentralized, each colony or territory within the British Empire had unique local rights, treaties, policies, and official which made the power and operations of censorship diffe ent in each area. In the upper map, the different colors delineating the degree of self-government in each region not only reveal the extent of the British Empire but emphasize the degree of separation between independent and dependent territories.

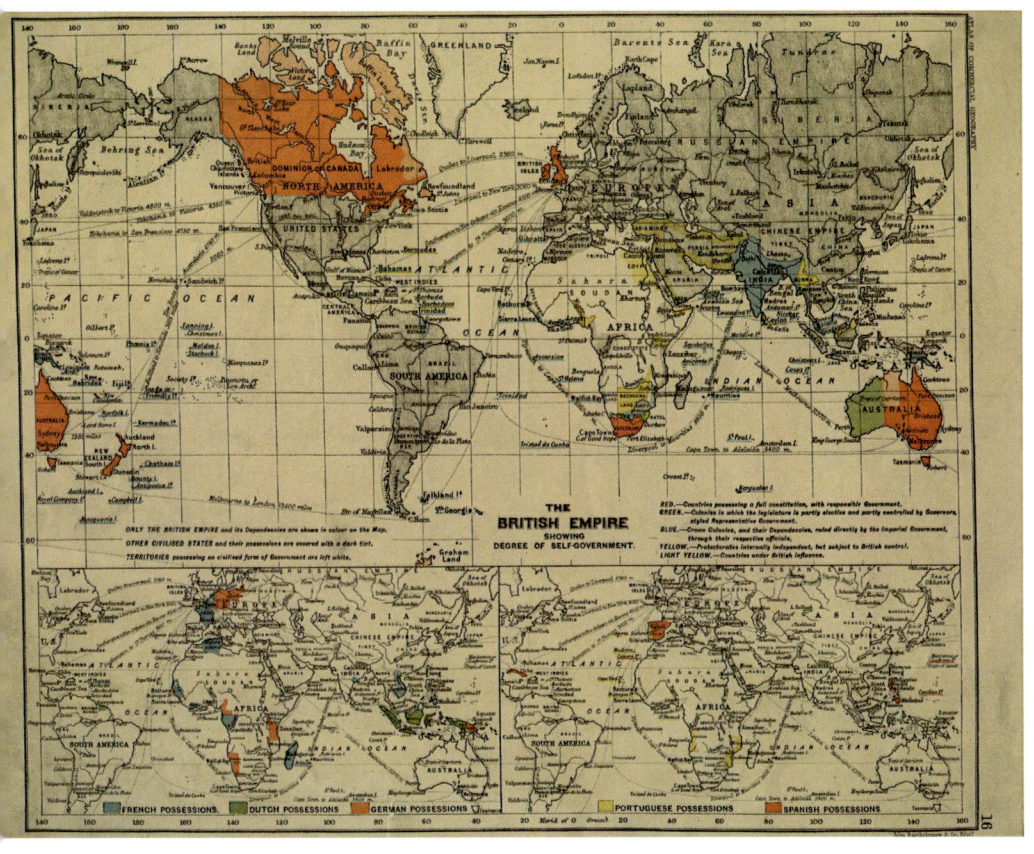

Not Pictured: *Jin zhi tu shu mu lu: Kang Ri zhi bu*, [Beijing: Xin min hui, 1939]. 9564 0278 Harvard Yenching/CJK.

20th Century Colonialism: During the Second Sino-Japanese War and World War II, the Japanese empire established a series of puppet states in China, including the Provisional Government of the Republic of China, which published this index of publications banned for containing anti-Japanese sentiment.

[173]

Not Pictured: Gustavus Lindquist (1886-1967), *A Handbook for Missionary Workers Among the American Indians,* New York: Home Missions Council, c. 1932.E98.M6L73 1932 Rare.

Curating Culture: This handbook aimed at Christian missionaries working among Native Americans describes, among instructions and strategies for conversion, the necessity of curbing the "communist" tendencies of the "Indian," and explains how native words could be altered to reflect Christian concepts. The missionary efforts outlined in this text are dually focused on Christianization and assimilation.

De-Censoring Education: Founded by the American Indian Movement in the 1970s, the "survival school" Red School House was a Native educational institution that attempted to combat the censorship of indigenous language and tradition that Native American children experienced in America's colonial education systems. The school aimed to foster a sense of community among Native American children, and to educate them about their cultural and linguistic heritage.

Facing: Report Cover, Proposal / Red School House, Native American Education Services. David Beaulieu Papers, 1954-1997, Box 2, Folder 8.

Below: Table, Goal Statement: I, II, III, IV, Native American Education Services. David Beaulieu Papers, 1954-1997, Box 2, Folder.

NATIVE HISTORY

OBJECTIVES	ACTIVITIES	EVALUATION/RESULTS

1.0 Maximum attendance due to culturally based curriculum.	1.1 Pre-Columbian history to include creation accounts and tribal origins
	
	1.2 Post-Columbian to 1873 (end of treaty-making period; alliances--Three Fires, Iroquois Confederacy, etc.)
	
	1.3 Federal Indian Policy
	  a. Treaties
	  b. Dawes Act (Severalty)
	  c. Snyder Act
	  d. Indian Reorganization Act
	  e. Relocation and Termination
	  f. Self-determination
	  g. Economic development
	
	1.4 Philosophy of Tribal Native Peoples
	  a. Traditional Values and Teachings (Trickster, cycle, etc.)
	  b. Pan-Indianism
	  c. Contemporary viewpoints
		·pre and post testing
		·collected samples of student work
		·written student and teacher observations
		·record of participation.

2.0 Increased family participation	2.1 Home visits to inform parents on student's strengths, weaknesses, and progress 2.2 Parent input and parents as guest speakers on tribal studies.	·written teacher observations ·collected, compiled and analyzed community survey.

Not Pictured: Photographs of Motion Picture Stills from the film *Redskin*, 1929. Motion Picture Stills Collection. Box 51, Folder 30. *Redskin* Stills. Photograph. 1929.

Hollywood Imagines Assimilation: A largely silent film with sections of sound and color, *Redskin* follows a Navajo boy named Wing Foot who is forcibly assimilated into the dominant culture at a residential school. Subjected to racism from white peers at university, Wing Foot returns to his people, but rejects their way of life and ends up an outcast in both the Navajo world and the white one. In a typical 1920s happy ending, Wing Foot discovers oil, makes the tribes rich, and gets the girl. Records suggest that no Native Americans were involved in the production, but the film's existence demonstrates some public awareness of the problems of forced integration.

ULTRA GASH INFERNO

erotic-grotesque manga by
Suehiro Maruo

Censoring Comics

> "The Law is a blunt instrument. It's not a scalpel. It's a club. ████████ If you accept—and I do—that freedom of speech is important, then you are going to have to defend the indefensible. That means you are going to be defending the right of people to read, or to write, or to say, what you don't say or like or want said. The Law is a huge blunt weapon that does not and will not make distinctions between what you find acceptable and what you don't."
> – Neil Gaiman, *"Why Defend Freedom of Icky Speech?"* 2008.

> "Comic books, traditionally what we think of, are for kids ████████ This is in a store directly across from an elementary school and it is put in a medium, in a forum, to directly appeal to kids. ████████ We're here to get this off the shelf."
> – ADA Nancy Ohan in the 2000 obscenity trial Texas v. Castillo

Comics and graphic novels face more censorship than text literature, for several reasons. First, comics are literally "graphic," and visual depictions of violence or sexuality spark stronger reactions than text. Second, many—not all—societies associate comic books with children, so comics with mature content are often considered a threat to young readers regardless of their intended audience. Third, political cartoons are a staple of political dissent, sparking reprisals from politicians and publics. Organizations such as Cartoonists Rights Network International and the Comic Book Legal Defense Fund work to protect artists—such as Ramón Esono Ebalé arrested and held without charge 2017-18 in Equatorial Guinea, and Atena Farghadani currently serving a twelve year jail sentence in Iran—as well as publishers, vendors, and readers. In the USA one can be fined or jailed for creating, selling, or owning "obscene" comics, and obscenity laws require the defense to establish that a supposedly-obscene work has redeeming "artistic merit," a vague criterion which leaves much room for bias. In Japan—a much larger producer of comics than the USA—a new restriction on comics "harmful to the youth" was passed as recently as 2011. More controversial comics—including the controversial French satirical newspaper *Charlie Hebdo*, target of the infamous 2015 shooting—appear in the Banned Bookcase section.

Facing: Suehiro Maruo, *Ultra Gash Inferno*, S.l.: Creation Books, 2001. *On loan from Ada Palmer.*

Below: *Demon Beast Invasion: the Fallen #2*, Bare Bear Press, New York, 1998, *On loan from Ada Palmer.*

Absolutely Not For Children: In 2000 in Dallas TX, comics shop worker Jesus Castillo was arrested and charged with obscenity for selling (in a clearly labeled adult section of the store) this extreme pornographic comic, *Demon Beast Invasion: The Fallen*. He was fined $4,000 and sentenced to 180 days in jail in a conviction upheld by the U.S. Supreme Court in 2002. Prosecutors echoed familiar claim that "Comic books, traditionally what we think of, are for kids." This copy was special ordered for this exhibit through a local Chicago comics shop, whose staff— ery conscious of the dangers all US comics store staff face on the front lines of censorship—kept the comic behind the counter, sealed in plastic, with paper pasted over the cover.

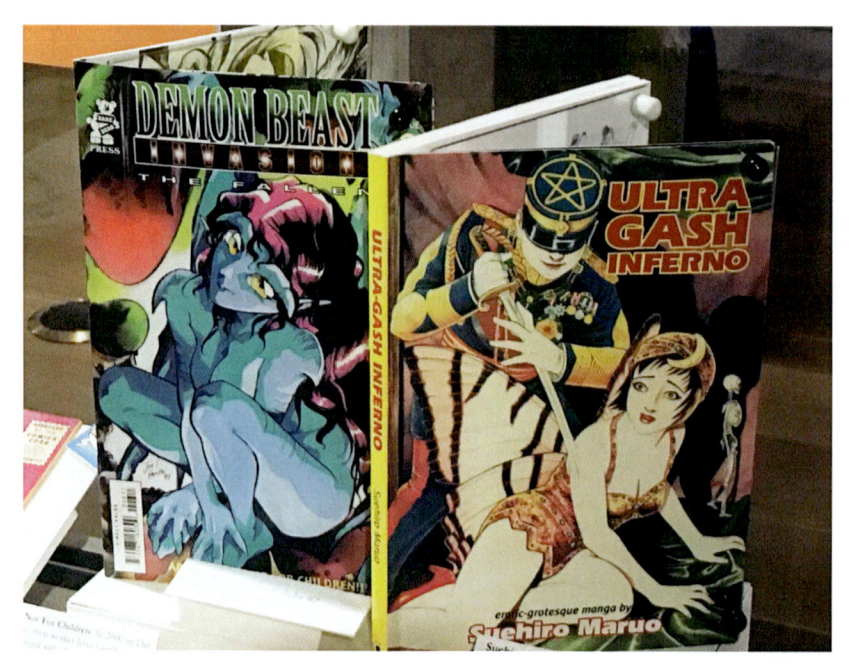

Defending "Icky Speech": Ero guro nansensu (ero "erotic" + guro "grotesque" + "nonsense") is a Japanese literary and artistic movement, originating in the 1930s, which explores eroticism, decadence, violence, and nihilistic hedonism. This example, *Ultra Gash Inferno*, is so extreme that the curator who wrote this label vomited while reading it. Twice. This is precisely the kind of material many people are comfortable censoring, but the last quarter of the volume is a social commentary protesting abuse of Japanese women by American occupation troops after World War II. This demonstrates how impossible it is to regulate "icky speech" without infringing political expression.

Nonexistent Victims: In 2011, Tokyo expanded an ordinance regarding "Healthy Development of Youths" to prohibit harmful depictions of "non-existent youths" or "depicted youths," i.e., drawings and comics depicting incest, sexual assault, and other "harmful" themes. So far the only works affected by the ban have been hardcore pornography most readers would find distasteful, but publishers and authors say the ordinance has had a "chilling effect," sowing fear and encouraging self-censorship. This *dōjinshi* (fan comic) protesting the bill was produced bilingually in Japanese and English, likely in hopes that America would pressure Japan to end the regulation.

Right: Takeshi Nogami, Takaaki Suzuki, Dan Kanemitsu, *Monkey Business: Idiot's Guide to Tokyo's Harmful Books Regulation*, Japan: Takeshi Nogami, 2010. *On loan from Ada Palmer.*

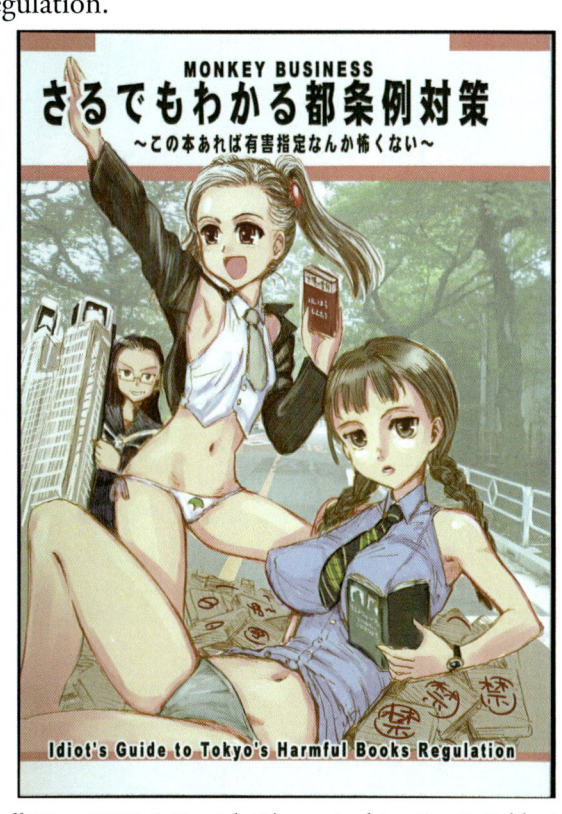

Not Pictured: *Sketchbook, Eightball 22*, ca. 2000-1, Daniel Clowes Archive, Box 9, Folder 1.

Protecting Children: The exhibit featured sketches from the creation Daniel Clowes's comic *Eightball 22, or Ice Haven*, a renowned and award-winning but also crude and mature alternative series. In 2007, Connecticut high school teacher Nathan Fisher lent a copy of *Eightball 22* to a thirteen-year-old student as a makeup summer reading assignment. The student's parents called the police in, characterizing the comic's depictions of a topless woman and a man's hand reaching up a skirt as "borderline pornography." Fisher resigned during the controversy, but no charges were pressed.

Book Burnings in America:
Wertham's 1954 *Seduction of the Innocent* blamed juvenile delinquency on comic books, citing evidence much of which was later demonstrated to be fabricated or manipulated. The book tapped into anti-comics fervor that had been building since the 1930s, and sparked comic book burnings and a Congressional inquiry. To dodge the First Amendment, the Senate asked publishers to self-censor, leading to the creation of a private "optional" censoring body, the Comics Code Authority. Vendors agreed to only sell comics that bore the CCA's seal, and its censors monitored, not only sex and violence, but dress, disrespectful depictions of police and politicians, and mandated that "in every instance good shall triumph over evil." Like many censoring bodies, the CCA was repurposed over time, and as the civil rights movement heated up, some artists reported the CCA giving them a hard time about depictions of African American characters, quietly discouraging representation. The CCA weakened over decades, and ended with the withdrawal of Marvel Comics in 2001 and DC and Archie Comics in 2011.

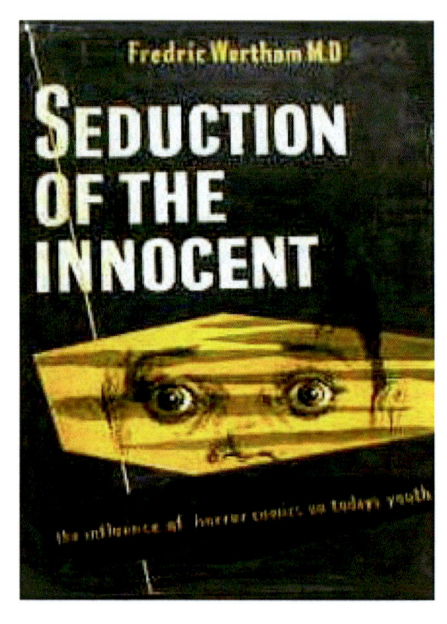

Above: Fredric Wertham (1895-1981), *Seduction of the Innocent*, London: Museum Press Limited, 1954. *On loan from Ada Palmer.*

Left: Catholic students burn 10,000 comic books in Binghamton, NY, 1948.

Holy Censorship, Batman! Wertham targeted Batman specifically in *Seduction of the Innocent*, alleging homosexual subtext between Batman and Robin. Here, the uncensored *Bat Man* #89 contrasts with the abrupt appearance of the Code seal on #90.

Right and Below: *Bat Man*, numbers 89 (left), 90 (right), New York: National Comics Publications, 1955. Walter C. Dopierala Comic Book Collection, Box 38, Folder 4.

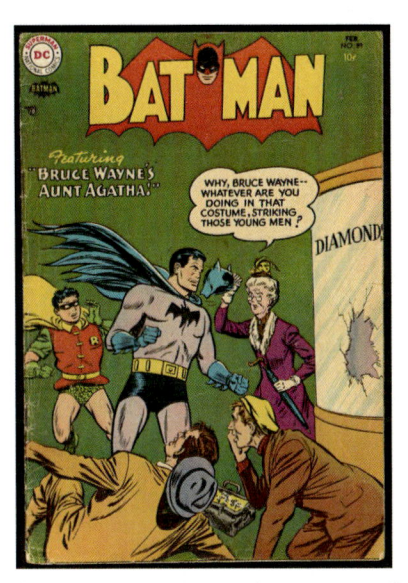

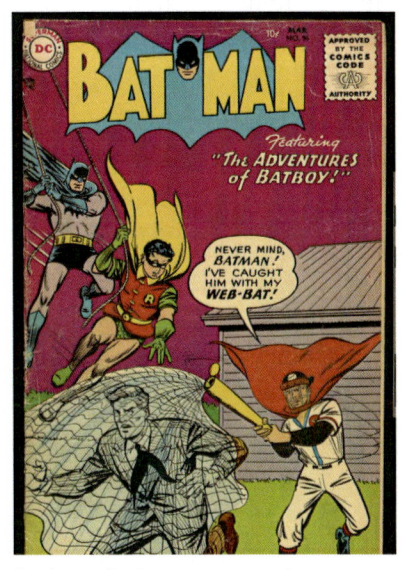

Below: Hergé (1907-1983), *Le Sceptre d'Ottokar*, [Belgium]: Casterman, 1947, PN6790.B43S247 1947. Historic Children's Book Collection.

Hidden Resistance: This eighth volume of Hergé's *Adventures of Tintin* was serialized in the children's section of a Belgian newspaper from 1938 to 1939. In it, the young reporter Tintin tries to stop a plot to overthrow the monarchy of the fictional Balkan country Syldavia, a satire of Nazi expansionism based on the annexation of Austria earlier in 1938. Hergé continued *The Adventures of Tintin* until Germany occupied Belgium in 1940. German occupiers banned the stories "Tintin in America" and "Tintin the Black Island"—set in the lands of Germany's enemies—but did not ban this one.

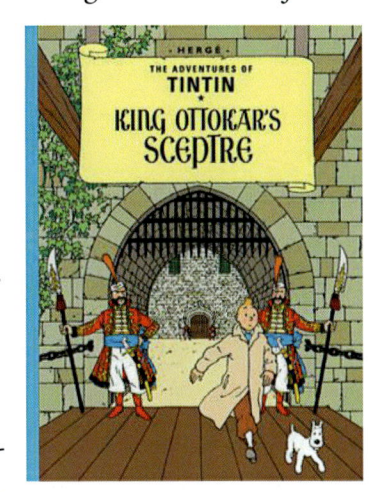

[181]

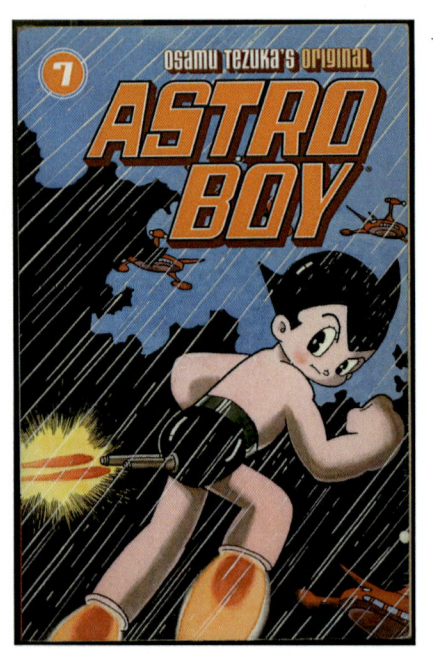

Childhood Without Books: During World War II, a generation of Japanese kids grew up in a broken school system, while censored presses produced only war propaganda. When the war ended, both the Japanese and American occupation governments suppressed discussions of the war, leaving these kids desperate—both for any children's literature—and for a way to understand the events which had shattered their world and families. Members of this generation vividly recount the arrival of the first bright, colorful books by "God of Manga" Osamu Tezuka. A fierce pacifist, Tezuka's iconic *Astro Boy* (Tetsuwan Atomu, 1952-68) depicted a robot civil rights movement, including robot voter suppression, anti-robot lynch mobs with KKK hoods, wars, nuclear bombs, and the robot-hating dictator "Hitlini." While being perceived as "for kids" often brings comics under fire, here censors ignored a mere science fiction comic, which let Tezuka kickstart the conversation about the mistakes of the past and the possibilities of a better future.

Above: Osamu Tezuka, *Astro Boy*, volume 7, Tokyo: Dark Horse Comics, 2002. *On loan from Ada Palmer.*

Right: Yoshihiro Tatsumi, *A Drifting Life*, Montreal: Drawn and Quarterly, 2009. *On loan from Ada Palmer.*

Making Room for Adults: One young reader who read and reread Tezuka's early manga until they fell apart was Yoshihiro Tatsumi, whose autobiography is displayed here. As Tatsumi himself began to publish manga in the 1950s-70s, Japan experienced its own wave of public and parental outrage about comics harming children. Since

[182]

manga literally means "whimsical pictures," critics argued that manga must be light and funny. Tatsumi coined the term *gekiga* ("dramatic pictures") adopted by a wave of serious and provocative authors. By the 1970s, the efforts of Tatsumi and his peers to make space for mature manga let the authors they had looked up to as children finally treat the war directly, in works such as Shigeru Mizuki's *Showa: a History of Japan*, Tezuka's *Message to Adolf*, and Buddhist epic *Phoenix*.

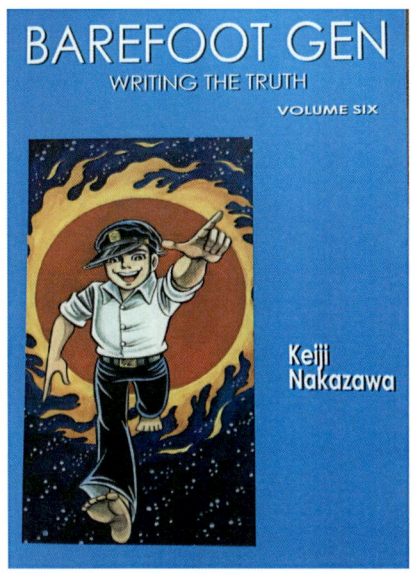

Above Right: Keiji Nakazawa, *Barefoot Gen, volume six*, San Francisco: Last Gasp, 2004. *On Loan from Ada Palmer.*

"For ten years after the atomic bomb was dropped there was so little public discussion of the bomb or of radioactivity that even the Chugoku Shinbun, the major newspaper of the city where the atomic bomb was dropped, did not have the movable type for 'atomic bomb' or 'radioactivity'. The silence continued so long because the U.S. Army Surgeons Investigation Team in the fall of 1945 had issued a mistaken statement: all people expected to die from the radiation effects of the atomic bomb had by then already died; accordingly, no further cases of physiological effects due to residual radiation would be acknowledged."
– Kenzaburō Ōe, Hiroshima Notes to the 1995 English translation of *Barefoot Gen*, originally published 1965

"I have to draw every one of these wretched people ▬ blasted away by the bomb & thrown away like so much garbage ▬▬▬ I'll draw them if it's the last thing I do."
– Keiji Nakazawa, *Barefoot Gen*, 1972-1973

Activism or Obscenity? Another of Tezuka's avid early readers was Hiroshima survivor Keiji Nakazawa, who found in art and manga hope for a universal medium that could let his pleas for peace and nuclear disarmament cross language barriers. Many of the grotesque images of gory melting faces in Nakazawa's harrowing autobiography *Barefoot Gen* are indistinguishable from the imagery in violent horror comics which critics so often denounce as harmful to children. Our impulse to place political works like *Barefoot Gen* in a separate category from graphic horror or pornography demonstrates why obscenity laws often resort to vague concepts such as "artistic merit" or "potential harm" rather than forbidding specific content.

The Price of Liberty: This engraving by printmaker Misch Kohn depicts a "fight for life" against the oppressive Chicago Police Department. It introduced the chapter on "Censorship" in *Pursuit of Freedom: A History of Civil Liberty in Illinois,* published in 1942 by the Chicago Civil Liberties Committee, an autonomous organization affiliated with the ACLU that formed to fight censorship and defend the rights of groups targeted by police. *Pursuit of Freedom* was meant as a public education tool, repeating the motto "Eternal vigilance is the price of liberty" (Wendell Phillips, *American Abolitionist,* January 28, 1852).

Art Censorship in Chicago

> "Why did they devise censorship? To show a world which doesn't exist, an ideal world, or what they envisaged as the ideal world. And we wanted to depict the world as it was."
> — Krzysztof Kieślowski, Index on Censorship 24(6), *1995*
>
> "I know it when I see it."
> – Supreme Court Justice Potter Stewart on obscenity, Jacobellis v. Ohio, 378 U.S. 184, 1964

On August 14, 1934 the newspaper *Variety* called Chicago's censorship "the worst in the country". This referred largely to censorship of motion pictures, and the city was brought to the Supreme Court twice by Times Film Corporation for denied movie permits. However, Chicago has a long and heated history of censoring many forms of art media, from newspapers and radio to film, theater, and public art. In 1958 and 1959, the UChicago student-run *Chicago Review* was prevented from publishing literature deemed "obscene." Recently, two faculty accused the School of the Art Institute of Chicago of censorship, Roxanne Assaf fired in 2010 after teaching the popular but controversial course "Palestine/Israel: US Media Myths"; and Michael Bonesteel, who taught outsider and comic book art, who resigned in 2017 when his courses were cancelled after Title IX complaints from students who called their content offensive. These and the other local cases examined below show how art's power to provoke and transgress constantly stimulates new public conversations about censorship, pushing Chicago to define and redefine the limits of acceptability.

Facing: Misch Kohn (American, 1916-2003), commissioned by the Works Progress Administration. Chapter IV: Censorship, from Pur- suit of Freedom, 1940. Wood engraving on ivory China paper. 75 x 101 mm (block); 145 x 179 mm (sheet). *The Art Institute of Chicago, Works Progress Administration Allocation,* RX20769/668.6.

Political Irrerevance

In 1988, the School of the Art Institute displayed the piece to the left, *Mirth and Girth* by David K. Nelson, a portrait of the then-recently deceased mayor Harold Washington clad in only women's undergarments. The painting triggered intense reactions from the African American community and local aldermen, who forcefully removed the painting and slashed it. This drew national media attention, and the ACLU brought suit to defend the artist's right to free speech—both were awarded $95,000 from the city.

Above: The photo to the right shows the painting being "arrested" by Chicago aldermen Allan Streeter and Ernest Jones, flanked by Chicago police officers. *Chicago Tribune*, 1988. Photograph by Val Mazzenga.

Facing: David K. Nelson, *Mirth & Girth*, 1988. Acrylic on canvas, 48 in × 36 in.

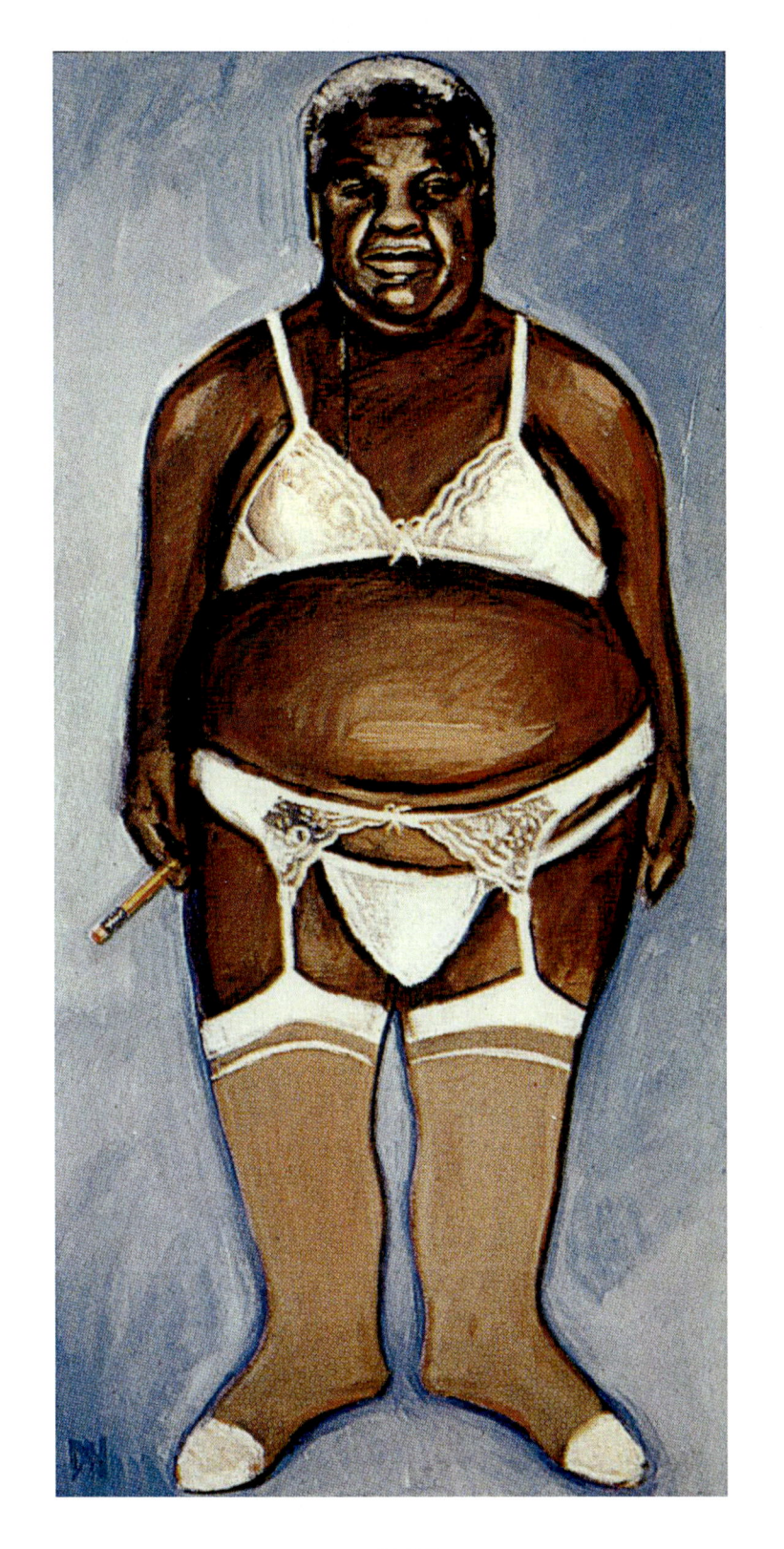

[187]

Protest Unwelcome

In 2014, Chicago artist Amie Sell was approached by the Milwaukee Avenue Arts Festival to create an installation. She created *Home Sweet Home*, a set of four blankets and a chair with the words "Home sweet home" sewn in five languages, criticizing M. Fishman & Co, a property management company with a history of forcing low income renters out of gentrified neighborhoods. The company had donated Sell's installation space and her art was removed without her permission before the festival began.

Amie Sell

Kitchen Space
August 3-24

Above and Below: Posters promoting the subsequent reinstallations of *Home Sweet Home,* by Amie Sell.

Lower Facing: The Balbo Monument in Burnham Park (as pictured on February 19, 2010). Photograph by J. Crocker.

Creating Reminders

Housed in the university's Smart Museum, this 1970 print, *Untitled (Censor)*, was part of a collaboration (Screen Prints 1970) between the School of the Art Institute of Chicago and the Advance Screen Company, facilitated by artist and professor Sonia Sheridan, whose work examined the transforming effects of new technologies in modern society.

Above: Kathleen Dulen (American), *Untitled (Censor)*, 1969-1970. 15 1/16 x 15 1/8 in. (38.3 x 38.4 cm). 1995.16.45. *David and Alfred Smart Museum of Art, University of Chicago, Purchase, Anonymous Gift.*

Mulitple Histories

This piece in downtown Chicago is a part of a current hot debate. A genuine Roman antiquity from the ancient port city Ostia, the object was gifted to the city in 1933 by Mussolini to honor the fascist Italian general Italo Balbo. Protesters have proclaimed it a monument to fascism itself, particularly since its corners bear decorative fasces. There are currently multiple petitions to remove the statue and rename Balbo Drive, but some see it as a historical reminder of relations between Italy and Chicago, and its cultural value as a Roman antique is substantial. Chicago mayor Rahm Emanuel, when asked about the monument, remarked "You don't have to ask me what my position is on fascism. Thank you. I'm against fascism. Take a chill pill, will you?"

[190]

Fake News is Not New

> "Any writer or journalist who wants to retain his integrity finds him-self thwarted by the general drift of society ▇ the concentration of the press in the hands of a few rich men, the grip of monopoly on radio and the films, the unwillingness of the public to spend money on books, making it necessary for nearly every writer to earn part of his living by hack work, the encroachment of official bodies ▇ and the continuous war atmosphere of the past ten years, whose distorting effects no one has been able to escape. ▇ What is really at issue is the right to report contemporary events truthfully."
>
> —George Orwell, "The Prevention of Literature," 1946.

Orwell's description above of threats to journalistic integrity might almost describe our own decade, since many controversies dogging the press today are new versions of old problems, reshaped by new information technologies. Terms such as "fake news," the German *lügenpresse* ("lying press"), and other allegations of libel have been used in many eras to delegitimize the press and manipulate public opinion. The reverse, genuinely false news reports (whether propaganda or honest error) are also a perennial problem, since tools created to restrict misinformation are easily repurposed to censor other things.

Facing: Sebastian Brant (German), *Winged Fama (Rumor)*, 1502. Woodcut illustration from the "Strasbourg Vergil," edited by Sebastian Brant: P*ublii Virgilii Maronis Opera cum quinque vulgatis commentariis expolitissimisque figuris atque imaginibus nuper per Se-bastianum Brant superadditis* (Strasbourg: Johannis Grieninger, 1502), fol. 215v, executed by an anonymous engraver under the direction of Brant. *Universitätsbibliothek Heidelberg.*

"Sweet knight, thou art now one of the greatest men in the realm."

Rumor's Smooth Comforts False: *Henry IV Part 2* opens with a monologue by personified Rumour, who causes misery by spreading false news, in this case about who won a battle. Fake news recurs in the scene illustrated here, when Pistol, reporting Henry IV's death, falsely proclaims that Falstaff—about to be exiled—is now one of the greatest men in the realm. In the sequel, *Henry V,* the wise young king refuses to believe which side has won the battle of Agincourt until the French ambassador tells him in person. These references show that false news was a familiar issue for Shakespeare's audience, and that the ability to disregard rumor and seek credible sources was one mark of a good leader.

ACT I

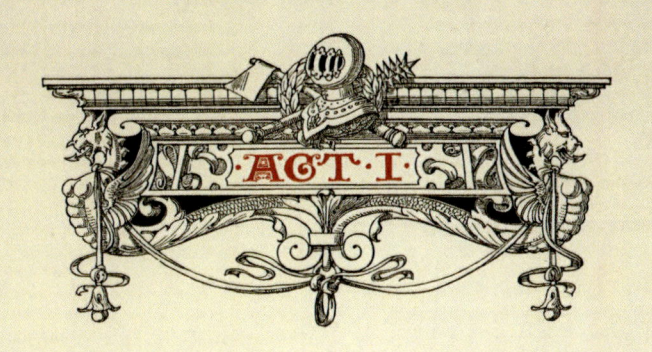

SCENE I.—*The Same.*

Enter Lord BARDOLPH.

L. Bard. Who keeps the gate here? ho!

The Porter opens the gate.

    Where is the earl?
Port. What shall I say you are?
L. Bard.   Tell thou the earl,
That the Lord Bardolph doth attend him here.
Port. His lordship is walk'd forth into the
    orchard:
Please it your honour, knock but at the gate,
And he himself will answer.

Enter NORTHUMBERLAND.

L. Bard.   Here comes the earl.
North. What news, Lord Bardolph? every
    minute now
Should be the father of some stratagem.
The times are wild: contention, like a horse
Full of high feeding, madly hath broke loose,
And bears down all before him.
L. Bard.   Noble earl,
I bring you certain news from Shrewsbury.
North. Good, an God will!
L. Bard.   As good as heart can wish.
The king is almost wounded to the death,
And, in the fortune of my lord your son,
Prince Harry slain outright; and both the Blunts
Kill'd by the hand of Douglas; young Prince
    John,
And Westmoreland, and Stafford, fled the field;
And Harry Monmouth's brawn, the hulk Sir John,
Is prisoner to your son. O! such a day,
So fought, so follow'd, and so fairly won,
Came not till now to dignify the times,
Since Cæsar's fortunes.
North.   How is this deriv'd?
Saw you the field? came you from Shrewsbury?
L. Bard. I spake with one, my lord, that came
    from thence;
A gentleman well bred, and of good name,
That freely render'd me these news for true.
North. Here comes my servant, Travers, whom
    I sent
On Tuesday last to listen after news.
L. Bard. My lord, I over-rode him on the way;
And he is furnish'd with no certainties,
More than he haply may retail from me.

Enter TRAVERS.

North. Now, Travers, what good tidings come
    with you?
Tra. My lord, Sir John Umfrevile turn'd me back
With joyful tidings; and, being better hors'd,
Out-rode me. After him came spurring hard
A gentleman, almost forspent with speed,
That stopp'd by me to breathe his bloodied horse.
He ask'd the way to Chester; and of him
I did demand, what news from Shrewsbury.
He told me that rebellion had ill luck,
And that young Harry Percy's spur was cold.
With that he gave his able horse the head,
And, bending forward, struck his armed heels
Against the panting sides of his poor jade
Up to the rowel-head; and starting so,
He seem'd in running to devour the way,
Staying no longer question.
North.   Ha!—Again.
Said he, young Harry Percy's spur was cold?
Of Hotspur, Coldspur? that rebellion
Had met ill luck?
L. Bard.   My lord, I'll tell you what:
If my young lord your son have not the day,
Upon mine honour, for a silken point
I'll give my barony: never talk of it.
North. Why should that gentleman, that rode
    by Travers,
Give then such instances of loss?

Facing and Above: William Shakespeare (1564-1616), *King Henry IV*, London: Cassell & Company, 1887, ffPR2809.A2D75 1887 Rare.

[193]

Early Instant News: Popular ballads—quick to print and usually penned to fit existing melodies—were a major news medium in Europe in the sixteenth to eighteenth centuries, disseminating sensational accounts of crimes, scandals, battles, politics, and miracles in formats accessible even to the semi-literate. These eighteenth century Italian ballads were collected by Bishop Walter Augustus Shirley, demonstrating how these disposable works crossed national and linguistic barriers.

ISTORIA NUOVA
D' UN CASO SUCCESSO IN VALENZA
DOVE S'INTENDE
COME
ANGIOLA CRUDELE
PRIVO' DI VITA IL PADRE, E LA MADRE
PER CAGION D'AMORE.

SE mi state, grata udienza, ad udire
Un caso, che vi farò maravigliare,
Che successo in Valenza io vi vò dire,
D' una Figlia crudel vi vò narrare,
Che non ebbe pietà, state a sentire,
Di suo Padre, che l' ebbe a generare,
Più crudele alla Madre la spietata,
Per cagion ch' era forte innamorata.

Molto era ricca, e di bellezza ornata,
Ma d' un suo camerier s' era invaghita,
S' accorse il Padre, o sorte spietata,
Che la Figlia d' amor era impazzita

CURIOSO CONTRASTO
NATO IN UNA CAMPAGNA
TRA LA MORTE
ED UN
SEMPLICISTA
il quale dopo voler sanare molta infermità con più erbe, convinto da essa, conosce, che il superar la Morte è il bene operare.

LUCCA)(Con Licenza.

ISTORIA
BELLISSIMA
DELLA VITA, E MORTE
DI PIETRO
MANCINO
CAPO DE' BANDITI
Dove s' intendono li ricatti, e uccisioni, che fece nel Regno di Napoli.

In Loreto: Per Sartorj Stamp. di S. Casa.

Con Licenza de' Superiori.

Above and Facing: *Italian Ballad Pamphlet Collection of English Churchman Walter Augustus Shirley,* [Italy]: s.n., [between 1810 and 1824]. PQ4222.B3I83 1810 Rare. *The George Williamson Endowment Fund.*

Right: Pierre Alexandre Du Peyrou, *Lettre à Monsieur-rélative à J.J. Rousseau: avec la réfutation de ce libelle,* [Lyon]: A Goa, 1765. PQ2043.D92 1765 Rare.

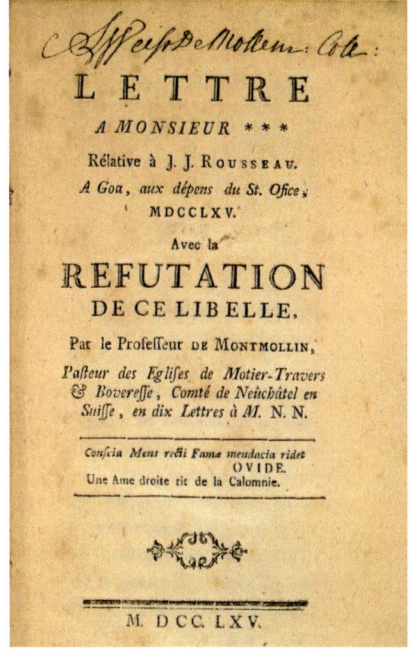

Forbidden to Defend One's Self: While some Enlightenment authors self-censored to avoid persecution, Rousseau naively published his radically deist *Emile* under his own name, and was immediately condemned in his native Geneva and in his new home, Paris. In exile, Rousseau sparred in print with Voltaire and other intellectuals, but was deeply hurt by the attacks and libels that dogged many condemned authors. As his own writings continued to be banned and burned, allies defended him in works like this, by his editor and executor Pierre Alexandre Du Peyrou.

[195]

"Freedom of the intellect means freedom to report what one has seen, heard, and felt, and not to be obliged to fabricate imaginary facts and feelings. ▮
▮ *Friends of totalitarianism in this country tend to argue that since absolute truth is not attainable, a big lie is no worse than a little lie."*
— Orwell, "The Prevention of Literature," 1946

"We need no other new Laws for the punishing of them ▮ *than what are already in force: As for example, if any Audacious Villain shall Publish Treason, he is already lyable to suffer as a Traytor; or if he Writes Scandalous Reflections upon the Government, I presume he is by the present Laws of the Land subject to a Fine and Imprisonment."*
— Charles Blount, *A Just Vindication of Learning*, 1678

The Press and Democracy: Friends or Foes? During World War II, the Commission on Freedom of the Press, led by University of Chicago President Robert Hutchins, sought to produce a report on how to balance freedom of speech with fears that an irresponsible press could be damaging to democracy. One page in the commission report defines wrongfully misleading information as "an intentional falsification of the evidence pertinent to a current argument" saying that "it isn't simply that the press lies but that the press lies in respect to public issues which the public is called upon to discuss and therefore is muddying the waters of opinion." In "People Speaking to Peoples," the commission discusses the importance of providing true information to counter ignorance and deceit, not simply more information. This distinction implies that false information should be censored in order to promote understanding. In "Self-Regulation of the Movies," the commission emphasizes that "practical provisions of the Code were empirically derived." Here, they show the similarities and agreements between the rulings of different censor boards and public audiences compiled in the "Don'ts and Be Carefuls" lists and the commission's own "Practical Applications of the Code."

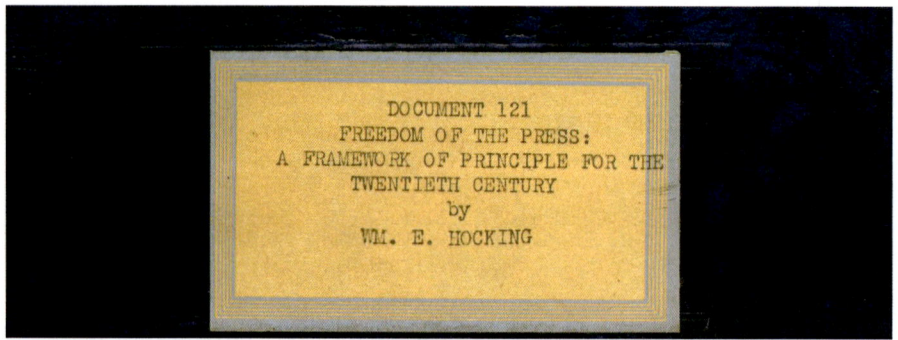

Above and Facing: *Freedom of the Press: A Framework of Principle for the Twentieth Century*, 1946. William E. Hocking, Commission on Freedom of the Press Records 1944-46, Box 9, Folder 3.

law needs revision. Are there interests to be protected which existing law does not protect? Are there defects in the performance of the press which law could remedy, or abuses which it ought to control? Has the community claims upon the output of the press which require or admit a measure of legal recognition? Originally, freedom of speech and press were liberties which chiefly concerned individuals who had opinions to utter; today it is their readers and hearers, the consumers of opinion, who are chiefly concerned. For the use of these liberties affects the mental diet of entire populations and qualifies the soundness of all democratic processes of thought. It shapes not alone the course of public life within communities, but becomes the one mass factor in the international field which affects issues of peace and war. To the press with its present scope and equipment thus attaches an unprecedented power. Shall this power be left not alone to the spirit of free enterprise but also to an unregulated spontaneity in the amount, veracity, and quality of its offering?

Here the problems begin to invade the background of principle from which our fundamental law itself emerged. We have to ask by what standards existing law can itself be judged. This nation was founded in liberty; have we learned something about the nature of liberty, its cost, and its responsibilities? Has the maxim of laissez faire, no longer adequate for a free economy, to be supplemented in the field of mass communication?

I. CRIMES AGAINST THE LAW
    These shall never be presented in such a way as to throw sympathy with the crime as against law and justice or to inspire others with a desire for imitation.
    1. Murder
        a. The technique of murder must be presented in a way that will not inspire imitation.
        b. Brutal killings are not to be presented in detail.
        c. Revenge in modern times shall not be justified.
    2. Methods of Crime should not be explicitly presented.
        a. Theft, robbery, safe-cracking, and dynamiting of trains, mines, buildings, etc., should not be detailed in method.
        b. Arson must be subject to the same safeguards.
        c. The use of firearms should be restricted to essentials.
        d. Methods of smuggling should not be presented.

Marginal notes:
- Sympathy for criminals (Be Careful #11)
- Technique for committing murder, by whatever method (Be Careful #7)
- Theft, robbery, safe-cracking and dynamiting of trains, mines, buildings, etc., (having in mind the effect which a too-detailed description of these may have upon the moron) (Be Careful #5)
- Arson (Be Careful #3)
- The use of firearms (Be Careful #4)
- Methods of smuggling (Be Careful #8)

Above and Facing: "Self-Regulation of the Movies," pages 115-117, Commission on Freedom of the Press, Records 1944-46, Box 3, Folder 8.

Below: "Peoples Speaking to Peoples," Document No. 62a, Page 2, Robert Leigh and Llewellyn White, Commission on Freedom of the Press Records 1944-46, Box 3, Folder 1.

    "The word 'true' poses a difficult problem. Truthful, conscientious, realistic, honest information? That is what is meant (cf. last paragraph on page 2) and is all that can be hoped for." -- Riezler.

    Staff sees difficulty but makes only slight suggestion for change. Prefers sticking by true with all its difficulty, but also its brevity. Can Commissioners suggest a better word? Paragraph now reads:

    On what, then, must the mass mind feed in order to be capable of reaching wise decisions? Not on propaganda, surely; fortunately an overdose of spoon-fed words and images has immunized the world against its most obvious forms, at least. The surest antidote for ignorance and deceit is the widest possible exchange of objectively realistic (or true)* information. True information, not merely more information. True information, not merely unhindered flow of information, as those who would have us simply write the First Amendment into international law seem to suggest! There is evidence that a mere quantitative flow of words and images across national borders may replace ignorance with prejudice and distortion, rather than with understanding.

    FOURTH PARAGRAPH, SECOND SENTENCE

    "This makes one tantalized to know what some of the most incredible instances were! Comment strictly frivolous." -- Clark.

    The sentence reads: Among the many examples of misunderstanding about America that have come to light during the war, the most incredible have involved, not Borneo bushmen, but Western Europeans who have seen dozens of Hollywood movies.

    White can supply a number of examples -- if the Commission feels their inclusion would strengthen the passage.

3. Illegal drug traffic must never be presented.

  The illegal traffic in drugs (Don't #3)
  The use of drugs (Be Careful #23)

4. The use of liquor in American life, when not required by the plot or for proper characterization, will not be shown.

II. SEX

The sanctity of the institution of marriage and the home shall be upheld. Pictures shall not infer that low forms of sex relationship are the accepted or common thing.

The institution of marriage (Be Careful #21)

1. Adultery and Illicit Sex, sometimes necessary plot material, must not be explicitly treated or justified, or presented attractively.
2. Scenes of Passion
   a. These should not be introduced except where they are definitely essential to the plot.
   b. Excessive and lustful kissing, lustful embraces, suggestive postures and gestures are not to be shown.

   Excessive or lustful kissing, particularly when one character or the other is a "heavy" (Be Careful #25)
   First-night scenes (Be careful #18)

   c. In general, passion should be treated in such manner as not to stimulate the lower and baser emotions.
3. Seduction or Rape
   a. These should never be more than suggested, and then only when essential for the plot. They must never be shown by explicit method.

   Rape or attempted rape (Be Careful #17)
   Deliberate seduction of girls (Be Careful #20)

   b. They are never the proper subject for comedy.
4. Sex perversion or any inference to it is forbidden.

   Any inference of sex perversion (Don't #4)
5. White slavery shall not be treated.

   White slavery (Don't #5)
6. Miscegenation (sex relationship between the white and black races) is forbidden.

   Miscegenation (sex relationships between the white and black races) (Don't #6)
7. Sex hygiene and venereal diseases are not proper subjects for theatrical motion pictures.

   Sex hygiene and venereal disease (Don't #7)
8. Scenes of actual child birth, in fact or in silhouette, are never to be presented.

   Scenes of actual childbirth-- in fact or in silhouette (Don't #8)

Left: Newspaper article (reproduction), *New York Times*, March 4, 1936.

"*Lügenpresse*" Hidden on Page Sixteen: In this *New York Times* update about affairs in Germany, a headline about fish and meat stocks hides a report of Germany stripping citizenship from twenty-five journalists, authors, actors, and other intellectuals. Jewish journalist Herbert Stahl is singled out for having "directed lying press (i.e. *lügenpresse*) attacks in American newspapers against Germany." These events were buried deep in the newspaper, in a moment when people still hoped Nazism would not lead America back into war.

A Rebirth of Fake News: In his 2016 campaign, then-candidate Donald Trump began levying "fake news" as a slur against sources critical of him and his campaign. Some of his supporters have also shouted "lügenpresse" at members of the media. Such discrediting labels act as de facto censorship—while the source is not banned it is drowned out, and when the public loses confidence in journalism authorities can step in to control the narrative.

[200]

> "But the press was then far from being enslaved as it is at present; the government exercised a censorship upon newspapers, but not upon books; a distinction which might be supported, if the censorship had been used with moderation: for newspapers exert a popular influence, while books, for the greater part, are only read by well informed people, and may enlighten, but not inflame opinion."
> – Germaine de Staël, *Ten Years of Exile*, written 1810-1817 about her experiences of the French Revolution

> "It is the press, above all, which wages a positively fanatical and slanderous struggle, tearing down everything which can be regarded as a support of national independence, cultural elevation, and the economic independence of the nation."
> – Adolf Hitler, *Mein Kampf*, 1925

Doublethink? Donald Trump's presidency kicked off with a strikingly Orwellian moment, when Trump told White House staff to disseminate the false information that his inauguration had garnered—as then-Press Secretary Sean Spicer put it—the "largest audience to ever to witness an inauguration, period—both in person and around the globe." Trump claimed that the press was falsely denying this fact, and that side-by-side photos of Obama's inauguration and his own were doctored.

Left: Two photos giving very different impressions of Trump's 2017 inauguration.

Small Changes in Technology: Below, victorious Truman laughingly shows off one of the most famous newspaper errors in US history. The 1948 election seemed to favor Dewey late into the night due to a worker strike, the *Tribune* had switched from linotype printing to a slower method which required finalizing their text several hours sooner than most newspapers in order to make their morning release.

Right: Truman Holding "Dewey Defeats Truman," Associated Press, Nov. 3, 1948.

[201]

Internet Censorship

> *"And though all the windes of doctrin were let loose to play upon the earth, so Truth be in the field, we do injuriously, by licencing and prohibiting to misdoubt her strength."*
> –Milton, *Aeropagitica*, 1644
>
> *"Of late years, the arguments of Milton and Mill have been questions, because truth does not seem to emerge from a controversy in the automatic way their [logic] would lead us to expect."*
> – Harold Nelson, *Freedom of the Press from Hamilton to the Warren Court,* 1967

The internet poses new challenges to and opportunities for efforts to control information. Cases, such as The American Digital Millennium Copyright Act, Egypt's 2011 internet shutdown, and the Right to Be Forgotten movement in the European Union demonstrate the rapid evolution of internet censorship and its relationship with governments, private companies, and individuals.

Right to be Forgotten

In 2014, the EU Court of Justice established the Right to be Forgotten, wherein European citizens can request that their personal information be removed from search results. Some opposed this as a violation of free speech while others welcomed it as a protection of privacy. By March 2015, Google had received over 200,000 requests to remove information, of which over 95% were about private personal information and roughly 50% were approved. Like much legislation of the internet, efforts to enforce the Right to Be Forgotten have run into barriers of technology itself, since some kinds of data archiving are difficult or short-term impossible to eradicate. As with cases when governments have demanded backdoors to encryption, legislators with little understanding of engineering or programming rarely believe "we can't" when they demand actions from developers.

DELETED FROM SEARCH RESULTS ON SUBJECT'S NAME	REJECTED, MAINTAINED IN SEARCH FOR NAME MAINTAINED IN SEARCH FOR NAME
A request to remove results detailing a patient's medical history.	Elected politician requesting removal of links to news articles about a political scandal he was associated with.
A request by someone incidentally mentioned in a story, a news report, but not the actual subject of the reporting.	Multiple requests from a single individual who asked to remove 20 links to recent articles about his arrest for financial crimes.
A woman requested removal of a decades-old article about her husband's murder, which included her name.	A public official asked to remove a link to a student organization's petition demanding his removal.
An individual asked to remove a link to an article covering a contest in which he participated as a minor.	A media professional requested removal of four links to articles reporting on embarrassing content he posted to the Internet.
The name on the membership list of a far-right party of someone who no longer holds such views.	Reports of a violent crime committed by someone later acquitted because of mental disability.
A request to remove five-year-old stories about exoneration in a child pornography case.	Request from a news outlet to remove content about it from another news outlet.
Links to "revenge porn"—nude pictures put online by an ex-boyfriend.	Request for removal of a news article about a child abuse scandal, which resulted in a conviction.

Above: Examples excerpted from "Results May Vary, Border Disputes on the Frontlines of the 'Right to Be Forgotten'," by Julia Rowples, *Slate*, 2015.

Digital Millennium Copyright Act

To update copyright for the digital era, in 1998, the United States introduced the Digital Millennium Copyright Act. Largely shaped by the interests of businesses rather than consumers, the act includes anti-circumvention and safe-harbor provisions, and aims to prohibit technologies that circumvent copyright control, and to protect corporate service providers from misuse by users. The DMCA also allows companies to demand content removal through "take down notices," a system intended to protect copyright but which—like the many previous information control systems explored in this exhibit—is easily repurposed. Many take down notice systems are automated and presume allegations of infringement are true until proved false, removing any content flagged by a user with no human oversight and a slow appeals process. This makes it easy for someone to flag legitimate content, and thereby instantly, if temporarily, silence users.

This file has been removed in response to a DMCA takedown notice.

Pursuant to the safe harbor provisions of **Section 512**[1] of the **Digital Millennium Copyright Act**[2], this file has been removed in response to a takedown notice[3] sent by the copyright owner to the Wikimedia Foundation. The takedown notice is archived here[4].

Click here to show further instructions[5]

Appeal: If you uploaded this file and believe it was wrongly removed due to mistake or misidentification, you may file a **DMCA counter-notice** here[6].

Català | Česky | Deutsch | English | Español | ‎العربية‎ | Suomi | Français | Magyar | 日本語 | 한국어 | Македонски | Português | Русский | ไทย | 中文 | 中文(简体) | 中文(繁體) | +/−

Egypt's 2011 Internet Shutdown

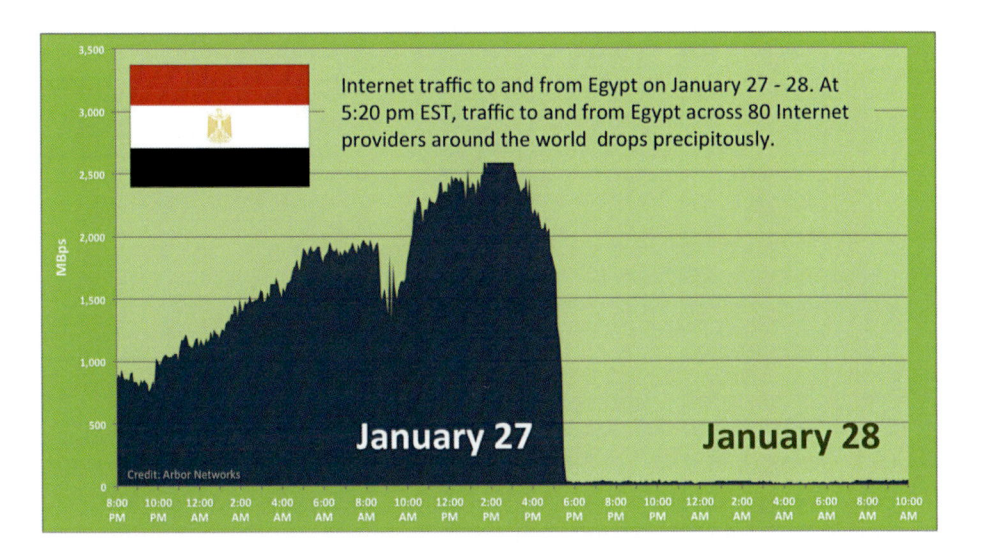

Above: Graph showing internet traffic to and from Egypt during the shutdown.

On January 28th, 2011, the Egyptian government shut down nearly all network access and cell phone service following a series of protests known as the January 25th Revolution. Within minutes, data traffic dropped by 90% for a nation of 80 million people. While many governments filter certain online content, the scale and speed of this act was unprecedented. Telecommunications company Vodafone claimed that it was "obliged to comply," whereas Google condemned the shutdown and launched a "speak-to-tweet" service that enabled Egyptians to tweet without an internet connection. Since the event, some internet service providers have sought to develop ways to reroute the internet to circumvent shutdowns during coups or tumults, while all internet developers have wrestled with various governments' efforts to create the means to demand shutdowns, or special access to private data in particular circumstances.

Appendix I:
Banned Bookcase:
Tour the Continents

> *"[O]pting your child out of reading this book doesn't protect him or her. They are still surrounded by the other students who are going to be saturated with this book."*
> – Macey France, "THIS Is Common Core-Approved for Children?"
> *politichicks.com*, 2015
>
> *"It's scary to think of books being removed from libraries because they're controversial. But it's even scarier to think of a country where books are so irrelevant, parents don't even care enough to complain."*
> – Eleanor Barkhorn, "Why We Want Parents to Try to Ban Books,"
> *The Atlantic*, 2010

Read a banned book! This appendix lists the books from the exhibit's "banned bookcase," which collected works that have been banned or censored, from nudist magazines and pornography to euthanasia literature and young adult books challenged in American classrooms. Ten items from each continent offer a tour of censorship as a global phenomenon, while books used in the University of Chicago's Core classes remind us how censorship touches our campus community and education today. We invite you to look up for yourself the history of each book.

Does It Belong On Library Shelves? Controversial materials like *Charlie Hebdo,* Nazi propaganda, or anti-vaccination literature are excellent examples of how libraries exercise teamwork. A library's collection policy spells out what criteria librarians should use in acquiring books. A small public library's policy usually focuses on books' current popularity and local needs—school books, books of legal or medical help—trusting special collections libraries to archive materials like *Charlie Hebdo* for the use of researchers and journalists. For this reason our Special Collections Research Center—like many such collections—is open to the public. Clear collection policies also help librarians respond to pressures to include or exclude books. Madonna's 1992 book *Sex* sparked a rash of demands that it be barred from libraries. Some libraries struggled to improvise responses to pressure from parents and local government, while others with clear collections policies such as "Purchase X copies of a book for every Y people on the waiting list," looked at their numbers and ordered more. Clear policies also help librarians choose which items should be removed to make space, and which donations should be accepted.

Africa

Things Fall Apart, by Chinua Achebe
L'Apartheid, by Nelson Mandela
When the Lion Feeds, by Wilbur Smith
Africa My Beginning, by Ingoapele Madingoane
Blame Me on History, by William Bloke Modisane
Waiting for the Barbarians, by J.M. Coetzee
Poets to the People: South African Freedom Poems, edited by Barry Feinberg
Jol'iinkomo, by Mafika Gwala
Our Friend the King, by Gilles Perrault
The Stone-Country, by Alex La Guma

Asia

Dragon Ball (Volume One), by Akira Toriyama
Persepolis, by Marjane Satrapi
The Kite Runner, by Khaled Hosseini
Mao: The Unknown Story, by Jung Chang and Jon Halliday
Beijing Comrades, by Bei Tong
The Satanic Verses, by Salman Rushdie
The Adivasi Will Not Dance, by Hansda Sowvendra Shekhar
So Far from the Bamboo Grove, by Yoko Kawashima Watkins
The Color of Earth (Volume One), by Kim Dong Hwa
Ruined City, by Jia Pingwa

Australia

The Peaceful Pill Handbook, by Philip Nitschke and Fiona Stewart
Marijuana Grower's Handbook, by Ed Rosenthal
Down Under the Plum Trees, by Felicity Mary Tuohy and Michael Thomas Murphy
Pierre et Gilles, by Jonathan Turner
Cleo New Zealand (magazine), August 1996
Naturist Life New Zealand (magazine), November 1994
Forever Amber, by Kathleen Winsor
Silent Hill: Homecoming (video game), by Double Helix Games
Upsurge, by J.M. Harcourt
Pictura Britannica Art from Britain, by Bernice Murphy

Europe

Harry Potter and the Sorcerer's Stone, by J. K. Rowling
The Second Sex, by Simone de Beauvoir
The Merchant of Venice, by William Shakespeare
Mein Kampf, by Adolf Hitler
Ulysses, by James Joyce
Mirror of the Polish Crown, by Sebastian Miczynski
Animal Farm, by George Orwell
Brave New World, by Aldous Huxley
The Decameron, by Giovanni Boccaccio
The Prince, by Niccolo Machiavelli

North America

The Awakening, by Kate Chopin
Little Bill series, by Bill Cosby and Varnette P. Honeywood
Saga (Volume Two), by Brian Vaughan and Fiona Staples
How to Make Disposable Silencers, by Desert and Eliezer Flores
To Kill a Mockingbird, by Harper Lee
This One Summer, by Mariko and Jillian Tamaki
Beloved, by Toni Morrison
Arming America: The Origins of a National Gun Culture, by Michael A. Bellesiles
Hallucinations: The Ill-Fated Peregrinations of Fray Servando, by Reinaldo Arenas
The Absolutely True Diary of a Part-Time Indian, by Sherman Alexie

South America

The House of the Spirits, by Isabel Allende
Memories of My Melancholy Whores, by Gabriel García Márquez

The Time of the Hero, by Mario Vargas Llosa
The Pedagogy of the Oppressed, by Paulo Freire
Canto General/General Song, by Pablo Neruda
El Libro Negro de La Justicia Chilena/The Black Book of Chilean Justice, by Alejandra Matus
The Zahir: A Novel of Obsession, by Paulo Coehlo
Libro de Manuel/A Manual for Manuel, by Julio Cortázar
El Hacedor/Dreamtigers, by Jorge Luis Borges
Feliz Ano Novo/Happy New Year, by Rubem Fonseca

University of Chicago Core Curriculum

Confessions, by Jean-Jacques Rousseau
Fun Home, by Alison Bechdel
Complete Works of William Shakespeare, by William Shakespeare
Discourse on Method and Meditations on First Philosophy, by Descartes
Luther's Catechetical Writings, by Martin Luther
The Bible, by Various
Candide, ou l'Optimisme, by Voltaire
Nicomachean Ethics, by Aristotle
The Advancement of Learning, by Francis Bacon
An Essay Concerning Human Understanding, by John Locke

Additional Case Studies

Invisible Man, by Ralph Ellison
The Brief Wondrous Life of Oscar Wao, by Junot Díaz
Down Second Avenue, by Es'kia Mphahlele
Like Water for Chocolate, by Laura Esquivel
The Talmud, by Various
Jacques the Fatalist, by Denis Diderot
Alice's Adventures in Wonderland, by Lewis Carroll
The Adventures of Huckleberry Finn, by Mark Twain
Charlie Hebdo, (newspaper)
The First Circle, by Aleksandr Solzhenitsyn

Why were these books banned? Sex, race, obscenity, politics, propaganda, misinformation, "facilitating crime," "protecting children"; we encourage you to look up these books' unique stories, and to compare the sorts of content and means of banning and silencing that characterize different regions and regimes.

Appendix II: Censor's Desk: Learn What Censoring Feels Like

What is it like *destroying* words for a living? The censors employed by the Inquisition and other famous censoring bodies were real human beings, many of them well-educated intellectuals. In this exhibit, we invited people to sit down and experience the physical act of censorship, and the complex act of destroying words.

We provided two sets of materials. One set allowed visitors to try an inquisitor's task, expurgating condemned sentences from a book in which the Inquisition has condemned a few lines but not the whole thing. The other set allowed one to try modern redacting, by blacking out with marker a US government document ordered to be purged of "content which might endanger national security" before it was released under the Freedom of Information Act.

Our modern document was Page 11 of the 2002 "National Intelligence Estimate," a redacted version of which was used in 2004 by the George W. Bush administration to justify its claim that Iraq possessed weapons of mass destruction; visitors were given an unredacted version released in 2014, which shows how the redactor's choices facilitated the deception.

Above: An inquisitor caught in the act of censorship. Visitors were given the following "instructions": *One of the first printed books burned by the Church, the* Nine Hundred Theses *by Italian humanist Giovanni Pico della Mirandola was a radical attempt to integrate elements of Platonism, Pythagoreanism, Judaism, Islam, and other religions and philosophies into Christianity. Pope Innocent VIII condemned thirteen of the theses, and later the whole book. In book 4, Pico advances radical ideas about magic, Kaballah, and defends the ancient theologian Origen who argued that damnation is finite and that even the souls in Hell will eventually be saved. Imagine that in this copy, kept for reference in a library used by young Inquisitors and Dominican monks, you have been instructed to cross out the most dangerous theses: 4.1, 4.2, 4.8, 4.9, 4.10, 4.14, 4.19., and 4.20.*

"When you have once corrected these misstatements and parted them with your Censor's wand from the faith of the Church, I may read what is left with safety, and having first taken the antidote need no longer dread the poison."
— St. Jerome, Letter LXXXIV to Pammachius and Oceanus, 399-400 CE

Do you ever think of the Censor? I don't mean from the point of view of muttonising your language, for it's obvious you don't do that. But do you ever think of him as rooms full of ladies and gentlemen, all engaged in the embarrassing occupation of reading other people's letters? What will they do when they can't be censors any longer ▬▬▬ Will they pine and languish and suddenly feel themselves cut off from humanity? ▬▬ Or will they demonstrate their freedom by never opening another envelope, not even envelopes addressed to them ▬▬▬"
— Letter from Sylvia Townsend Warner to Paul Nordoff regarding Britain's wartime censorship of civilian letters, November 17, 1940

..6. The intuition of God's knowledge is not directed formally at creatures as primary or sec of theologians says, but contemplating himself only, and nothing but himself prim elevated manner, and with more than the power equal to the task, he knows all thing ▬▬▬ no ▬▬▬ God ▬▬▬ exists ▬▬▬

of theologians says, but contemplating himself only, and nothing but himself primarily or secon elevated manner, and with more than the power equal to the task, he knows all things. ▬▬▬ ~~no~~ ▬▬▬ God ▬▬▬ exists ▬▬▬
7. The three transcendentals in which the image consists do not rightly signify different concepts, and ~~be defined~~ or described.

Cutting to the Point: In the top image, we see a visitor took the opportunity to make the already scandalous document more scandalous. A subsequent visitor, however, expressed their disapproval and in the lower image above, we see they crossed out the "no," leaving "…God…exists." Below, we see another example of what a nuisance negation can be; here, another visitor strategically expurgated no's and not's to make this document approvable.

4.6. The intuition of God's knowledge is ~~not~~ directed formally at creatures as primary or secondary objects, as the common school of theologians says, but ~~contemplating himself~~ only, ~~and nothing but himself primarily or secondarily, in a ~~~~ and~~ elevated ~~manner, and~~ with ~~more than the~~ power equal to the task, he knows all things.
Corollary: There is ~~no~~ multiplicity of understandings in God, ~~nor ~~~~~~, as things understood, exist numerically in the divine essence as something understood, but in the innermost sense there exists ~~but~~ one most simple understanding.
4.7. The three transcendentals in which the image consists do not rightly signify different concepts, and especially none that can be defined or described.
4.8. Christ did ~~not~~ truly and in respect to his real presence descend into Hell as Thomas and the common way propose, ~~but only in~~ ~~effect~~.
4.9. Although it seems probable to me, it should ~~not be pertinaciously~~ asserted that the soul of Christ could ~~not~~ have descended into hell in ~~a mode unknown to us~~.

[212]

Appendix IV:
Contributors Listed by Case

Censorship: Expectations and Reality: Ada Palmer
How Do YOU Define Censorship?: Carolyn Hirsch, Morley Musick, Olivia Palid & Augustin Vannier
Plural Inquisitions: Julian Borda, Michael Hosler-Lancaster, Caitlin Hubbard, Jillian Lepek, Metha Gautama, Jasmine Mithani, Samantha Truman, Julia Walker, Peyton Walker & Stuart McManus
Birth of Copyright Law: Katherine Surma & Sam Koffma
Universal Acids, Toxic Ideas: Clio Sophia Koller & Julia Tomasson
Censoring the Classics: Timothy Cunningham & Lauren Scott
Censorship in Translation: Peter Chen, Hannah Dorsey, Caitlin Hubbard, Sam Koffman, Gautama Mehta, Hannah Trower & Victoria Xing
Censorship in the Soviet Union: Kiril Shishkin
The Great Firewall of China: John-Paul Heil & Ada Palmer
Censorship in New Zealand: What Does the First Amendment Really Do?: Ada Palmer
Colonial Censorship: Peter Chen & Anna Christensen
Censoring Comics: Peter Chen, Nathaniel Eakman, Sarah Larson & Ada Palmer
Art Censorship in Chicago: Jillian Lepek & Peyton Walker
Fake News Is Not New: Adam Biesman, Jamie Ehrlich, Max Freedman & Katherine Surma
Internet Censorship: Sam Koffman, Sarah Larson & Sam Gersho
Banned Bookcase: Tour the Continents: Peter Chen, Hannah Dorsey, Jasmine Mithani, Olivia Palid, Victoria Xing, Nate Eakman, Julia Walker & John-Paul Heil
Censor's Desk: Learn What Censorship Feels Like: Ada Palmer, in consultation with Joshua Craze

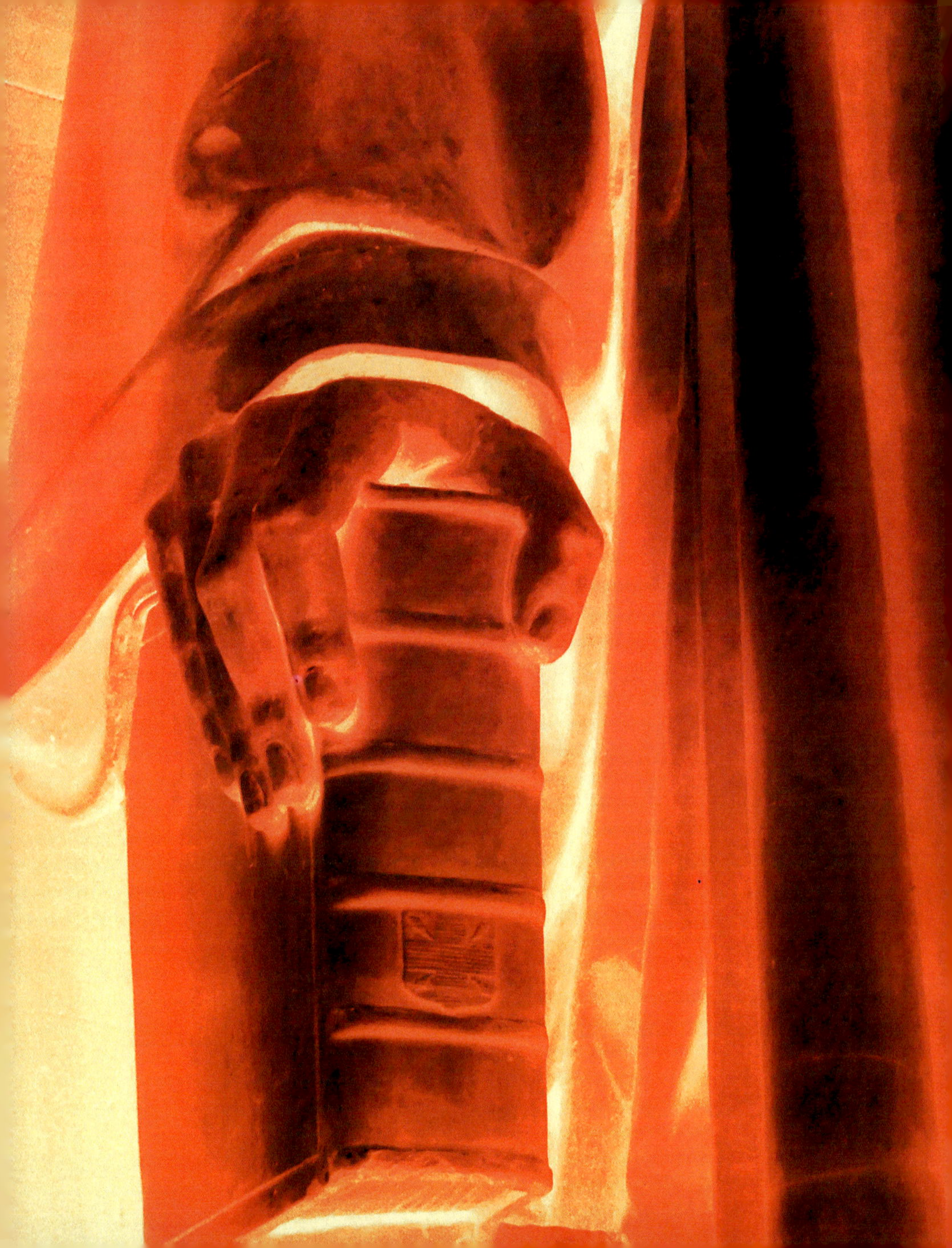

Appendix IV:
Further Reading

Anderson, Nate. *The Internet Police: How Crime Went Online -- and the Cops Followed.* New York: W.W. Norton & Company, 2013.
Aron-Beller, Katherine and Christopher Black. *The Roman Inquisition: Centre Versus Peripheries.* Leiden: Brill 2018.
Barlow, John Perry. "Declaration of the Independence of Cyberspace." Eff.org. https://www.eff.org/cyberspace-independence (retrieved 8/12/2018.
Bayly, C. A. *Empire and Information: Intelligence Gathering and Social Communication in India, 1780-1870.* Cambridge Studies in Indian History and Society 1. Cambridge; New York: Cambridge University Press, 1996.
Black, Christopher F. *The talian Inquisition.* New Haven: Yale University Press, 1941.
Blair, Ann. *Too Much to Know: Managing Scholarly Information before the Modern Age.* New Haven [Conn.]: Yale University Press, 2010.
Cardon, Dominique. "Inside the Mind of PageRank: A Study of Google's Algorithm." *La Découverte* 177 (2013): 63-95.
Cavallo, Guglielmo, Roger Chartier, and Lydia G. Cochrane eds. *A History of Reading in the West.* Oxford: Polity Press, 1999, esp. 179-237.
Choldin, Marianna T., Maurice Friedberg, and Barbara Dash, eds. *The Red Pencil: Artists, Scholars, and Censors in the USSR.* Special Study of the Kennan Institute for Advanced Russian Studies, the Wilson Center. Boston: Unwin Hyman, 1989.
Christoffe, Paul. *Censored: a Short History of Censorship in New Zealand.* Wellington, N.Z.: Research Unit, Department of Internal Affairs, 1989.
Chuchiak, John F., ed. *The nquisition in New Spain, 1536-1820: A Documentary History.* Baltimore: Johns Hopkins University Press, 2012.
Coleman, E. Gabriella. *Coding Freedom: The thics and Aesthetics of Hacking.* Princeton: Princeton University Press, 2012.
Copeland, David. *The edia's Role in Defining the ation: the Active Voice.* New York: Peter Lang 2010.
Copeland, David. *The dea of a Free Press: the Enlightenment and its Unruly Legacy.* Evanston: Northwestern University Press, 2006.
Culp, Robert, Eddy U, and Wen-hsin Yeh eds. *Knowledge Acts in Modern China: Ideas, Institutions, and Identities.* Berkeley: Institute of East Asian Studies, University of California Berkeley, 2016.
Craze, Joshua. "Excerpts from a Grammar of Redaction." (From "Grammar of Redaction," New Museum Temporary Center for Translation 2014.) In *Archival Dissonance: Knowledge Production and Contemporary Art,* ed. Anthony Downey. London: I.B. Tauris/Ibraaz, 2015.
Darnton, Robert. "An Early Information Society: News and the Media in

Eighteenth-Century Paris." *American Historical Review* 105 (2000): 1-35.

Darnton, Robert. *Censors at Work: How States Shaped Literature*. First edition. New York, NY: W.W. Norton & Company, 2014.

Doctorow, Cory. *Content: Selected Essays on Technology, Creativity, Copyright, and the Future of the Future*. 1st ed. San Francisco: Tachyon Publications, 2008.

Doctorow, Cory, Amanda Palmer, and Neil Gaiman. *Information Doesn't Want to Be Free: Laws for the Internet Age*. San Francisco: McSweeney's, 2014.

Doniger, Wendy. "Banned in Bangalore," The New York Times, March 5, 2014.

Doniger, Wendy. "India: Censorship by the Batra Brigade," The New York Review of Books, May 8, 2014.

Edwards, Paul N. *A Vast Machine: Computer Models, Climate Data, and the Politics of Global Warming*. Cambridge, Mass: MIT Press, 2010.

Eisenstein, Elisabeth. *The Printing Press as an Agent of Change*. Cambridge: Cambridge University Press, 1980.

Eliot & Rose eds. *A Companion to the History of the Book*. Malden: Blackwell, 2007, esp. 207-31.

Ettinghausen, Henry. *How the Press Began: the Pre-Periodical Printed News in Early Modern Europe*. Coruña, Spain: Universidade da Coruña, 2015.

Evans, James. "Electronic Publication and the Narrowing of Science and Scholarship." Science July 18, 2008 (321: 5887): 395-399.

Findlen, Paula and Hannah Marcus. "Science under Inquisition: Heresy and Knowledge in Catholic Rome." Isis 103 (2012), 376-382.

Foucault, Michel. "What is an Author?" The Essential Foucault, ed. Paul Rabinow and Nikolas Rose. New York: New Press, 2003: 377-91.

Friedman, Andrea. *Prurient Interests: Gender, Democracy and Obscenity in New York City, 1909-1945*. Chapter 2: "'The Habitats of Sex Crazed Perverts': Campaigns Against Burlesque," 62-94.

Gaiman, Neil. "Why Defend Freedom of Icky Speech?" Neil Gaiman's Journal. http://journal.neilgaiman.com/2008/12/why-defend-freedom-of-icky-speech.html (retrieved 6/15/2016)

Gitelman, Lisa. *Paper Knowledge: Toward a Media History of Documents. Sign, Storage, Transmission*. Durham: Duke University Press, 2014.

Glaeser, Andreas. "Power/Knowledge Failure: Epistemic Practices and Ideologies of the Secret Police in Former East German." Social Analysis 47:1 (Spring 2003): 10-26.

Grafton, Anthony. *The Culture of Correction in Renaissance Europe*. The Panizzi Lectures 2009. London: British Library, 2011.

Hajdu, David. *The Ten-Cent Plague: The Great Comic-Book Scare and How It Changed America*. 1st ed. New York: Farrar, Straus and Giroux, 2008.

Harrison, S. J., ed. *Expurgating the Classics: Editing out in Latin and Greek*. London: Bristol Classical Press, 2012.

Heins, Marjorie. *Not in Front of the Children: "Indecency," Censorship, and the Innocence of Youth.* 1st ed. New York: Hill and Wang, 2001.

"History of Comics Censorship." Comic Book Legal Defense Fund. cbldf.org/resources/history-of-comics-censorship/ (retrieved 8/12/2018).

Homer, Thomas Hobbes, Eric Nelson, and Thomas Hobbes. *Translations of Homer.* The Clarendon Edition of the Works of Thomas Hobbes, vol. 24-25. Oxford; New York: Clarendon Press, 2008.

Howsam, Leslie, ed. *The Cambridge Companion to the History of the Book.* Cambridge Companions to Literature. Cambridge: Cambridge University Press, 2014.

Hunt, Lynn Avery, ed. 1993. T*he Invention of Pornography: Obscenity and the Origins of Modernity, 1500-1800.* New York: Zone Books.

Hunter, Michael Cyril William, and David Wootton, eds. *Atheism from the Reformation to the Enlightenment.* Oxford : Oxford ; New York: Clarendon Press ; Oxford University Press, 1992.

Ivins, William Mills. *Prints and Visual Communication.* Da Capo Press Series in Graphic Art, v. 10. New York: Da Capo Press, 1969.

Johns, Adrian. *Death of a Pirate: British Radio and the Making of the Information Age.* 1st ed. New York: W.W. Norton & Co, 2011.

———. "The Information Defense Industry and the Culture of Networks." A Modern 2 (2013).

———. *Piracy: The Intellectual Property Wars from Gutenberg to Gates.* Chicago: University of Chicago Press, 2009.

———. *The Nature of the Book: Print and Knowledge in the Making.* Chicago: University of Chicago Press, 1998.

Karaganis, Joe, ed. *Media Piracy in Emerging Economies.* New York, NY: Social Science Research Council, 2011.

Katherine Aron-Beller, and Christopher Black. T*he Roman Inquisition Centre versus Peripheries. Catholic Christendom, 1300-1700.* Brill, 2018.

Kelty, Christopher M. *Two Bits: The Cultural Significance of Free Software. Experimental Futures.* Durham: Duke University Press, 2008.

Kors, Alan Charles. *Atheism in France, 1650-1729.* Princeton, N.J: Princeton University Press, 1990.

———. *Epicureans and Atheists in France, 1650-1729.* Cambridge, United Kingdom: Cambridge University Press, 2016.

———. *Naturalism and Unbelief in France, 1650-1729.* Cambridge, United Kingdom: Cambridge University Press, 2016.

Lawton, Philip. "For the Gentleman and the Scholar: Sexual and Scatological References in the Loeb Classical Library." In Expurgating the Classics: Editing Out in Greek and Latin, edited by Stephen Harrison and Christopher Stray. London: Bristol Classical Press, 2012.

Liebman, Seymour B. *The Jews in New Spain: Faith, Flame, and the Inquisition.* Coral Gables, Fla: University of Miami Press, 1970.

Marcus, Hannah. "The Mind of the Censor: Girolamo Rossi, a Physician and Censor for the Congregation of the Index." Early Science and Medicine, v. 23 (1-2) 2018,14-33.

Matytsin, Anton M. *The Specter of Skepticism in the Age of Enlightenment.*

Baltimore: Johns Hopkins University Press, 2016.

McKitterick, David. *Print, Manuscript and the Search or Order, 1450-1830*. Cambridge: Cambridge University Press, 2003.

McLuhan, Marshall. *Understanding Media: The Extensions of Man*. 1st MIT Press ed. Cambridge, Mass: MIT Press, 1994.

Milton, John. *Areopagitica*. Clarendon Press Series. Oxford: Clarendon Press, 1894.

Moretti, Franco. *Distant Reading*. London: Verso, 2013.

Nelson, Eric. "General Introduction," in Thomas Hobbes, Works vol. XXIV, Translations of Homer: Introductions; Iliad. Oxford: Clarendon Press, 2008.

Nesvig, Martin Austin. *Ideology and Inquisition: The World of the Censors in Early Mexico*. New Haven: Yale University Press, 2009.

Nicholson, Steve. *The Censorship of British Drama, 1900-1968*. Exeter: University of Exeter Press, 2003-2014.

Orwell, George. "The Prevention of Literature," in Orwell's Nineteen Eighty-Four, ed. Irving Howe. London: Harcourt, 1963, 262-273.

Office of Film & Literature Classification (of New Zealand). "The Classification Criteria" classificationoffice.govt.nz/about-nz-classification/the-classification-criteria/

Patterson, Lyman Ray. *Copyright in Historical Perspective*. Nashville: Vanderbilt University Press, 1968.

Pettegree, Andrew. *The Book in the Renaissance*. New Haven [Conn.]: Yale University Press, 2010.

Priolkar, Anant Kakba, Gabriel Dellon, and Claudius Buchanan. *The Goa Inquisition: Being a Quatercentenary Commemoration Study of the Inquisition in India*. Bombay: Bombay University Press, 1961.

Reynolds, Leighton Durham and N. G. Wilson. "The Latin West," in Scribes and Scholars: a Guide to the Transmission of Greek and Latin Literature. Oxford: Clarendon, 1991, 80-122.

Rheingold, Howard. *The Virtual Community: Homesteading on the Electronic Frontier*. Rev. ed. Cambridge, Mass: MIT Press, 2000.

Rice, Eugene F. *The Foundations of Early Modern Europe, 1460-1559*. New York: W. W. Norton, 1970, 1-10.

Rocke, Michael. *Forbidden Friendships: Homosexuality and Male Culture in Renaissance Florence*. Studies in the History of Sexuality. New York: Oxford University Press, 1996.

Savage, William W. *Comic Books and America, 1945-1954*. 1st ed. Norman: University of Oklahoma Press, 1990.

Sinnreich, Aram. *Mashed Up: Music, Technology, and the Rise of Configurable culture*. Amherst: University of Massachusetts Press, 2010.

Sinnreich, Aram. *The Piracy Crusade: How the Music Industry's War on Sharing Destroys Markets and Erodes Civil Liberties*. Amherst: University of Massachusetts Press, 2013.

Schodt, Frederik L. *Manga! Manga! The World of Japanese Comics*. 1st ed. Tokyo : New York : New York, N.Y: Kodansha International ; Distributed in the U.S. by Kodansha International/USA through Harper & Row, 1983.

Sheppard, Kenneth. *Anti-Atheism in Early Modern England 1580-1720: The Atheist Answered and His Error Confuted.* Studies in the History of Christian Traditions, volume 176. Leiden ; Boston: Brill, 2015.

Slauter, Will. "Upright Piracy: Understanding the Lack of Copyright for Journalism in Eighteenth-Century Britain," Book History, 16 (1), 34-61

Soll, Jacob. T*he Information Master: Jean-Baptiste Colbert's Secret State Intelligence System. Cultures of Knowledge in the Early Modern World.* Ann Arbor: University of Michigan Press, 2009.

Stow, Kenneth R. "The Burning of the Talmud in 1533, in the Light of Sixteenth Century Catholic Attitudes toward the Talmud." Bibliothèque d'Humanism et Renaissance, t. 34, N. 3 (1972), 435-59.

Strasser, Bruno. "Collecting Nature: Practices, Styles, and Narratives." Osiris 27 (2012): 303-40.

Strasser, Bruno. "Data-driven sciences: From wonder cabinets to electronic databases." Studies in the History and Philosophy of Biological and Biomedical Sciences, 43 (2012): 85-87.

Sundram, Ravi. *Pirate Modernity: Delhi's Media Urbanism. Asia's Transformations.* Milton Park, Abingdon, Oxon ; New York, NY: Routledge, 2010.

"The Classification Criteria" Office of Film & Literature Classification. classificationoffice.govt.nz/about-nz-classification/the-classification-criteria/ (retrieved 8/20/2018).

"Top Ten Most Challenged Books Lists," American Library Association, March 26, 2013. http://www.ala.org/advocacy/bbooks/frequentlychallengedbooks/top10 (retrieved August 28, 2018).

Turner, Fred. *From Counterculture to Cyberculture: Stewart Brand, the Whole Earth Network, and the Rise of Digital Utopianism.* Chicago: University of Chicago Press, 2006.

Vivo, Filippo de. *Information and Communication in Venice: Rethinking Early Modern Politics.* Oxford ; New York: Oxford University Press, 2007.

von Hayek, Friedrich. "The Use of Knowledge in Society." American Economic Review 35:4 (September 1945): 519-30.

Walton, Charles ed. *Into Print: Limits and Legacies of the Enlightenment: Essays in Honor of Robert Darnton.* University Park: Pennsylvania State University Press, 2011.

Warner, Michael. T*he Letters of the Republic: Publication and the Public Sphere in Eighteenth-Century America.* Cambridge, Mass: Harvard University Press, 1990.

Vaidhyanathan, Siva. *Copyrights and Copywrongs: the Rise of Intellectual Property and How it Threatens Creativity.* New York: New York University Press, 2001.

Yates, JoAnne. *Control through Communication: The Rise of System in American Management.* Studies in Industry and Society 6. Baltimore: Johns Hopkins University Press, 1989.

Zamyatin, Yevgeny Ivanovich, and Mirra Ginsburg. *A Soviet Heretic.* Chicago: University of Chicago Press, 1970.